Language, Lore a[nd]
Lyrics
Reduced £15

£80

Books Collectable 19
£15.00
0 013450 000018
Oxfam Ireland
19

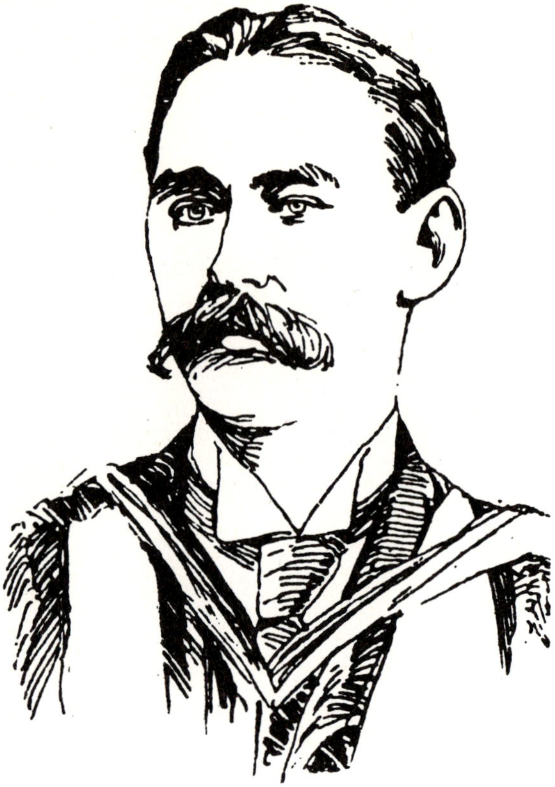

Language, Lore and Lyrics

ESSAYS AND LECTURES

Douglas Hyde
An Craoibhín Aoibhinn

EDITED WITH A PREFACE AND INTRODUCTION BY
Breandán Ó Conaire

IRISH ACADEMIC PRESS

The typesetting of this book — in 11 on 12pt Plantin —
was input by Gilbert Gough Typesetting and
output by Computer Graphics Ltd, Dublin for
Irish Academic Press, Kill Lane, Blackrock, County Dublin

Printed in Ireland

First edition 1986
Douglas Hyde material © beneficiaries of the Douglas Hyde Estate 1986
Other material © Breandán Ó Conaire 1986

British Library Cataloguing in Publication Data

Hyde, Douglas, 1860-1949
Language, lore and lyrics: essays and lectures
1. Folklore — Ireland
I. Title   II. Ó Conaire, Breandán
398'.09415   GR153.5

ISBN 0-7165-2372-8
ISBN 0-7165-2373-6 Pbk

Contents

List of Illustrations	6
Preface	7
Introduction	11
Smaointe : Thoughts	54
The Unpublished Songs of Ireland	66
A Plea for the Irish Language	74
Some Words about Unpublished Literature	81
Irish Folk-lore	93
Gaelic Irish Songs	104
Some Words on Irish Folk-lore	122
On Some Indian Folk-lore	135
The Irish Language	145
The Necessity for De-Anglicising Ireland	153
The Gaelic Revival	171
The Great Work of the Gaelic League	193
Index	200

List of Illustrations

A sketch of Douglas Hyde, from the first issue of *Fáinne an Lae*	*frontispiece*
A page from Hyde's diary, December 1878	*page* 9
A page from Hyde's diary, January 1891	10
The title page of Lhuyd's *Archaelogia Britannica* (Oxford, 1707)	23
The title page of Brooke's *Reliques of Irish Poetry* (Dublin, 1816)	24
The title page of O'Halloran's *History and Antiquities of Ireland* (London, 1772)	25
The title page of Walker's *Historical Memoirs of the Irish Bards* (Dublin, 1818)	26
The title page of the catalogue of the O'Daly auction (Dublin, 1878)	31
Title pages of four books written or published by John O'Daly	32
The title page of Hyde's *Leabhar Sgeulaigheachta* (Dublin, 1889)	39
A page from the manuscript of Hyde's Rathmines lecture, Dublin 1889	40
A letter from Hyde to Eoin Mac Néill, 26 June 1893	47
Eoin Mac Néill, Seán Pléimeann, Eoghan Ó Gramhna and Dáithí Ó Coinnín	48
A page from Canon Bourke's edition of Gallagher's *Sermons*	60
The title page and a text page of O'Molloy's *Lucerna Fidelium* (Rome, 1676)	61
The title page of Cleaver's anthology	147
The title page of the second edition of *The Annals of the Four Masters* (Dublin, 1856)	148
An advertisement for Hyde's Carnegie Hall lecture, November 1905	173
Tomás Ó Concheanainn; and a sketch of Hyde addressing crowds in Dublin, 1903	174

Preface

The nineteenth chapter of Lady Gregory's autobiography, *Seventy Years 1852-1922*, begins thus:

I think it was in 1896 that I suddenly became aware of the change that had come about in Ireland in those first years after Parnell's death. My twelve years of married life had been the years of the Land War, tenant struggling to gain a lasting possession for his children, landlord to keep that which had been in trust to him for his. All the passion of Ireland seemed to be thrown into that fight, it obscured the vision beyond it of the rebuilding of a nation. Then, at last, had come the breaking of Parnell's power and his death, the quarrel among his followers that pushed politics into the background, and with the loss of that dominance of his, there came a birth of new hope and interests, as it were, a setting free of the imagination. First among the builders of the new Ireland I had already set the name of Douglas Hyde.

Douglas Hyde (1860-1949), who was later to become the first President of his country, having spent more than two decades as professor of modern Irish at University College, Dublin, produced the seminal essays and lectures collected in this volume at the outset of his unique and multifaceted career. They contain the ideas and insights which fired his own imagination and were to make him famous in his time. These ideas fueled and sustained the cultural and political movements of his day culminating in the traumatic events which convulsed the nation in the first two decades of the twentieth century. Many of these ideas were subsequently enshrined in the practices and philosophies of the new state founded after the departure of the British in 1922.

Third son of Protestant rector Arthur Hyde and archdeacon's daughter Elizabeth Oldfield, Douglas Hyde was born in Castlerea, Co. Mayo and spent his early years in Kilmactrine, Co. Sligo. His most formative years however, between 1867 and 1880, were spent in the Breac-Ghaeltacht barony of Frenchpark, Co. Roscommnon, an area in which 5,735 Irish speakers were registered in the Census of 1861. It was amongst these people that he acquired his personal affection for and sympathetic insights into aspects of traditional Irish life — his 'vision of something great' — which was to guide and mould his later life and greatly influence the lives of his fellow countrymen. To put Professor Gerard Murphy's phrase in its original context:

he had a vision of something great which was a personal discovery of his own.

He had the power too of communicating that vision to others. And his lifelong fidelity to that vision was such that, long before he died, what was once personal to himself had become the common property of all his countrymen and changed the national outlook in a way that would have seemed incredible in the late eighties of the last century (*Studies*, September 1949).

Thirteen volumes of Hyde's personal diaries, which now reside in the National Library of Ireland, provide a valuable picture of the pattern and accomplishments of his life over a period of almost forty years: March 1874 to September 1912.[1] This present collection of public lectures and essays reveals the direction of his thought and energies in the crucial years between his entry as an undergraduate to Trinity College, Dublin in 1880 and the founding of Conradh na Gaeilge (the Gaelic League) in 1893. The final lecture and interview (pp. 175-199), given at the beginning and end respectively of an extensive tour of the U.S.A. which Hyde undertook in 1905-06, illuminate the successful thrust of the policies and philosophy of Conradh na Gaeilge as formulated over the preceding decade.

This work should help to acquaint the modern reader with part of the rich legacy and creative insights of Dr Douglas Hyde. It may also serve to encourage constructive discussion and timely debate on the many important issues to which these lectures and essays address themselves, doing so in the generous spirit of their wise, gifted and learned begetter.

---

1 See *The Young Douglas Hyde*, Dominic Daly (Irish University Press, Dublin, 1974) xii-xiii.

Diary of Douglas Hyde: December 1878

Diary entry for January 1891

Introduction

The most renowned speech of Dr Hyde's illustrious public career is undoubtedly that entitled 'The Necessity for De-Anglicising Ireland'. Described by various commentators as 'historic', 'momentous', 'resounding', 'epoch-making', it was delivered at a meeting of the recently founded Irish National Literary Society at the Leinster Hall, Molesworth Street on 25 November 1892. Hyde's diary records his preparation and the event itself:

14.11.1892	Lá fliuch. D'fhanas san tigh ag sgríobhadh ar mi-shacsanughadh Éireann.
21.11.1892	Lá an-fhliuch. Bhí Máire Bláca le teacht andiú acht bhí sé ró-fhliuch. Ag sgriobhadh deuntúis air Éirinn mi-sagṡ.
25.11.1892	Ag obair ar feadh an lae san Ardsgoil ag sgriobhadh mo leictiúir. Rinne mé an leictiúir do thabhairt uaim san Alla Laighean i Sr. Molesworth. Os cionn 100 duine ann. Sgillin ar an ticéad. 'Ar mi-shacsanughadh an Chinidh Éireannaigh'. Miss Purser agus na Gwinnes, Hannraoi Frionnsa, Miss Rowley 7c. agus Miss L'Estrange ann ag éisteacht liom. Mhair sé timcioll 1.20. Budh mhaith é, creidim. Bhí mé molta go mór.*

The lecture may be viewed as the culminating point of two independent developments, one individual and personal, the other social and cultural. Firstly, it embodies Hyde's own personal stand against the long history of cultural suppression and propaganda promoted by the English colonial power in Ireland, which he opposed on intellectual, social, economic and affective grounds. Secondly, it represents a major landmark in the progress of a movement, comprised of various groups and individuals, which had begun to clearly emerge in the eighteenth century, with gathering force in the nineteenth, and which concerned itself, directly

---

* Wet day. I remained in the house writing on de-anglicising Ireland.

Day very wet. Mary Blake was to arrive to-day but it was too wet. Writing composition on Ireland de-anglicised.

Working all day at the Academy writing my lecture. I delivered the lecture at the Leinster Hall in Molesworth Street. Over 100 people present. A shilling for a ticket. 'On the de-anglicisation of the Irish Race'. Miss Purser and the Gwynnes, Henry French, Miss Rowley etc. and Miss L'Estrange there listening to me. It lasted about 1 hour 20 mins. It was good, I believe. I was highly praised.

or indirectly, with the existence, and in some cases the rehabilitation and reclamation of native Irish learning and literature, history and art, music, custom and lore. The strands, some disparate, some overlapping, of this movement will be discussed later.

THE COLONIAL BACKGROUND

Hyde put forward in this speech what has been described by Professor David Greene as a 'radical and revolutionary'[2] policy. It was in effect a statement of ultimate resistance to the long tradition of legal, quasi-legal and social repression and denigration of the vernacular and indigenous culture of the people, carried on over many centuries. This colonizing strategy which apart from closing down possibilities of personal advancement and civil rights had gradually induced into the Irish psyche a pernicious form of self-contempt whose psychological effects were potentially more destructive than any harm suffered from purely external restrictions.

This psycho-linguistic or cultural aggression had operated from all the major power-centres of the colonial administration — religious, legal, educational, civil etc. — and had a long history. As early as 1285 the recently arrived Dominicans and Franciscans were being reported to the English king for making much ('faciunt multa') of the native language of the people.[3] J.F. Lydon in *The Lordship of Ireland in the Middle Ages* states: 'The fact is that officially the Gaelic race, and its language and institutions, indeed its whole culture, was regarded as at best second class, and often as depraved: the typical attitude of the conqueror towards the conquered. . . . In official eyes contact with Gaelic culture was a contamination.'[4]

In 1366 the well-known Statutes of Kilkenny were enacted, decreeing:

and if any English or Irish living amongst the English use the Irish language amongst themselves contrary to this ordinance and thereof be attaint, that his lands and tenements, if he have any, be seized into the hands of his immediate lord until he come to one of the places of our lord the King and find sufficient surety to adopt and use the English language and then that he have restitution of his said lands by writ to issue out of the same place. In case that such person have not lands or tenements, then his body shall be taken by some of the officers

---

2 'The Founding of the Gaelic League', David Greene in *The Gaelic League Idea*, ed. Seán Ó Tuama (Mercier Press, Cork, 1972) 18.
3 See 'Medieval Dominicans and the Irish Language', Conleth Kearns in *Irish Ecclesiastical Record* (July, 1960) 19; *The Church in Gaelic Ireland: 13th to 15th centuries*, Canice Mooney (Gill and Macmillan, Dublin, 1969) 2-3.
4 (Gill and Macmillan Dublin, 1972) 155, 186.

of our lord the King and committed to the next gaol, there to remain until he or another in his name find sufficient surety in the manner aforesaid.[5]

Professor Lydon remarks: 'the legislation of 1366 had been anticipated by a host of earlier enactments from 1297 onwards: bans on Irish dress, language, games, and so on, on marriage with the Irish enemy, on making treaties with them, on keeping rhymers or brehons, on trading with the Gaelic areas — none of this was new in the mid-fourteenth century.'[6] The Kilkenny statutes, though directed specifically at the *degenerate* (i.e. hibernicized) English, in effect outlawed the entire Irish speaking population of the island, the *natio Hibernica* ('the meere Irish, commonlie called the wild Irish' in the words of a later writer, Richard Stanihurst). In his *History of Medieval Ireland* Edmund Curtis writes:

Of the Irish who did not live among the English, or were able to defy their jurisdiction and live ... under their own chiefs, ... they were refused the threefold rights of *ius connubii, ius suffragii, ius commerciandi*, that is, they were legally forbidden to trade, marry, and enjoy citizen rights with the colonial race.

and

...to be proved of 'Irish and Irish nation' entailed, even for those who might have peacefully lived among the English, denial of civil rights and equality with their colonial neighbours. Numerous cases can be given of this, right up to Tudor times.[7]

The ascent of the Tudors to the English throne brought with it an added virulence in the prosecution of this policy. Professor Brian Ó Cuív states:

The State Papers ... show us that the extirpation of that language remained the state policy. Again and again we find plans put forward for this purpose, statutes passed, or orders sent from the King himself, such as the following found in a letter from Henry VIII to the town of Galway in 1536: 'that every inhabitaunt within the saide towne indevor theym selfe to speke Englyshe and to use theym selffe after the Englyshe facion; and specyally that you, and every of you, do put forth your childe to scole, to lerne to speke Englyshe'.[8]

---

5 *Irish Historical Documents 1172-1922*, ed. Edmund Curtis and R. B. McDowell (Methuen, London, 1968) 53.
6 *op. cit.* 187.
7 (Methuen, London, 1978) 235, 416. In fact, the appellation 'Irishman' itself could be classed as a legal insult. A Waterford enactment of 1382 decreed a specified fine (13s 4d) to be imposed on any person found guilty of referring to a fellow-citizen as 'Irishman'. (*Vid. Historical Manuscripts Commission X* (London, 1885) 292, para. IV).
8 *Irish Dialects and Irish-speaking Districts* (Dublin Institute for Advanced Studies, Dublin, 1971) 12; See also *A Literary History of Ireland*, Douglas Hyde (London, 1967) 608-13; 'Irish poets, historians, and judges in English documents, 1538-1615', T. F. O'Rahilly, *PRIA* 36 (1922) 86-120.

A general ordinance in Henry's reign

enacted that every person or persons, the King's true subjects, inhabiting this land of Ireland, of what estate, condition or degree he or they be, or shall be, to the uttermost of their power, cunning and knowledge, shall use and speak commonly the English tongue and language....[9]

Curtis makes an interesting point with regard to the original colonisers at this period:

The affection of the "Old English' for the native tongue and culture was scarcely less now than that of the native chiefs themselves. And this affection, which at first had been a necessity, soon became a passion, as the Tudor Reconquest degenerated into a crusade against not only the old-time liberties of Gaelic and Norman lords, but against the language, lore, culture, and faith of most Irishmen. The Irish language then became the symbol of a patriotism which now England's first colonists had no less embraced than the 'Old Irish' themselves.[10]

Tomás Ó Fiaich sums up the position thus:

The Tudor political advance and the suppression of the Irish language now went hand in hand. Irish was cut off from its patrons, the chieftains of both Gaelic and Anglo-Irish descent, who were decimated in a series of wars and confiscations. It was deprived of its poets and learned men, who were hunted and imprisoned by Sir John Perrot throughout Munster — we know the names of only a few who were hanged, for the bardic schools did not survive to treasure their martyrology. It was destroyed in the pages of ancient manuscripts, which were the special target of Sir George Carew. It was killed on the lips of children by the Court of Wards, which brought the sons of Irish noblemen to England, so that they might later return as loyal subjects, in language as in political allegiance.[11]

The thinking behind this cultural terrorism is revealed in some writings of the time.[12] Richard Stanihurst (1547-1618) in his *Treatise conteining a plaine and perfect Description of Ireland* (1577) wrote:

---

9   *Conradh na Gaeilge agus an tOideachas Aosach*, S. Mac Mathúna & R. Mac Gabhann (Cló Chois Fharraige, 1981) 1. James Hardiman in his *Irish Minstrelsy* (1831) remarked that 'most grants of land from the Crown, in the reigns of Henry and his successors to Charles I, contained special provisoes, for the disuse of the native, and the encouragement of the English tongue' (xxx). A report commissioned by Queen Elizabeth I, last of the Tudors, recommended 'that all brehons, carrages, and bardes ... be tryed and executed as in the case of treason' and suggested means for 'enlardging the Englysshe tong and extinguishing the Irish in as shorte a tyme as conveniently may be.' (*Vid.* 'Ireland's Manuscript Heritage' Brian Ó Cuív in *Éire-Ireland* (Spring 1984) 98-99; also *Historical Memoirs of the Irish Bards* I, J.C. Walker (Dublin, 1818) 197-9.
10 *op. cit.* 370.
11 'The Language and Political History', Tomás Ó Fiaich in *A View of the Irish Language*, ed. Brian Ó Cuív (Stationery Office, Dublin, 1969) 104.

First therefore take this with you, that a conquest draweth, or at the leastwise ought to draw to it three things, to wit, law, apparell, and language. For where the countrie is subdued, there the inhabitants ought to be ruled by the same law that the conqueror is governed, to weare the same fashion of attire wherwith the victor is vested, and speake the same language that the vanquisher parleth. And if anie of these three lacke, doubtlesse the conquest limpeth. Now whereas Ireland hath bin by lawfull conquest brought under the subjection of England ... is it decent (thinke you) that their [the English] owne ancient native toong shall be shrowded in oblivion, and suffer the enimies language, as it were a tettar or ringworme, to harbor it selfe within the iawes of English conquerors? No trulie ...[13]

The English poet and planter Edmund Spenser (1552-1598), private secretary to Lord Grey in 1580, gives us an insight into the mentality of the colonist in his oft-quoted remark: 'the woordes are the Image of the mynd, soe as, they proceeding from the mynd, the mynd must needes be affected with the woordes. Soe that the speache being Irish, the harte must needes be Irish'. In *A View of the Present State of Ireland* presented in the form of a dialogue, he wrote:

Irenaeus: And first I have to finde fault with the abuse of language, that is, for the speaking of Irish amongest the English, which as it is unnaturall that any people should love anothers language more then theyr owne, soe it is very inconvenient, and the cause of many other evills.

Eudox: It seemeth straunge to me that the English should take more delight to speake that language then theyr owne, wheras they should (me thinkes) rather take scorne to acquaynte theyr tonges therewith: for it hath bene ever the use of the conquerors to dispise the language of the conquered, and to force him by all meanes to learne his.[14]

The Law
Sir John Davies (1569-1626) was attorney-general for Ireland under James I, speaker of the Irish House of Commons, promoter of the plantation of Ulster and author of *Discovery of the True Causes why Ireland was never Entirely Subdued* (1612). He was instrumental in instituting a system of regular assizes and an informer-reports network in order the better to control, anglicise and penetrate the 'fastnesses' of the Irish. He explained the success of these measures:

For the Under-Sheriffes and Bayliffes errant, are better guides and Spies in the time of peace, then any were found in the time of war. Moreover, these

---

12 See e.g. *Elizabethan Ireland: A Selection of Writings by Elizabethan Writers on Ireland*, ed. James P. Myers Jr. (Archon, 1983).
13 *Holinshed Chronicles* (1808) 5.
14 *Complete Works* (Macmillan, London, 1871) 638.

civil assemblies at Assises and Sessions, have reclaymed the Irish from their wildenesse, caused them to cut off their Glibs and long Haire; to convert their Mantles into Cloaks; to conform themselves to the maner of England in al their behaviour and outward formes.

And because they find a great inconvenience in moving their suites by an Interpreter, they do for the most part send their Children to Schools especially to learne the English language: so as we may conceive an hope that the next generation will in tongue & heart, and every way else, become *English*; so as there will bee no difference or distinction but the Irish Sea betwixt us. And thus we see a good conversion, & the *Irish Game turned againe*.[15]

In their Introduction to the *Catalogue of the Books and Manuscripts comprising the library of Sir J. T. Gilbert* (1918) the editors, Douglas Hyde and D. J. O'Donoghue, referring to Davies' *Reports of Irish Law Cases* (1615) wrote: 'Sir John Davies was, first, Solicitor-General for Ireland, and afterwards Lord Chief Justice of England, and there is no possibility of fining down or explaining away the naked facts as his law cases show them, that an Irishman was *ipso facto* deprived of all legal rights and a lawful victim to every Englishman who desired to prey upon him.' Gilbert's own *Calendar of Ancient Records of Dublin* (1894) furnishes relevant example of the cultural exclusiveness of the country's premier municipal assembly, citing from their 1657 Laws, Orders and Constitutions:

whereas by the lawes all persons of this land ought to speake and use the English tongue and habitt, contrarie whereunto, and in open contempte whereof, there is Irish commonlie and usuallie spoken, and the Irish habitt worne not onelie in the streetes, and by such as live in the countrie and come to this cittie on market dayes, but alsoe by and in severall families in this cittie, to the great discontentment of the right honorable his highness councill for the affaires of Ireland, and the scandalizinge of the inhabitants and magistratts of the cittie ... (p. 118).

Towards the end of the following century the antiquarian Edward Ledwich reiterated the concept regarding the relationship between the tongue and the heart, between linguistic-cultural eradication and psychological domination:

While the Irish preserved their native language and dress there was no hope of civilizing them, or bringing them to an acquiescence in English dominion or English laws. Aware of this, the British princes endeavoured early to reduce by very penal laws, the Irish to a conformity with their other subjects.[16]

---

15 *op. cit.* 271-2. Neil McLeod describes Davies as 'the prime mover in exterminating native (Irish) Law', *Studia Celtica* XVI/XVII (1981-2) 66. See also *Sir John Davies and the Conquest of Ireland*, Hans H. Pawlisch (Cambridge, 1986).

16 *Antiquities of Ireland* (Dublin, 1790) 346. See *Irish Dialects Past and Present*, Thomas F. O'Rahilly (Dublin Institute for Advanced Studies, Dublin, 1972) 8-9.

These laws, together with confiscation, plantation, transportation, religious persecution, deliberate devastation and military intimidation assisted in the process of reducing the native population, in the words of O'Rahilly, 'to a condition bordering on serfdom.'[17]

A striking and opposite reminder of their distressing effects was give in the year Conradh na Gaeilge was founded, when in the course of a speech to the Irish National Teachers Annual Congress Mr M. Ó Mainnín, from the Gaeltacht region of West Kerry, outlined his personal experience of their application on the Irish-speaking community:

> how often I have seen in courts of law our Irish-speaking peasantry greviously wronged, non-suited, abused, and kicked off the bench, because they would not undertake to state their cases in a language (English) of which they practically knew next to nothing.[18]

Education
In the field of education, Parish schools instituted under an Act of 1537, specifically to introduce and diffuse the English language, and Charter schools funded from 1733 'as one of the most effectual means of converting and civilising the Irish natives', were superseded in 1831 by a new system of 'National' schools, 'under the rigorous inspection of the central educational authority, and their aim was to produce good law-abiding British subjects'.[21] Neither Irish history, Irish music nor the Irish language were taught in these schools. In reply to a query from George Trevelyan MP, chief secretary for Ireland, as to 'whether there was any special provision made in the early foundation of the National System of Education in 1831 or 1832, for the education in the Irish Language of those children who spoke Irish only', the Commissioners of National Education replied that 'no provision of the kind was made at the institution of the National System. As well as the Commissioners can trace the proceedings of that early period, the anxiety of the promoters of the National System was to encourage the cultivation of the English language and to make English the language of the schools' (20 February 1884).[22] A request make in 1844 to the Commissioners of National Education by the parish priest of Gaoth Dobhair seeking permission to have Irish taught in his local school, in the heart of the

---

17 *ibid.* 2.
18 *Irisleabhar na Gaedhilge*, Vol IV No. 46 (July 1893) 220.
19 Ó Cuív (1971), *op. cit.* 19.
20 *The Hedge Schools of Ireland*, P. J. Dowling (Mercier Press, Cork, 1968) 28.
21 'The Decline of the Irish Language', Maureen Wall in *A View of the Irish Language, op. cit.* 87.
22 *British Parliamentary Papers* Vol. 61 (1884): National Schools (Ireland) (Teaching of Irish) 9.

Donegal Gaeltacht, received a response which clearly demonstrated the position and status of the language as envisaged by the founders and executives of this system:

> Ordered, that the Commissioners decline to comply with this request, as it forms no part of the objects they have been appointed to accomplish.[23]

One of the objects to be accomplished however can be gleaned from the well known verse 'that used to hang in every National School...:

> I thank the goodness and the grace
> That on my birth have smiled,
> And made me in these Christian days
> A happy English child.'[24]

As Professor Joseph Lee explains: 'the government certainly intended the national school system to perform a massive brain-washing operation, obliterating subversive ancestral influence by inculcating in the pupils a proper reverence for the English connection and proper deference for their social superiors...'[25] Professor Heinrich Wagner speaks about the spoken language 'being strangled systematically by the educational policies of the central ... Government.'[26] Earlier in the century Charles Orpen had quoted a colonial case against teaching the language. It had little to do with education:

> Teaching Irish will excite disaffection to the King, and disincline to English connection; it will impede the amalgamation of the two classes in this country, those who speak Irish, and those who speak English; there are, therefore, many political motives against teaching it.[27]

---

23 Minutes of the Board, 7 June 1844. See 'An Bord Náisiúnta agus an Ghaeilge', T. Ó Raifeartaigh in *IER* 12/ 1949; 'The Irish Language in the 19th century', P. Ó Loingsigh in *Oideas* 14 (Spring 1975) 9-10; *The Fortunes of the Irish Language*, Daniel Corkery: 'All down the eighteenth century, the law of the land had presumed that the Catholic Irish people did not exist: such a presumption simplified legislative problems. The new Board of National Education simplified their own special problem by presuming that the Irish language did not exist. As a matter of fact, there were probably more people speaking Irish in 1831, when this scheme appeared, *than ever before.*' (C.J. Fallon, Dublin, 1954) 114.
24 'Education and the People', D. Kennedy in *Social Life in Ireland 1800-45*, ed. R.B. McDowell (Mercier Press, Cork, 1973) 65; Mac Mathúna & Mac Gabhann (1981), *op. cit.* 5.
25 *The Modernisation of Irish Society 1848-1918* (Gill and Macmillan, Dublin, 1973) 28.
26 *Proceedings of the Sixth International Congress of Celtic Studies*, ed. Gearóid Mac Eoin (DIAS, Dublin, 1983) 108.
27 *The Claim of Millions ...*, Charles E. H. Orpen (Dublin, 1821) 45.

Douglas Hyde painted the following picture of the system as it operated in practice among the Irish-speaking population:

> People who knew no Irish were appointed all over the island to teach people who knew no English. The results were horrible beyond description, for this process going on for two generations stupified and stultified, almost out of all recognition, one of the cleverest races in Europe. The fathers and mothers (denied schooling for their children in their own language, and driven to despair in their endeavour to get them to understand the schooling which they were receiving in English) tied sticks round the necks of the children to keep them from talking Irish, and every time they spoke a word a notch was cut in the stick, and when they went to school next morning they were beaten in proportion to the number of notches. This was popularly called the score or the tally. There was scarcely a child in the Irish-speaking parts of Ireland who did not undergo this treatment, and I have myself spoken to scores of men — and not such very old men either — who were treated in this way.[28]

Vivid accounts of the operation of this linguistic hegemony in the school system are preserved in the published works of Gaeltacht writers and in the archives of the Department of Irish Folklore, University College Dublin. Canon Ulick J. Bourke, MRIA, PP Claremorris, cited instances of the use of *bataí scóir* in Connacht, in an essay written 1873-4:

> The writer has seen within the past eight years several children — one a young girl from the village called Garrdha Mór within eight miles of the town of Tuam — who was beaten by a pedagogue named Corcoran because she spoke her native language. I have seen and spoken to several Ecclesiastics who suffered this inhuman and unnatural method of flagellation for uttering the language which nature taught them to articulate. His Grace the Archbishop of Tuam has several times assured this writer that he suffered stripes for speaking while a boy his mother tongue. Could any system more horrible be conceived! ... The sad result of this torturing system has been ruinously felt to this day. (MS. 12Q13, RIA).

P.H. Pearse, recalling an incident he encountered in Connemara of a child having been cruelly caned by a teacher because he had spoken Irish to the Schools' Inspector, commented:

> If these things happened in Poland or in Finland or in Alsace-Lorraine these islands would ring with denunciations. The British and the West British and — for aught I know — the North British press would report the facts under scare headings. We should hear of the 'Language War in Finland', or of the 'Reign of Terror in Polish Schools', or of 'German Aggression in Alsace-Lorraine'. But when Connacht is the theatre of tyranny the outside world hears nothing, for England controls the press agencies (*Guth na Bliadhna*, 1905).

---

28 Ms. 17, 756 N.L.I., 26-27. See also Greene (1972), *op. cit.* 10-11; 'Bataí Scóir', Seán Ó Súilleabháin in *Féil-sgríbhinn Eóin Mhic Néill*, ed. John Ryan (Dublin, 1940).

In the final analysis the ages-old colonial policy, abetted by other forces, largely achieved its desired results: a widespread language shift to English, a stigma of ignoble 'primitiveness' and poverty — both material and intellectual — attached to Irish, a general ignorance of the Irish language, history, music and literature, and an Irish speaking population who were unable to read or write their own language. An even more malign outcome was the inculcation of the seeds of shame and inferiority in the minds of Irish speakers for their own language,[29] and the fostering of an attitude of disdain, antipathy and contempt in others towards 'the barbarous tongue in which they converse',[30] a tongue described by a celebrated priest of Trinity College Dublin, John Pentland Mahaffy (1839-1919), who was himself ignorant of the language, as 'a most difficult and useless tongue — not only useless but a mischievous obstacle to civilisation.'[31] There are few phenomena more frequently reported from Irish-speaking Ireland in the latter half of the nineteenth century than the association of *náire** and *drochmheas*** with the language. Hyde was keenly aware of the psychological and intellectual dimensions of the conquest, referred to in his monumental *Literary History of Ireland* (1899) to 'the far-reaching and deliberate efforts of the National Board of Education to extirpate the national language' (606), and wrote: 'The children are taught, if nothing else, to be ashamed of their own parents, ashamed of their own nationality, ashamed of their own names' (634). Dr George Sigerson in a letter to *The Nation*, 13 September 1890, praising the Welsh Eiseddford, wrote:

The Welsh people have thus shown an honourable sentiment of self-respect widely different, I regret to say, from the slavish indifference of our Irish population to the preservation of their ancestral tongue. I have said 'indifference' — I, perhaps, should have said hostility. Up to the year 1850, or thereabouts, the Irish language was the prevalent language spoken at fairs, markets, in the field, by the priest at the altar, by the travellers whom you met on the public cars and coaches in Munster. Since that period its decline has been rapid. The last examination in the Irish catechism in the parish I inhabit took place in 1865 — just a quarter of a century ago. At the present time the elder members of the peasantry around me can speak Irish; but they do not speak it to their children, who, as a rule, know no more of it than they do of Greek. Conversing with a middle-aged farmer last week, I told him that,

---

29 For an example of a similar phenomenon in Gaelic Scotland *vid. Language Death*, Nancy C. Dorian (Pennsylvania, 1981) and review in *Scottish Gaelic Studies* XIV 1 (Winter 1983) 123-9. See also *The Colonizer and the Colonized*, Albert Memmi (London, 1975).

30 Orpen (1821), *op. cit.* 21.

31 'The Modern Babel' in *Nineteenth Century* 1896. See also *Writing in Irish Today*, D. Greene (Mercier Press, Cork, 1972) 13.

*shame   **contempt

so far as my own slight knowledge of the language extended, I took care to teach it to my grandson. He replied that when the lad grew up he would find nobody to understand him if he spoke Irish; complacently adding, 'it is gone.' The quiet satisfaction with which our peasantry allow the noble old tongue of their country to die out betrays an element of baseness, which is sometimes emphasised in the jaunty way in which the juniors will reply to a sentence or a question in Irish by saying: 'I hasn't any Irish', as if their disgraceful ignorance was something to be proud of.

Hyde speaks of a similar phenomenon among higher society in his Preface to *Beside the Fire* (1890):

In most circles in Ireland it is a disgrace to be known to talk Irish; and in the capital, if one makes use of an Irish word to express one's meaning, as one sometimes does of a French or German word, one would be looked upon as positively outside the pale of decency.

Although Irish had already been in decline, the Great Famine (1845-48) and its aftermath dealt a traumatic blow to the spirit of the people and to the strength and survival of the language. Seán de Fréine graphically describes the subsequent widespread retreat and the phenomenon of the 'great silence':

Irish speakers commonly became the butt of ridicule and contempt. Parents who knew no English used violence to prevent their children from speaking the only language to which they had natural access. Children were set to spy on one another, even on their brothers and sisters, to catch them unawares in speaking Irish, so that they could be punished for doing so. Children admitted to speaking Irish, as a sin, in the confessional. In many places they were forced to wear the notorious tally stick. This was usually a piece of wood tied round the neck which any adult who heard them lapsing into Irish was expected to notch, so that they could be beaten later by their parents or teachers for every mark on the stick. Irish manuscripts, formerly held in high regard, were thrown out as rubbish, used to wrap groceries, cut up for tailors' patterns, dismembered to provide ornamentation for scrap books, given to children to scribble on, and burnt in superstitious ignorance as books of black magic.

Irish speakers became as elusive as the Abominable Snowman. The census of 1851 indicates a widespread denial of a knowledge of Irish.[32]

REBIRTH AND DISCOVERY

The antithesis to this history of cultural colonialism and decline is most notably represented by a burgeoning interest displayed by various groups and individuals during the eighteenth and nineteenth centuries in Irish

---

[32] *The Great Silence* (Mercier Press, Cork, 1978) 73. Corkery (1954) *op. cit.* also refers to this post-famine 'unbroken silence' (p. 117).

history, music, language, customs etc. These fields of interest may be summarised as follows:

1. *Comparative and historical linguistics* Eoin Mac Néill traces this important strand back firstly to George Buchanan's history of Scotland (1583)[33] and subsequently to the *Archaeologia Britannica* (1707) of Edward Lhuyd.[34] This new scholarship awakened a sustained academic interest in the importance of Irish for philological research and in the study of the origins and affinities of peoples and languages, literatures and traditions.

2. *Religion* The *Aibidil Gaoidheilge et Caiticiosma* of John O'Kearney (1571), Uilliam Ó Domhnuill's *Tiomna Nuadh* (New Testament, 1603) and *Leabhar na nUrnaightheadh gComhchoidchoind* (Book of Common Prayer, 1608) mark the beginning of the utilisation of the printing press in the propagation of religion in Ireland. Elizabeth I had an Irish type specially cast for this purpose and some Evangelical Protestant bodies sought to use the language as a means of obtaining converts among the Irish-speaking communities. The London Hibernian (1806) and the Baptist (1814) Societies both made use of Irish, but the Irish Society for Promoting the Education of the Native Irish through the Medium of their Own Language (1818) was the best known of these organisations, and in 1838 under its auspices a professorship of Irish was funded at Trinity College, Dublin, for this purpose. The catechism of Bonaventura Ó hEoghusa (Antwerp, 1611), Flaithrí Ó Maolchonaire's *Sgáthán an Chrábhaidh* (Louvain, 1616) and *Sgáthán Shacramuinte na hAithridhe* (Louvain, 1618) by Aodh Mac Aingil saw the beginning of the Catholic response to this initiative.[35] Although this movement resulted in the printing and distribution of both religious matter (homilies, prayer books, sermons, poetry, catechisms, books of the Bible) and secular texts (spelling books, primers, dictionaries) and provided employment for those literate in Irish,[36] the Protestant missionary effort 'succeeded in provoking a reaction against the reading of the Irish bible, or, indeed, any material in Irish at all, which was to do much harm to the already weakened status of the language.'[37] Pádraig de Brún remarks that 'the

---

33 See *The Irish Review* December 1913 (Eoin Mac Néill).

34 *Phases of Irish History*, Eoin MacNeill (Gill, Dublin, 1968) 6; *Life and Letters of Edward Lhuyd*, R. T. Gunter (London, 1945); *Celtica V* 218-28, *XI* 34-42; *Collectors of Irish Manuscripts* N. Ní Shéaghdha (D.I.A.S., 1985) 8-10.

35 See *Aodh Mac Aingil agus an Scoil Nua-Ghaedhilge i Lobháin*, Tomás Ó Cléirigh (An Gúm, Dublin, 1935); *Irish Spirituality*, ed. M. Maher (Veritas, Dublin, 1981) chap. 7.

36 See 'The Irish Society's Bible Teachers 1818-27', Pádraig de Brún in *Éigse XIX* (1983) 287.

37 'The Irish Language Movement', David Greene in *Irish Anglicanism 1869-1969*, ed. M. Hurley SJ (Allen Figgis, Dublin, 1970) 111. See *The Voice of Ireland*, ed. W. G. Fitzgerald (Dublin, 1924) 444-6.

Archæologia Britannica,

GIVING SOME ACCOUNT
Additional to what has been hitherto Publish'd,
OF THE
LANGUAGES, HISTORIES and CUSTOMS
Of the Original Inhabitants
OF
GREAT BRITAIN:

From Collections and Observations in Travels through
Wales, Cornwal, Bas-Bretagne, Ireland and *Scotland.*

By EDWARD LHUYD M.A. of *Jesus College,*
Keeper of the ASHMOLEAN MUSEUM in OXFORD.

VOL. I.
GLOSSOGRAPHY.

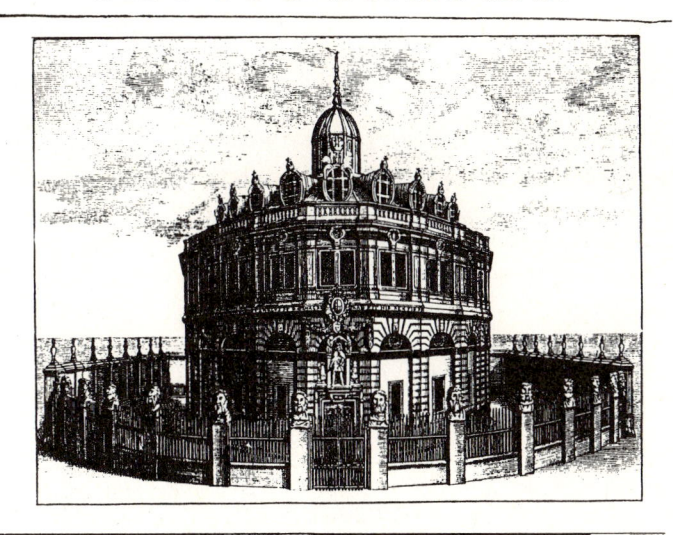

OXFORD,
Printed at the THEATER for the Author, MDCCVII.
And Sold by Mr. *Bateman* in *Pater-Noster-Row, London:* and *Jeremiah Pepyat*
Bookseller at *Dublin.*

RELIQUES

OF

IRISH POETRY:

CONSISTING OF

HEROIC POEMS, ODES, ELEGIES, AND SONGS,

TRANSLATED INTO ENGLISH VERSE:

With Notes explanatory and historical;

AND

THE ORIGINALS IN THE IRISH CHARACTER.

TO WHICH IS SUBJOINED AN IRISH TALE.

BY MISS BROOKE.

TO WHICH IS PREFIXED,

A MEMOIR OF HER LIFE AND WRITINGS,

BY AARON CROSSLY SEYMOUR, ESQ.

AUTHOR OF " LETTERS TO YOUNG PERSONS," &c. &c.

A Oiriṅ, ar biṅ liṅ do rgeala.—Caṫ Ꝼabṗa.
Melodious, Oisin, are thy strains to me.

DUBLIN:

PRINTED BY J. CHRISTIE, 17, ROSS-LANE.

1816.

AN INTRODUCTION

TO THE STUDY OF THE

HISTORY AND ANTIQUITIES

OF

IRELAND:

IN WHICH THE ASSERTIONS OF

Mr. HUME AND OTHER WRITERS

ARE OCCASIONALLY CONSIDERED.

ILLUSTRATED WITH COPPER-PLATES.

ALSO

TWO APPENDIXES:

CONTAINING

1. ANIMADVERSIONS ON AN INTRODUCTION TO THE HISTORY OF G. BRITAIN AND IRELAND, BY J. MACPHERSON, Esq.

2. OBSERVATIONS ON THE MEMOIRS OF GREAT-BRITAIN AND IRELAND, BY SIR JOHN DALRYMPLE.

By SYLVESTER O HALLORAN.

LONDON:
PRINTED FOR J. MURRAY, N° 32, FLEET-STREET.
M.DCC.LXXII.

HISTORICAL MEMOIRS

OF THE

IRISH BARDS;

AN

HISTORICAL ESSAY

ON THE

Dress

OF THE

ANCIENT AND MODERN IRISH;

AND

A MEMOIR

ON THE

Armour and Weapons

OF

THE IRISH.

BY JOSEPH C. WALKER, ESQ.

MEMBER OF THE ROYAL IRISH ACADEMY, CORRESPONDENT FELLOW OF THE ANTIQUARIAN SOCIETY OF PERTH, AND HONORARY MEMBER OF THE ETRUSCAN ACADEMY OF CORTONA.

IN TWO VOLUMES.

VOL. I.

Second Edition.

DUBLIN:

PRINTED BY J. CHRISTIE, 170, JAMES'S-STREET.

1818.

condemnation of the reading of all Irish books, apparently widespread later in the [nineteenth] century, was presumably due to the reinforcement of Anglicising attitudes among the [Catholic] clergy by the fears and frustrations produced by the Bible campaign.'[38]

3. *Literature* The publication of the products of the forger James Macpherson (1736-1796) in the 1760s sparked controversy and attention in early Irish literature and manuscripts. His *Fragments of Ancient Poetry Collected in the Highlands of Scotland and Translated from the Gaelic or Erse Language* (1760), *Fingal* (1762), *Temora* (1763), described as 'ancient epic poems', and *The Works of Ossian* (1765) gave a strong impetus to the Romantic movement, and were followed by *Specimens of the Poetry of the Antient Welsh Bards* by Evan Evans (1764) and Bishop Thomas Percy's *Reliques of Ancient Poetry* (1765). Charlotte Brooke (1740-1793), encouraged by Percy, produced *Reliques of Irish Poetry* (1789)[39] which was favourably reviewed and which introduced many English readers for the first time to a variety of native Irish poetic compositions. Forty years later James Hardiman (1782-1855) achieved similar fame with his *Irish Minstrelsy; or Bardic Remains of Ireland with English Poetical Translations* (1831). A strain of ersatz Celticism displayed in Thomas Moore's *Melodies* (1808-   ), in Thomas Gray's 'The Bard' (1755) and in the exegeses of Matthew Arnold (1866-7) and Ernest Renan (1823-92) also found favour among important sections of society. As Hyde says with reference to Moore: 'He had rendered the past of Ireland sentimentally interesting without arousing the prejudices of or alarming the upper classes.'[40]

4. *History* Due primarily to the work of gentlemen scholars such as Charles O'Conor of Belanagare (1710-1791), author of *Dissertations on the ancient History of Ireland* (1753), Dr Silvester O'Halloran (1728-1807), General Charles Vallancey (1721-1812) and Joseph Cooper Walker (c. 1762-1810) Irish history and the study of antiquity was given a new lease of life in the eighteenth century. Their collective aim was to propagate a more truthful version of Irish history, especially of the pre-Norman era, by acquainting themselves and others with the native Irish sources. Vallancey, whose enthusiasm frequently overran his scholarship, has been described by Arthur Griffith as 'the first man of weight and influence in Anglo-Ireland to espouse the claim of the despised native Irish to an illustrious place among the nations ... the first champion

---

38 de Brún (1983) *op. cit.*, 285 n 24.
39 See 'Two Eighteenth-Century Irish Scholars', R. A. Breathnach in *Studia Hibernica* 5 (1965).
40 'Irish Language Movement: Some Reminiscences' *Manchester Guardian Commerical* 10 May 1923. See also *Mise agus an Connradh* Dubhghlas de hÍde (An Gúm, Dublin, 1937) 14.

of the Irish language in the house of its enemies.'[41] This movement also resulted in the translation into English of works by native Irish historians, Ruairí Ó Flaithearta (1629-1718), Seán Ó Linsigh (c.1599-c.1670), Seathrún Céitinn (c.1580-c.1644) and Mícheál Ó Cléirigh (c.1575-1643), and helped to spread a knowledge of Ireland's past that had hitherto lain shrouded in obscurity.

Societies
One of the results of these developments was the founding, principally in the capital and in Belfast, of a number of learned societies e.g. the (Royal) Irish Academy (1782), the Gaelic Society of Dublin (1807), Belfast Harp Society (1809), the Iberno-Celtic Society (1818), the Ulster Gaelic Society (1830), th Irish Archaeology Society (1840), the Celtic Society (1845), the Kilkenny Archaeological Society (1849) and the Ossianic Society (1853), whose activities required the services of native Irish scholars, scribes, teachers and collectors, and whose *raison d'être* rested, in the majority of cases, on the existence of the Irish language, 'since without a rediscovery of the language all the doors would have remained closed.'[42] The generation of brilliant scholars, headed by O'Donovan (1806-1861) and O'Curry (1794-1862), thus employed were augmented later in the century by equally eminent Celticists from the continent — Dottin, Gaidoz, de Jubainville, Meyer, Nigra, Windisch, Thurneysen, Zimmer — who, following the researches of Franz Bopp, Hermann Ebel and Johann Caspar Zeuss, had begun to investigate the rich fields of Irish literature and philology.

Little of this scholarly research and antiquarian activity touched the lives of the ordinary people, however, the majority of whom, according to T.W Moody, comprised 'a nation long accustomed to subjection, stamped with crippling inferiority, and largely unconscious of its ancient roots in the past.'[43] The beneficial effects however included some diminution of the pall of ignorance and prejudice which governed the treatment of and attitudes to Irish culture and history. Regarding the learned societies Tomás Ó hAilín rightly points out that they helped to vindicate native Irish learning, to make the academic study of Irish respectable, and most importantly 'they played no small part in the slow growth of a national awareness of the significance of the language and of its value to the Irish people.'[44] They began to uncover the evidence

---

41 *Evening Telegraph*, 15 March 1913.

42 *Irish Literature in English: The Romantic Period* Vol. 1, Patrick Rafroidi (Colin Smythe, Gerrards Cross, 1980), 167.

43 'Thomas Davis and the Irish Nation', T. W. Moody in *Hermathena* CIII (Autumn 1966) 20.

44 'Irish Revival Movements', Tomás Ó hAilín in *A View of the Irish Language, op. cit.* 91.

from the past upon which a distinct and independent future could be built.

The Romantic Movement
The burgeoning Romantic spirit and its empathy with the past, allied to European movements for national-cultural self-government, was to have an increasingly important role in developments in both the literary-historical and the political arenas. On the influence of Romanticism in Ireland Professor Rafroidi writes:

> With its taste for Celtism, it made of Ireland a fashionable subject that, in its absence, the natives would not have dreamed of exploiting.... Concerned with local cultures, Christian and Medieval traditions, it prompted a treasure hunt which all obscurely knew to be in this case as fruitful as it was essential, since it led to the rediscovery of lost identity.[45]

Regarding Romanticism's love of the past, he adds:

> ... the past is the necessary condition for resurrection.... The Irish of the present would find sustenance for the most intimate and unconquerable part of their being in times long past. And the return to their roots was not just a folkloric reconstruction, it was an ascesis.... For small, indomitable, dispossessed and humiliated states, groaning under the yoke of a foreign invader ... for Ireland, the past and freedom became synonymous.[46]

In mid-century the figure of Thomas Davis (1814-1845), Protestant liberal intellectual, and the Young Ireland newspaper *The Nation* (1842-) come to the fore. Emphasising the potential of the past as a source of inspiration and pride, Davis regarded Irish music, folklore, nomenclature, heroes, customs, characteristics, dress, literature and especially history and language, as a dynamic reservoir to which all Irish people had unique access and responsibility. He sought to combine material advancement with intellectual-spiritual growth, spoke against the debilitating forces of 'Anglicisation'[47] and replaced O'Connell's utilitarian attitude to the language with the manifesto that: 'A people without a language of its own is only half a nation. A nation should guard its language more than its territories.... To lose your native tongue, and learn that of an alien, is the worst badge of conquest — it is the chain on the soul.'[48]

---

45 Rafroidi (1980), *op. cit.* xxvi.
46 *ibid.* xxvi, 148-9.
47 *Vid. Essays by Thomas Davis*, ed.D. J. O'Donoghue (Dundalk 1914) 388.
48 'Our National Language' in *The Nation* 1 April 1843. Moody (1966), *op. cit.* remarks that Davis 'had an intuitive sense of the significance of the language as a unique expression of Irishness, as a vehicle of the Gaelic spirit, and as one of the richest elements

Two years after the early death of Thomas Davis at the age of thirty, Seán Ó Dálaigh (1800-1878) lectured on 'The decline of the Irish Language and Means suggested for its Revival'. He lauded the principles enunciated by Davis and said:

> To revive the language and make it general is not so difficult a task as one would imagine at the first glance. Let there be a respectful Memorial presented to the Commissioners of National Eduation to have Irish classes in their schools throughout the country, and this, once established, we might have some hopes of part of the labour being done. This, along with the classes already formed in the Clubs would go very far towards remedying the evil ...[49]

Ó Dálaigh, a native speaker from Waterford, was a collector of manuscripts, a bookseller, a publisher, an editor, founder-member and secretary of the Ossianic Society established in 1853, all of whose council members, president and vice-presidents, were requied, by rule, to be Irish scholars, and which specialised in issuing modern texts — poems and prose from the *Fianaíocht* — for a more general audience than that catered for by other learned societies. Hyde, who knew him as an elderly man and purchased some of his most valuable books and manuscripts at the auction held after his death, described him thus:

> 'Ní raibh éinne, lena linn, do rinne níos mó ar a shlí féin chun Gaeilge do leathnú agus do shaothrú.'[50]

However, other matters occupied centre stage during the following decade: the brutal effects of the Great Famine (1845-48), the sequel to the attempted insurrection of 1848, the agitation for tenant rights. The 1860's saw the countryside organising of the Fenians, building on the national and historical consciousness raised by Davis and Young Ireland. Though vanquished in the abortive rising of 1867 their influence continued on into the successful Home Rule electoral successes in the 1870's. Some of the Fenian leaders, John Devoy, John O'Mahony and in particular O'Donovan Rossa — who made a tour through Connacht in 1864, and was much admired by Douglas Hyde — were favourably

---

in the national inheritance .... his attitude to the Irish language was implicit in his whole concept of Irish nationality' (22-23). See also *Irish Historical Studies VI* (3/1949) 199-205.

49 8 November 1847; G 416 N.L.I.

50 de hÍde (1937), *op. cit.* 17. (There was nobody, in his time, who did more in his own way to extend and cultivate Irish.) He produced self-instruction primers (1846, 1853, 1871), two volumes of laoithe Fianaíochta (1859, 1861) for the Ossianic Society, edited prose and poetry texts for *The Nation*, the *Pious Miscellany* of Tadhg Gaelach Ó Súilleabháin (1858, 1868), and three poetry anthologies with English metrical versions by Edward Walsh, James Clarence Mangan and George Sigerson; *Reliques of Irish Jacobite Poetry* (1844, 1866) and *Poets and Poetry of Munster* (I 1849, II 1860), and *The Irish Language Miscellany* (1876).

CATALOGUE

OF

BOOKS AND MANUSCRIPTS,

ON

IRISH HISTORY AND ANTIQUITIES,

POETRY AND MUSIC, TOPOGRAPHY, PHILOLOGY, RARE TRACTS,

Maps and Autographs,

COLLECTED BY THE

LATE MR. JOHN O'DALY, BOOKSELLER,

No. 9, ANGLESEA STREET,

TOGETHER WITH

MISCELLANEOUS, STANDARD, AND ILLUSTRATED WORKS,

WITH VARIOUS EFFECTS ON ANOTHER ACCOUNT,

TO BE

Sold by Auction,

BY

JOHN FLEMING JONES,

AT HIS LITERARY AND GENERAL SALEROOMS,

No. 8, D'OLIER STREET,

ON MONDAY, 19th AUGUST, and Five following days,

COMMENCING EACH DAY AT ONE O'CLOCK.

DUBLIN:

1878

FÉIN-TEAGASG GAOIDEILGE.

SELF-INSTRUCTION IN IRISH;

OR,

THE RUDIMENTS OF THAT LANGUAGE

BROUGHT WITHIN THE COMPREHENSION OF THE ENGLISH READER,

WITHOUT THE AID OF A TEACHER.

BY

JOHN O'DALY.

THIRD EDITION, IMPROVED AND ENLARGED.

"Biaú an Gaoiðeilge fa mear mór,
A n-Áṫ-Cliaṫ na b-fleargg b-fion óil."
The Gaelic shall be in great esteem,
In Dublin of the goblets of rosy wine.
O'MOLLOY, A.D. 1677.

DUBLIN:
JAMES M'GLASHAN, UPPER SACKVILLE-STREET;
AND SOLD BY ALL BOOKSELLERS.
1853.

THE POETS AND POETRY OF MUNSTER:

A SELECTION OF IRISH SONGS

BY THE POETS OF THE LAST CENTURY,

WITH POETICAL TRANSLATIONS

BY THE LATE

JAMES CLARENCE MANGAN,

NOW FOR THE FIRST TIME PUBLISHED.

With the Original Music,

AND

BIOGRAPHICAL SKETCHES OF THE AUTHORS.

BY JOHN O'DALY,

Editor of "Reliques of Irish Jacobite Poetry," "Kings of the Race of Eibhear;"
Author of "Self-Instruction in Irish," and Assistant Secretary to the
Celtic Society.

DUBLIN:
JOHN O'DALY, 7, BEDFORD ROW.
MDCCCXLIX.

THE PIOUS MISCELLANY,

And other Poems,

BY

ταòg gaolach,

OR

TIMOTHY O'SULLIVAN.

NOW FOR THE FIRST TIME COLLECTED.

DUBLIN:
JOHN O'DALY, 9, ANGLESEA-STREET.
1868.

THE IRISH LANGUAGE MISCELLANY:

BEING

A Selection of Poems

BY

THE MUNSTER BARDS OF THE LAST CENTURY.

COLLECTED AND EDITED

BY

JOHN O'DALY.

DUBLIN:
JOHN O'DALY, ANGLESEA-STREET.
1876.

disposed towards the language.[51] The Fenians were active in Frenchpark and John Lavin, Hyde's Irish-speaking friend and neighbour was a member of the organisation. Some of Hyde's early compositions exhibit a strong nationalist-separatist outlook.[52] At the beginning of the 1870's the question of the Irish language in the National Schools began to surface at the annual conventions of the newly founded Irish National Teachers Organisation (INTO, 1868-), a number of whose members then prepared, in 1874, a Memorial to be submitted to the Commissioners of National Education.[53] The following year the Royal Historical and Archaeological Society of Ireland unanimously passed a resolution, proposed by the Rev. James Graves, at their April meeting in Kilkenny 'that in order to raise up scholars to translate the priceless Irish manuscripts, and to preserve the Irish language from being entirely lost, we ... strongly recommend to the Commissioners of Education the importance of paying for the teaching of Irish by the National School teachers, similar to Latin and French.'[54] One year later the Society for the Preservation of the Irish Language (SPIL, 1876-1915), was founded, composed of a judicious amalgam of willing, committed idealists ('hardworking humble men without much influence or aristocratic connections')[55] who undertook the necessary spadework, and the patricians of various hues who supplied the essential academic, social and political ballast for effective action. The SPIL developed the INTO Memorial idea and succeeded, in 1878, in having Irish placed on the National School's programme— as an optional extra subject — and, under the guise of 'Celtic', on the programme of the Intermediate Board 'as a philological subject'. If it achieved nothing else this minimum possible concession, in David Greene's words, 'brought about the abolition of the *scoreen* and of floggings for speaking Irish'.[56]

51 See 'The Gaelic Cultural Movements and the New Nationalism', Brian Ó Cuív in *The Making of 1916*, ed. K. B. Nowlan (Stationery Office, Dublin, 1969) 5; Ó Fiaich (1969), *op. cit.* 109-110.
52 See 'The Young Douglas Hyde', D. Ó Dálaigh in *Studia Hibernica* 10 (1970).
53 See *Irisleabhar na Gaedhilge* Vol. *III* No. 26 (1887) 18; Vol. *III* No. 29 (1888) 76-77; Vol. *IV* No. 33 (1889) 1-4.
54 B.P.P. (1884) *op. cit.* 11.
55 Phrase of R.J. O'Mulrennin, Hon. Secretary, Gaelic Union in letter 26 February 1888: Ms. 3253 N.L.I. See 'Risteard Ó Maoilbhréanainn', M. Ní Mhuiríosa in *Feasta* Iúil 1971; *1882-1982 Breathaisnéis a hAon* D. Breathnach, M. Ní Mhurchú (Clóchomhar, 1986) 86-7.
56 Greene (1972) *op. cit.* 17.

EARLY WRITINGS

Both the SPIL and its offshoot the Gaelic Union (1880-) produced simple cheap lesson books, headline copies, reading books and textbooks for the new school programmes. The GU, whose original stated aims included 'the preservation and cultivation of the Irish language, and its consequent extension as a spoken tongue' and the encouragement of 'the production of a modern Irish literature',[57] initiated a system of prizes to promote the teaching and study of Irish and launched in 1882 *Irisleabhar na Gaeilge/The Gaelic Journal* (1882-1909) which was to provide an important platform for writers, students and scholars for over a quarter of a century. Douglas Hyde was a member of SPIL and later a council member of GU. Dáithí Ó Coimín/David Comyn, a friend of Hyde's and a founder member of both groups,[58] had succeeded in establishing regular Irish-language sections in a number of newspapers. Hyde was one of his more important and consistent contributors[59] and it was in 'Fáinne an Lae' (The Dawning of the Day), the Gaelic Department of *The Irishman* that his 'Smuainte' (Thoughts) was published on 16 and 23 October 1880. It is in essence a public letter addressed to Ó Coimín and to various named correspondents of the column, in which he sets forth his own ideas and anxieties concerning the current public perception of the language, the possibilities for its advancement — 'leathnú ár dteanga i measc na ndaoine' (the extension of our language among the people) — and the responsibilities of the educated and wealthy classes in regard to the fostering of Irish culture. He seeks to encourage writing in Irish, castigates writers for their laziness and especially for unnecessary use of old, antiquated and complex vocabulary and constructions in place of clear, simple, plain diction — 'teanga na ndaoine' (the language of the people).

Hyde himself was an assiduous student of languages. Before he was nineteen years old he had already some knowledge of Latin, Greek, French and German. He also had a good grounding in Irish, as he relates in his diary:

do thosaigh me beagán de d'foghlam vivâ voce o Séumas O Hart an fear choimeáda na ppurtach 7 sul fuair se bás do bhi cuid mhaith agam, acht amháin nach raibh me abalta morán do thuigsint nuair chuala me da labairt é. Gidh

---

57 *The Gaelic Union for the Preservation and Cultivation of the Irish Language.* Council, Object, Rules, Means, Associations, Class Rules etc. (Dublin, 1882) 8.

58 See 'Dáithí Ó Coimín agus bunú Irisleabhar na Gaeilge', Breandán Ó Conaire in *Comhar* Aibreán, Bealtaine 1980; *Réamh-Chonraitheoirí*, Máirín Ní Mhuiríosa (Clódhanna, Dublin, 1968).

59 See e.g. 'Aguisín le Clár Saothair an Chraoibhín', Tomás de Bhaldraithe in *Galvia IV* (1957), 18-24.

go raibh me abalta gac uile focal bunáite do beith teastál uaim do radh, me fein. Acht anuair fuair Seumas bocht bás, fear-tíre is mo measamhlacht ⁊ cneastacht chonnarcas airiamh, ⁊ fear da tugas nios mo meais ⁊ grádh 'na thugas do aon duine-tire go foil ⁊ 'na bhéarfadh go deó, nuair fuair seision bás san mbliadhan 1875 san mí 28ú Nollaig shaoil me go mbeith mo Gaedheilg imtighte as mo cuimhne, acht ann sin tosaigh ag caint le bean Uilliam O Connele nuair thainic si chum na mbo do bhleaghan ann san trathnona, ni raibh me le fada ag caint léithe go bfuair me biseac mór ann mo teanga Gaedhelge mar rinne sí níos mo uasáid dam 'na Séumas, air mbeith do Seumas ro contrálta uaibhreach ionnos gur b'eagal liom iomarcuid trioblóide do chur air. Ar uairibh mar an gcéadna fuair mé focla ⁊ eolas o Seán o Laimhin ⁊ a bhean, ⁊ o dhaoine do chasfaoi orm ⁊ misi amuigh ag éunlaitheóracht ⁊c. Ní fada go raibh mé abalta tuigsint ⁊ labhart* (December 1878).

Although he had begun to attempt to use Irish in the diary by March 1874 it was not until he acquired — by 1876 — a copy of the New Testament that he began to master the written language. A sedulous student and an indefatigable book-buyer, he had amassed an impressive collection of books (Irish, Scottish, Gaelic and Anglo-Irish) and Irish manuscripts by the age of twenty.[60] His diary also reveals that his instinct and talent as a collector and rescuer from oblivion of unique aspects of Irish tradition was active by 1875 when fragments of tales and songs from oral sources begin to appear. In fact some lines from the poet Raftery's 'Cill Aodáin' were jotted down as early as 1873.[61]

Hyde's early essays in English, 'The Unpublished Songs of Ireland' and 'A Plea for the Irish Language', published 1885-86, are the early fruits of a stimulating alliance between, on the one hand, his informed reading, study and personal contact with the native Irish literary and folk traditions and his participation in the affairs of the Society for the Preservation of the Irish Language and the Gaelic Union and, on the

---

* I began to learn a little of it *viva voce* from Seamas Hart, keeper of the bogs, and before he died I had a good amount, except that I was unable to understand a great deal when I heard it spoken, although I was able to say almost every word I wanted myself. But when poor Seamas died, the most estimable and kindly countryman I ever saw, and a man to whom I gave more respect and affection than I have given to any countryperson up to the present nor that I will ever give, when he died in the year 1875 in the month of (28 December) I thought my Irish would go out of my memory, but then I began talking with William Connelly's wife when she came to milk the cows in the evening. I wasn't long talking to her before I found a great improvement in my Irish as she was more useful to me than Seamas — Seamas being too contrary and arrogant, so that I feared bothering him overmuch. Sometimes, as well, I got words and information from John Lavin and his wife, and from people I would encounter when I was out fowling. It wasn't long before I was able to understand and speak it.

60 See 'Printíseacht an Chraoibhín i Litríocht na Gaeilge', D. Ó Dálaigh in *Éigse* XIV (Samhradh 1971).
61 *Abhráin atá Leagtha ar an Reachtúire/Songs ascribed to Raftery* (Irish University Press, Shannon, 1973), Introduction (D. Daly).

other hand, the regular round of soirée, debate and discussion in which he took an active part especially from 1884 onwards at the Young Ireland Society, the Contemporary Club, the Mosaic Club, the Pan-Celtic Society, the Historical and Theological Societies, Trinity College Dublin, as well as the more informal get-togethers in student rooms and at the homes of his friends in the capital.[62] His diary is littered with references to these bodies, especially to the Contemporary Club founded in 1885 by Charles Hubert Oldham (1860-1926) who also founded and managed the *Dublin University Review*. Of the debates which took place at the Club W.B. Yeats remarked:

In Ireland harsh argument which had gone out of fashion in England was still the manner of our conversation, and at this club Unionist and Nationalist could interrupt one another and insult one another without the formal and traditional restraint of public speech. Sometimes they would change the subject and discuss Socialism, or a philosophical question, merely to discover their old passions under a new shape.[63]

Hyde, who had enrolled at Trinity College Dublin in 1880, did not take rooms there until 1883 and emerged in 1887 with degrees in divinity, modern literature and law and numerous prizes for prose and verse composition. Professor Edward Dowden described him in 1891 as 'one of the most brilliant and distinguished scholars of recent years.'

In 'Ireland after Parnell' (*The Trembling of the Veil*, Book II) Yeats recalls his first impressions of the young Connachtman:

I had met Dr Douglas Hyde when I lived in Dublin, and he was still an undergraduate. I have a memory of meeting in college rooms for the first time a very dark young man, who filled me with surprise, partly because he had pushed a snuffbox towards me, and partly because there was something about his vague serious eyes, as in his high cheek-bones, that suggested a different civilization, a different race. I had set him down as a peasant, and wondered what brought him to college, and to a Protestant college, but somebody explained that he belonged to some branch of the Hydes of Castle Hyde, and that he had a Protestant Rector for father. He had much frequented the company of old countrymen, and had so acquired the Irish language, and his taste for snuff, and for moderate quantities of a detestable species of illegal whiskey distilled from the potato by certain of his neighbours.[64]

In August 1885 the *Dublin University Review* published a short article, 'The Irish Language and Literature' written at the invitation of the editor by Justin Huntly McCarthy MP, novelist and historian, who appealed

---

62   There is also reference to a proposal to establish an Irish language debating society at Mr Hyde's rooms in the Minutes of the *Gaelic Union* 6 March 1886.
63   *Autobiographies* (Macmillan, London, 1956) 93.
64   *idem.* 216-7.

'to all young Irishmen to learn something at least of the language ... and to become familiar with the splendid stories of legendary Irish history'.[65] This was followed in the October issue by 'The Unpublished Songs of Ireland', which marked Hyde's public debut as a writer on Irish 'folklore'. Here he presents a varied selection of verses from the gleanings of 'several summers in central Connacht', offers practical advice to prospective collectors and discusses the subject matter, structure, provenance, genres and artistic features of these songs from the oral tradition, while emphasising the point that their fate was inextricably linked with the fortunes of the language.[66] It is a cautious and plaintive introduction to a subject in which he himself was to labour and excel in later years as a collector, editor and translator. Five years hence another essay on the same subject, 'Gaelic Folk Songs', printed in *The Nation*, April-May 1890, was to launch his major project on the Songs of Connacht, of which Chapters 4 (Love Songs), 5 (Raftery), 6 and 7 (Religious Songs) were subsequently published in book form. Chapters 1-3 (O'Carolan, Songs in Praise of Women, Drinking Songs) have recently appeared in this format for the first time.[67]

In his second article in the *Review* Hyde confronted for the first time in public the issue of the language. 'A Plea for the Irish Language' was composed in response to some editorial remarks printed in the issue for June 1886. In the 'Notes of the Month' section the functions of the Royal Irish Academy were under discussion and the absence of a 'scholarly Irish dictionary ... obtainable by students of our national tongue' was bemoaned by the editor T.W. Rolleston, who then continued:

But we should like to see more definiteness or more common-sense in the aims of *An Chraoibhín Aoibhinn* and his friends. Do they wish to make Irish the language of our conversation and our newspapers? Impossible, and wholly undesirable. Do they wish to make us a bi-lingual people in the sense that everybody should know two languages? But peasantry and artisans cannot be

---

65 Hyde's diary entry under 2 June 1885 reads: Leictiuiridhe 7 grindál. Bhí mé go diabhalta tuirseach. Chaith mé an oidhche i rúmaibh Oldham le Cherri Yeats Gregg éigin, Stocli Aine 7 Ó Cobhthaigh 7 Stokes éigin, ag déunadh cómhairle air spiorad Éirionnach náisiuntach do thabhairt asteach ann san 'Revue'. Chuaidh mé ann mo leabuidh 12.30 7 mé an tsaruighthe. (Lectures and grinding. I was devilish tired. I spent the night in Oldham's rooms with Cherry, Yeats, someone called Gregg, the elder Stockley, and Coffey and someone called Stokes, discussing how to introduce an Irish national spirit into the Revue. I went to bed 12.30 exhausted).

66 This latter point is supported by modern musicologist and folklorist Breandán Breathnach in his *Folk Music and Dances of Ireland* (Cork, 1977): 'One may deduce a rule ... that there is an innate relationship between folksong and language which inhibits adoption by way of translation' (31).

67 *The Songs of Connacht: Amhráin Chúige Chonnacht* Douglas Hyde, ed. Breandán Ó Conaire (Irish Academic Press, Dublin, 1985).

expected to know two languages except at the expense of both. Would they separate Ireland into an English-speaking country with an Irish-speaking country? But how seriously this would affect the free circulation of thought:

> 'Shooting in pulses of fire, ceaseless, to vivify all.'

What is there left except to treat Irish as a classic, and leave it to the Universities? Sufficient endowments will secure their attention to its interests.

The item then ends with this arresting non-sequiter:

Meantime it is rapidly gaining ground in Eastern Ireland. In Antrim, Down, and the City of Dublin the number of Irish-speaking people has more than trebled in the last ten or twelve years.

His biographer, Dominic Daly, describes Hyde's reply as 'an article of major significance in the study of Hyde's political and cultural development.'[68] To claim however, as Dr. Daly does, that it was in effect 'the manifesto of the future president of the Gaelic League'[69] is both inaccurate and premature. While enumerating the merits, suitability and value of the ancestral tongue, and presaging the radical loss and impoverishment of the distinctive characteristics and integrity of the Irish nation consequent on its destruction, the overtly defensive and occasionally pessimistic tone of the essay[70] exemplify the environment in which it was composed and presented, and its carefully restricted argument base illustrates the hostile social climate in which the young scholar wrote these first cautious words of advice and warning to those with influence in the intellectual-cultural affairs of the nation at a time when the vision of Home Rule was distinctly visible on the political horizon.

Large sections of this essay are reprinted, with some important additions, three years later as an appendix to his pioneering collection of folkstories *Leabhar Sgeulaigheachta* (1889). On account of his academic achievements, his family background, his personal courage and his first-hand experience of the living language, Hyde had both the knowledge and the confidence to take on any opposition in the capital, whose patronising or hostile attitudes, based he believed on ignorance or social-racial prejudice, he instinctively reacted against. The opening remarks this time also revealed his increasing irritation with the halfway-house position:

68   *The Young Douglas Hyde* (Irish University Press, Dublin, 1974) 64.
69   *idem.* 69.
70   The Minute Book of the Gaelic Union records: 'The article in the *Dublin University Review* was criticised freely, it being the general opinion that the Craobhín Aobhinn (*sic*) had yielded weakly to the materialistic argument and had not made the most of his position' (7 August 1886).
   For references to Hyde as 'a practitioner of art of the possible . . . trimming his sails to the prevailing winds' *vid.* Daly (1974) 213.

> Bronnta air an leabarlan Náisiúnta i
> Sráid ... Dáis, leis an ...
> ... ughdar ...

Leabhar Sgeulaigheachta

cruinnighte agus curtha le céile

le

Dubhghlas de h-Íde.

(An Craoibhín Aoibhinn)

.i. Douglas Hyde, LL.D.

ball de Chómhairle Aondachta na Gaedhilge,
ball de'n Chumann Pan Cheilteach, &c.

Baile-Átha-Cliath.

Clóbhuailte le Gill, Sráid Uí Chonaill.

1889.

The title page of a signed copy of **Leabhar Sgeulaigheachta** *presented to the National Library of Ireland by the author* good deal of management to get him to tell his stories. I always start by half a glass of whiskey and a pipe of tobacco, and perhaps a story of my own. One must be careful to start with half a glass of whiskey only, I have several times after much trouble and long journies prostrated my own intent by giving them a whole glass which generally puts them off their heads, but half that glass as a rule makes them go on famously.

Now if you start to take down the story verbatim with a pencil and paper, as an unwary collector will do you destroy everything. You will make the shanachie irritable, he will not wait for you to write down your sentence, and if you call out "stop stop! wait till I get this down,

A page from the manuscript of Hyde's Rathmines lecture, December 1889

It seems ridiculous that we cannot publish a book in our own language without introducing more or less of English into it. I had determined to publish these stories just as they are, without any commentary, such seeming to me unnecessary; but certain friends pointed out to me the advisability of adding some explanatory observations on the text which should prove useful to any who may use this book to learn Irish.

I accordingly write — reluctantly enough — this and the following notes in English....

The new concluding paragraph was equally forthright:

I do not think there is much to add to what I have said here, except to observe that it is a national duty — I had almost said a moral one — for all those who speak Irish to speak it to their children also, and to take care that the growing generation shall know it as well as themselves: and in general, that it is the duty of all Irish-speakers to use their own language amongst themselves, and on all possible occasions, except where it will not run. For, if we allow one of the finest and richest languages in Europe, which, fifty years ago, was spoken by nearly four millions of Irishmen, to die out without a struggle, it will be an everlasting disgrace and a blighting stigma upon our nationality.[71]

In the meantime 'Some Words about Unpublished Literature' was presented in *The Gael* (7/1/1888). Here he offers examples of 'those few folk-songs composed in English, which have spontaneously sprang up and taken root amongst the peasantry' and which he had noted in the course of his researches into the Irish oral tradition.

Folklore
Hyde's diary for December 1889 records the occasion of his lecture in Rathmines on Irish folklore. The entry for the 10th reads:

Ar léigheadh agus ag sgríobhadh gan dul amach. Chríochnuigh mé mo dheuntús air sean-sgeuluigheacht Gaedheilge. Dínéar leis an tSiothchanach. Buideal pórt, almas seampéin, glainne brandaidh. Dínéar maith. Annsin chuadhmar ag iarraidh an áit ag Rath-maighin 'n áit a raibh mo leictiúr le bheith. 80 Duine ann no mar sin. Labhair mé mo leictiúr gan a léigheadh,

---

71   *Leabhar Sgeulaigheachta* cruinnighthe agus curtha le chéile le Dúbhghlas de h-Íde (Baile Átha Cliath 1889) 213-29, 'Note 1: On the reasons for keeping alive the Irish Language'. Some six years hence, in 1894, he repeated this warning at the conclusion of a lecture given before the members of the Irish Literary Society of London, and subsequently published under the title: 'The Last Three Centuries of Gaelic Literature':

For if we neglect to preserve now for the Ireland of the future, the most interesting and valuable portion of our race heritage, generations yet to come shall curse our supineness.

But I believe the old Irish race has yet enough of common sense, of patriotism, of firmness to see to it, that our half million of Irish speakers shall never grow less, but continue to hand down for the delight of multitudes in a free and prosperous Ireland of the Future, the speech and accents of a great and historic Past.

uair agus ceathramha 'gá labhairt — an-mhaith. Mórán molta air gach taoibh dham. Abhaile ag an 11.30.*

The previous year Yeats had presaged the emergence of Hyde as a pioneering figure in the field of Irish folklore when in the Introduction to his *Fairy and Folk Tales of the Irish Peasantry* (1888) to which Hyde had contributed three tales and much advice, he wrote:

Mr Douglas Hyde is now preparing a volume of folk tales in Gaelic, having taken them down, for the most part, word for word among the Gaelic speakers of Roscommon and Galway. He is, perhaps, most to be trusted of all. He knows the people thoroughly. Others see a phase of Irish life; he understands all its elements. His work is neither humorous nor mournful; it is simply life.

The publication of *Leabhar Sgeulaigheachta* (1889) and *Beside the Fire* (1890) confirmed his growing stature both as a collector and scholar. Terence McCaughey describes him as a 'researcher of quite extraordinary concentration when it came to the study of the oral tradition which 19th century prejudice could scarcely bring itself to dignify with the status of scholarship' (*Hibernia*, 26 April 1974). In endeavouring 'to be a little more accurate than my predecessors, and to give the *exact language* of my informants, together with their names and various localities'[72] he brought more truthful and 'scientific' criteria to bear on the collecting, study and presentation of Irish folklore. His careful, stylish and idiomatic translations were also highly praised. In his review of *Beside the Fire*, 'Dr Hyde's incomparable little book', Yeats remarked: 'He has caught and faithfully reproduced the peasant idiom and phrase. In becoming scientifically accurate, he has not ceased to be a man of letters. His fifteen translations from traditional Gaelic originals are models of what such translations should be.... The result is many pages in which you can hear in imagination the very voice of the sennachie, and almost smell the smoke of his turf fire' (*National Observer*, 28 February 1891). Professor Alan Bliss has described these translations as 'the first use of Anglo-Irish as a literary medium.'[73]

---

* Reading and writing without going out. I finished my composition on old Irish storytelling. Dinner with Sheehan. A bottle of port, ulmas champagne, a glass of brandy. A good dinner. Then we set off to look for a place in Rathmines where my lecture was to be held. 80 people, or thereabouts. I spoke my lecture without reading it, speaking for an hour and a quarter — very good. Much praise on every side for me. Home at 11.30.

72 *Beside the Fire: a collection of Irish Gaelic folk stories* edited, translated, and annotated by Douglas Hyde, LLD, MRIA (An Chraoibhín Aoibhinn) . . . (London 1890) xvii.
73 'The Language of Synge' in *J.M. Synge: Centenary Papers*, ed. M. Harmon (Dolmen Press, Dublin, 1972) 36. Lester Connor speaks of these stories having 'influenced every Irish short story writer thereafter, including Yeats himself, Padraic Colum, James Stephens, Frank O'Connor and more.' (Yeats International Summer School, Sligo, 1971).

It was in 1890 also that he initiated his project to publish the Songs of Connacht.[74] The enterprise began with the first three chapters appearing in *The Nation* (17 May — 29 November), preceded by the essay 'Gaelic Folk Songs'(26 April-10 May) in which he introduces his readers to the *genre*, distinguishes between the literary productions of the professional poets, the classical songs and the genuine folk songs, and pays particular attention to the Love songs and Drinking songs which he illustrates with over two dozen extracts accompanied by his own skilful verse translations.

Hyde spent the 1890-1891 academic year (October-May) as interim professor of modern languages, teaching English, French and German, at the University of New Brunswick, Fredericton, Canada. During the Christmas vacation he set out on a hunting trip which furnished him with further folklore material, and which he describes in his diary:

On St. Stephen's day I started on a hunting expedition with dá ógánach as an mbaile seó darbh ainm Chesnutt agus Randolph, ceannuighthe saidhbhir agus an dara fear aca ag dul a' pósadh inghine an Phremier, and three Indians or half breeds, for a place called Guspereaux between forty and 50 miles from Fredericton where there were said to be lots of caribou. We brought with us a tent and lots of provisions and taboggans. We drove with a team of horses on a big sleigh 42 miles and though we started at 8 in the morning we only got to the last house in the settlement at midnight. Thainig an fear an tighe, D'Arcy no Uilliam O Dorchuidh sean Éireannach as chondaé Cillcainnigh amach ague é lom nocht gan sgríd air. We invaded the house, hunted the daughters who were sleeping in the kitchen round the stove, and passed the night there. Next day we started in a snow storm for a point some miles further in among the woods. We were hauled in by another team, and pitched our tent.... Ní dhearnamar mórán nuair bhíomar ann san gcampa acht ag ithe an iomarcuidh. I shot a couple of partridge or ruffed grouse and three large porcupines weighing 25 or 30 lbs each with rifle bullets, but that was all.

We used to spend the evenings smoking and telling stories. I got many stories from the Indians and told them many, and learned a couple of hundred Milicete words, but did not get far enough to reduce the language to any kind of grammar, or even learn the conjugation of verbs. D'íoc mé dollar agus ceathramhadh do'n Indiach do bhí liom gach lá agus chosain an turas uile $45 dom no mar sin. I left the others behind me and came home for the opening of the college on Jan 8 (?)*

---

74 See *Amhráin Chúige Chonnacht/The Songs of Connacht* Dubhghlas de hÍde (Irish Academic Press, Dublin, 1985), Introduction (B. Ó Conaire).

* ... with two young men from this town named Chesnutt and Randolph, a rich merchant, and the second man of them about to marry the daughter of the Premier..., The man of the house, D'Arcy or William D'Arcy, and old Irishman from County Kilkenny, came out and he stark naked without a screed on him.... We did not do much while we were in the camp except to eat excessively.... I paid a dollar and a quarter to the Indian who was with me every day, and the entire trip cost me $45 or thereabouts.

The following month he lectured on folklore at the Presbyterian kirk ('Spoke for an hour and 10 minutes, it went off well'), and subsequently had his essay 'On Some Indian Folklore' published by the *Providence Sunday Journal* (12 April 1891).[75] A previous essay 'Some Words on Irish Folklore' had also appeared in this journal (24 August 1890).[76]

New York Lecture, 1891
On his journey home Hyde sojourned with friends in Boston (3-9 June 1891) and in New York (10-25 June), in the course of which he met Fenian leader O'Donovan Rossa, Patrick Forde, editor of the *Irish World* and language activists O'Neill Russell[77] and Pádraig Ó Beirn;[78] was wined and dined ('Feustaidh agus uile shórt') by the New York Gaelic Society to whom he delivered a forceful address, 16 June 1891, on 'the present condition and future prospects of the Irish language as a spoken tongue'. His diary sets the New York scene:

15.6.1891 Lá áidhbheul-theith, glaine 113 san ngréin, 95 san sgáile. Cheannuigh mé gunna piléir le Colt agus peilleiridhe 7c air $20 agus ticéad go Niagara agus air ais air $16. Sgríobh mé labhairt air stáid na Gaedheilge 7c. Chuaidh mé san tráthnóna go Cumann na Gaedheilge. Tugadar féis air mo shon-sa. 15 nó 20 duine ann. Ag labhairt Gaedheilge. Suipeur deas aca. Fíon le leac oidhre tríd agus puinnse. D'ólamar go leor. Bhí sé labhairt ann san nGaedheilg agus an oiread nó níos mó i mBeurla agus iad uile dom mholadh-sa. D'fhanamar ag caint 's ag ól go di a 3 air maidin. Ní raibh mise air meisge acht do bhí mo sháith ólta agam. Tháinig seisear aca abhaile don teach ósta liom ag an 4 a.m.

75 In his annual synopsis for 1891 Hyde wrote: 'Níor sgríobh mé mórán and bhl(iain) so. Sgríobh mé aon artiogal nó dó air sgéuluigheacht na Milisíteach, ach níor sgríobh mé acht cuig nò sé de dhántaibh beaga 7 sórt deuntúis air Chéiting. Thainig mo leabhar 'Cois na Teineadh' amach le Nutt san Earrach. Thosaigh mé ag fóghlaim Anglo-Saixís 7 rinneas cuid mhaith de sin. Sé an nidh is fearr do rinneas.' (I did not write much this year. I wrote an article or two on the story-telling of the Milicetes, but I wrote only five or six small poems and a sort of a piece on Keating. My book 'Beside the Fire' was brought out by Nutt in the Spring. I began learning Anglo-Saxon and did a good deal of that. That was the best thing I did).

76 This essay and the Rathmines lecture provide the main substance of the Preface to *Beside the Fire* (1890). Some other of his American articles are detailed in 'From the Little Branch to the New Island', H. Reynolds in *Dublin Magazine* (Oct.-Dec.) 1938.

77 See *Réamhchonraitheoirí* Máirín Ní Mhuiríosa (Clódhanna, Dublin, 1968) 39-52; *Mise agus an Connradh, op. cit.* 44-6, 162-7.

78 See 'Pádraig Ó Beirn: Fear a d'fhill', Breandán Ó Conaire in *Go Meiriceá Siar*, eag. S Ó hAnnracháin (Clóchomhar, Dublin, 1979).

16.6.1891 Tháinig an Ruiseullach faoi mo dhéin agus rug sé leis mé go Mlle. Carusi gan aon bhiadh d'ithe. Labhras léithe agus d'fháisg sí mo lámh go carthanach agus go gradhamhuil agus thug rós dam. Luidh mé air mo leabuidh i meadhon laé. Glaine aimsire 100 san sgáile. Stoirm ann sin. Cruinniughadh mór ag Cumann na Gaedhilge san tráthnóna. Rinne mise labhairt i mBeurla agus i nGaedheilge. Colman san gcathaoir. Bhí duine ann do phóg mo lámh, agus chraith gach aon aca lámha liom. Abhaile ag an 12. Deochanna.*

Two years later, in response to an invitation from Eoin Mac Néill to what turned out to be the inaugural meeting of Conradh na Gaeilge, the Gaelic League, Hyde recalled this important lecture:

Go raibh maith agad ar son do litre cineálta. Tá mé ar aon intinn leat ar fad. Níl aon nidh ar bith is mó teastál le deunamh anois ná an Ghaedheilg do chongbháil *dá labhairt* ameasg na ndaoine.B'fheárr liom-sa, mo thaoibh féin, muirighin 5 daoine d'fheicsint ag labhairt Gaedheilge 'na measg féin ná deich ndaoine d'fheicsint ionánn a léigheadh.

Do labhair mé ar an gceist seo trí bliadhna ó shoin i Nuadh-Eabhrac i láthair cruinnighthe mhóir daoine agus dubhairt mé nach raibh aon chaoi eile leis an nGaedheilg do chongbháil beo, acht dream de dhaoinibh toghtha do shiúbhail ar fud na tíre ó thigh go tigh go díreach mar do rinne Riobard Stepháin nuair bhí sé ag cur na Féinne ar bonn, tar éis Éire do bheith fágtha mar chorp marbh ar chlár bog déal faoi sgín na ndochtúir. Chuaidh Stepháin ar fud an oileáin ann sin, ó bhaile go baile agus ó thigh go tigh, agus tháinig anam úr ann sna daoinibh. Is é mo mheas-sa, (agus dubhairt mé an rud céudna an lá cheana ag mo leictiúr don Chuman Litirdhea Éireannach i dtosach an tseisiúin) nach bhfuil aon chaoi eile leis an nGaedheilge d'aithbheódhughadh ná sin do dheunamh. Bhí gach uile dhuine ar aon inntinn liom i Nuadh Eabhrac

15.6.1891 * Extremely hot day, the glass at 113 in the sun, 95 in the shade. I bought a Colt revolver and bullets etc. for $20 and a return ticket to Niagara for $16. I wrote a speech on the state of the Irish language etc. I went to the Gaelic Society in the evening. They gave a reception in my honour, 15 or 20 people there. Speaking Irish. They had a nice supper (prepared). Wine with ice through it and punch. We drank plenty. There were six speeches in Irish and a similar number or more in English and all praising me. We remained talking and drinking until 3 in the morning. I was not drunk but I had my full of drink. Six of them accompanied me back to the hotel at 4 a.m.

16.6.1891 Russell came for me and took me with him to Mlle. Carusi. I had eaten no food. I spoke with her and she squeezed my hand kindly and lovingly and gave me a rose. I lay on my bed at mid-day. Weather glass 100 in the shade. A storm (broke out) then. A big meeting of the Gaelic Society in the evening. I gave a speech in English and Irish. Coleman in the Chair. One person there kissed my hand, and everyone shook hands with me. Home at 12. Drinks.

acht ní bhfuaireas aon airgead uatha leis an gcómhairle seo do thabhairt chun cinn. Acht más féidir cumann nó cuideacht do cur ar bonn leis sin do chur i ngníomh béidh dóthchas mór agam as, agus ní riachtanach a rádh go dtiubhraidh mé gach uile chongnamh dó is féidir liom (26 June 1893)[79].*

Later on, in his autobiography *Mise agus an Connradh* (1937), he referred to the *Gaelic American* (27 June 1891) report of his speech and its central message:

Deir an páipéar san gur labhair mé ar feadh leath-uaire i nGaedhilg sul ar chas mé ar Bhéarla do labhairt, agus ag seo cuid de théacs mo chainte mar fuaireas ins an bpáipéar sin é, agus é clóbhuailte i nGaedhilg:

Anois a dhaoine uaisle, má's mian libh an Ghaedhilg do chongbháil beó in bhur measg ní'l aon tslighe ná aon mhódh eile le sin do dhéanamh acht amháin í do labhairt i gcómhnuidhe — i gcómhnuidhe adeirim, eadraibh fhéin. Leanaigí mo shompla-sa impidhim orraibh. Tá mé faoi gheasaibh mar dubhairt siad ins an tSean-Gaedhilg, tá mé faoi gheasaibh nó faoi mhóid, gan aon fhocal Béarla do labhairt a-choidhche ná go deó, acht amháin an uair nach dtuigfidhear mé i nGaedhilge .... deirim-se libh-se, agus deirim arís é nach bhfuil aon rud eile leis an teanga do chongbháil beó, acht amháin í do labhairt eadraibh féin...

Ba soisgéal nua an soisgéal sin saoilim — bhí sé nua i nÉirinn ar chuma ar bith óir bhí go leór cumann ann ó am go ham, mar thaisbeán mé cheana, chum Gaedhilg do léigheadh nó chum láimhsgríbhinní do chlóbhualadh innti — acht

---

[79] Ms 10874(2) N.L.I. In an editorial on the founding of Conradh na Gaeilge Eoghan Ó Gramhna, editor of *Irisleabhar na Gaedhilge/Gaelic Journal* and professor of Irish at Maynooth since October 1891, commented: 'The idea of making our movement more popular and practical has long been in the air. It was put forward by Dr Hyde in New York two years ago. Since that time it has been touched upon more than once in the *Gaelic Journal*. It has now at length taken tangible shape and found for itself a local habitation and a name'.

* Thank you for your kind letter. I am in complete agreement with you. There is nothing at all which most needs to be done than that Irish be kept spoken among the people. I would prefer, for my own part, to see a family of 5 speaking Irish among themselves than to see 10 people able to read it.

I spoke on this question three years ago in New York in the presence of a large gathering of people and I said that there was no other way to keep Irish alive than that a select group of people should travel throughout the country from house to house, exactly as Robert (James) Stephens did when he was founding the Fenians, when Ireland had been left for dead on a soft deal board under the knife of the doctors. Stephens went throughout the island then from town to town and from house to house, and a new spirit came into the people. It is my opinion (and I said the same thing the other day in my lecture to the Irish Literary Society at the start of the session) that there is no other way to revive Irish than that. Everyone agreed with me in New York but I received no money from them to implement that advice. But if a society or an association can be founded to put that into action I will have great hopes for it, and it is not necessary to say that I will assist it in every way I can.

Letter to Eoin Mac Néill, 26 June 1893

48 LANGUAGE, LORE AND LYRICS

Eoin Mac Néill

Seán Pléimeann

Eoghan Ó Gramhna

Dáithí Ó Coimín

í do labhairt, ba rud nua é sin. An cumann chum Gaedhilg do bhuan-choimeád ní raibh ann acht cumann acadamhail nuair d'fhág lucht na nAontachta é. Ní chuala mé éinne aca ag labhairt Gaedhilge riamh. Bhí an Aondacht níos fearr. Do labhruigheadh an Cíosógach agus Seán Pléimeann í, agus dá mbeadh sé ar chumas na mball eile úsáid do dhéanamh dí go furasta, is dóigh go ndéanfaidís é. Acht ní raibh aon chumann ann chum na daoine féin do chur 'gá labhairt gur cuireadh Cumann na Gaedhilge ar bun.*

At the beginning of the 1890s, and prior to Hyde's 1892 Presidential address to the National Literary Society, notable contributions to the language-culture debate were made by a number of eminent politicians and scholars. In November 1890 Eoghan Ó Gramhna's essay on 'The National Language' appeared in the *Irish Ecclesiastical Record*, noting the contribution of distinguished Protestant and foreign scholars in the realm of Irish learning and challenging the educated Catholic classes to remedy their ignorance and lack of appreciation of 'the language and literature of their ancestors.'

'Does Education mean Anglicisation?', he asked. 'Can education, which ought to be a development of the power of the mind, have anything in common with a system which neglects and practically scorns that great power of speaking a magnificent language which children have in the Irish-speaking counties — a power which our foreign friends, after years of study, are glad to obtain even imperfectly.' Earlier that year, in a letter to his friend Seán Mag Fhloinn of the *Tuam News*, he had expressed staunchly optimistic hopes for the future prospects of the language:

Adeir an sean-scoláire, Seaghan Pléimion, nach raibh an speur chomh geal, geallamhnach dár dteangain le na chuimhne. Tá leabhra nuadha ag teacht

---

* The newspaper says that I spoke for a half hour in Irish before I turned to English, and the following is part of the text of my speech as I found it in that newspaper, printed in Irish type:

Now, dear people, if you desire to keep Irish alive in your midst there is no other way nor method to accomplish that except by always speaking it — always, I say, among yourselves. Follow my example, I implore you. I am under *geasa* (prohibitions) as they said in the Old Irish, I am under *geasa* or vows never to utter an English word except when I would not be understood in Irish. . . . I say to you, and I repeat it, that there is no other way to keep the language alive than by speaking it among yourselves. . . .

That was a new message (gospel) I think — it was new in Ireland in any case, for there had been many societies from time to time, as I have shown previously, for the reading of Irish or to publish Irish manuscripts — but to speak it, that was something new. The SPIL was merely an academic society when the GU people left it. I never heard any of them speaking Irish. The GU was an improvement. (Michael) Cusack and (John) Fleming used speak it, and if the other members had been able to use it fluently, they would probably have done so. But no society existed to put the people themselves to speaking it until the Irish Society (= Gaelic League) was founded.

amach go minic.... Ní bhfuightheá acht corr-dhuine (agus ba chorr an tÉireannach é) a chuireas in aghaidh na teangan anois. Gheobhaidh tú mórchuid daoineadh lé'r mian an teanga d'fheicsin faoi chaithréim arís, agus dá labhairt air aonach, air margadh agus air gach cruinniughadh eile ... creidim go daingean, dílis, gur féidir í shábháil, agus go ndéanfar í shábháil freisin, má dhéanann gach uile dhuine againn a dhualgas.*[80] (11/7/1890).

In 1891 the chair of Irish in Maynooth was re-established, and in December, six months after Hyde's New York speech, another vigorous article 'Why and How the Irish language is to be preserved' was published, also in the *IER*. Its author, Eoin Mac Néill, directly addressed the Irish clergy as the single most influential body in the country with power to cause 'the Irish language to flourish or languish or perish all over Ireland.' Emphasising the unique effectiveness of 'action and example' he set forth selected arguments aimed at winning the support of the clergy, 'who alone practically can carry out what the laity can only aspire to, or but weakly and partially effect. The laity who commonly speak Irish, are powerless to this end. The students of Irish are usually men of little means and much work. The leisured classes do nothing, and nothing is expected of them....'

In May of the following year two forceful speeches gave added impetus to the movement. In the House of Commons in London T.M. Healy MP attacked the 'gross absurdity' of the 'so-called system of (National) education', and assailed those who looked down upon the 'illiterate' Irish:

I denounce as an atrocity passing under the name of education a number of absurd rules the pundits have got together in the Education Department. If children are to be compulsorily educated, let it be in their own language; but to oblige them to read in a language they cannot understand and do not speak, is an absurdity.... When I hear of the Irish illiterate peasant, I cannot help saying that if I were compelled to live on a desert island with either an Irish

---

80 Ms. 3253(2) N.L.I. The activities of many diverse individuals and organisations, in addition to those already mentioned, may have contributed to the emergence of this climate of energetic optimism, e.g., the founding of the Gaelic Athletic Organisation (1884), the publication by Rev. E. Cleaver of *Duanaire na Nuadh-Ghaedhilge* (1885), the literary-historical writings of Standish James O'Grady and the folk-studies of Lady Wilde, the establishment of the National Library of Ireland (1887) and the public support for the language of Michael Davitt etc.

* The old scholar, John Fleming, says that the sky has not been so bright and promising for our language as long as he can remember. New books are frequently coming out.... You would only get the odd person (and it's an odd Irishman he would be) who opposes the language now. You'll find many people who wish to see the language successful again, and being spoken at fair, at market and at every other meeting (place).... I firmly and truly believe that it can be saved, and what's more that it will be saved, if every one of us does his duty.

illiterate peasant or an Irish Chief Secretary, I would prefer the Irish illiterate peasant (laughter). These people are not uneducated in any sense of the word. They have just as much intelligence, just as much shrewdness, as you have, and the system of denouncing them adopted by English prigs and Philistines is utterly galling and destestable to me. Not so very long ago you put the same price on the head of a wolf as you did on the head of a schoolmaster. It suits you now to take another line.

Earlier in the month William O'Brien MP had delivered an address of considerable power to the Cork National Society in which he proclaimed that the battle for the language would be won 'upon the day when the half a million of people who still understand the language are made to feel that a knowledge of Irish is not an encumbrance or a reproach, but an accomplishment to be proud of, to be envied for, and to be transmitted to their children as religiously as old family silver.'[81]

Six months later Douglas Hyde delivered his own grand salvo before the National Literary Society. Reports of the immediate reception accorded the ideas expressed on his speech are strikingly contrasting. In *Mise agus an Connradh* Hyde recalls a friend overhearing dismissive remarks on his way out of the Hall, and the Chairman at the following evening's meeting of the Contemporary Club adopting a similar attitude. However, in a letter to *United Ireland* W.B. Yeats spoke of 'some enthusiastic members of Dr Hyde's audience call(ing) it the most important utterance of its kind since '48' (i.e. 1848, the year of the Young Ireland insurrection). The paper's editorial writer, with whom Yeats voiced his complete agreement, stated: 'I have no hesitation in saying that it was one of the best, and, what is better, one of the most practical lectures on a National topic I have heard for a long time' (3 December 1892). The *Irish Daily Independent* praised 'this excellent lecture' and recommended its publication.[82] The *Freeman's Journal* referred to the 'extremely able and interesting lecture' (26 November 1892) and the *Irish Times* was predictably hostile.[83] W.P. Ryan wrote that the speech 'might almost be described as sensational in its effect. It certainly deserved to be so, going as it did to the heart of a national evil which was preying on Irish life like a cancer.'[84]

---

81 *Irisleabhar na Gaedhilge* Vol. IV No. 42 (July 1892) 157-60; No. 43 (December 1892) 162-5.
82 It was published in 1894 along with addresses by Sir Charles Gavan Duffy and Dr George Sigerson in a booklet entitled *The Revival of Irish Literature*. The lecture was originally titled: 'The Necessity of De-Anglicizing the Irish Nation' [*I na G* No. 43 Vol.IV (December 1892) 175].
83 *Vid. Mise agus an Connradh op. cit.* 34n.
84 *The Irish Literary Revival* (London, 1894) 129.

Hyde repeated the speech in Cork the following January and many times subsequently.[85] By March Mac Néill's 'A Plea and a Plan for the extension of the movement to preserve and spread the Gaelic language in Ireland' had appeared in *Irisleabhar na Gaedhilge/The Gaelic Journal* and at a meeting on 31 July Conradh na Gaeilge was founded,[86] electing Hyde as its President four days later. Thus was established the next essential phase in the progress of the movement. And much more was to follow. A modern historian, discussing the 'many important but rather undramatic things' which grew out of the political vacuum created by the demise of Charles Stewart Parnell, recently stated:

The most important, perhaps, of all these post-1891 new departures was the Gaelic League. The league was the ideological breeding-ground of an entire generation of political leaders, agitators, publicists and administrators; it is scarcely an exaggeration to state that the league created the political elite of independent Ireland.[87]

Although Hyde went on to accomplish further *gníomhartha gaisce** during his lifetime — as scholar, poet and dramatist, resourceful campaign leader and fund raiser, literary historian and senator etc. — this famous oration served to kindle and inspire the social, intellectual, linguistic and education movement which, in the phrase of a contemporary, 'he blasted out of the rock of Anglo-Irish prejudice',[88] and firmly planted the early seeds of the 'psychical revolution'[89] which

---

85   See *Mo Thurus go hAmerice*, An Craoibhín Aoibhinn (An Gúm, Dublin, 1937) 19.

86   Although specifically setting out to promote in the Irish people a spirit of initiative, self-reliance and self-respect, to support and revive Irish manufacture and industry, to create employment and to halt emigration, the Conradh's point of departure was the survival and development of the language, as evidenced by its two initial and major objectives.

1. The preservation of Irish as the National language of Ireland, and the extension of its use as a spoken tongue.
2. The study and publication of existing Irish literature, and the cultivation of a modern literature in Irish.

In his introduction to the 1967 edition of Hyde's *Literary History of Ireland* Professor B. Ó Cuív comments that 'there is no doubt that the founding of the Gaelic League in 1893 by Hyde and a handful of enthusiasts was one of the most important events in the history of modern Ireland'.

87   Tom Garvin *Irish Times* 10 June 1986. Greene (1970) *op. cit.* refers to the League as the organisation which 'changed the face of Ireland' (114).

*deeds of valour

88   *George Moore,* Susan Mitchell (Maunsel, Dublin, 1916) 83-84.

89   This term is used by Professor Donnchadh Ó Floinn in his pamphlet *The Integral Irish Tradition* where he says:

Our people do not yet appreciate what a key-figure in our history Dr Douglas Hyde was. At a time of deep depression, it was he alone who saw that Ireland's most urgent need was not material but phychical. Hyde's psychiatry for the nation was to get Ireland to return to her own mind, to know herself as she had been, and to be herself again. . . .

was to germinate and regenerate vital areas of Irish life and letters in the twentieth century, vindicating the judgement expressed by his co-religionist from Co. Antrim, Ernest Blythe (1889-1975), some three-quarters of a century later:

Hyde rendered unique service to the nation because of his clear vision in regard to essentials, and because of his devotion and of his literary and oratorical gifts.... Few citizens of any nation have done more than Douglas Hyde to conquer apathy, revive true national pride, to turn the tide of affairs and set their people on a new course.[90]

BREANDÁN Ó CONAIRE

Do not associate Hyde's name only with the language revival. The revolution that Hyde caused among Irishmen was mental. He saw that the language was a symbol of that revolution and that there could be no sincere revival without it. . . .

It must seem like an exaggeration, until one tries to think of individual facts that would overthrow it, that everything that has been done in Ireland for over seventy years that had a smatch of honour in it came from Hyde's mental revolution, which was a mental restoration. The language revival; whatever was fresh in literature, whether in Irish or English; art; industry; social fashion and pastimes; most vitally of all, politics: the Hyde movement wrought a revival in all the chief departments of the natural life of the 20th-century Irishman. (3).

90 *The Gaelic League Idea, op. cit.* 39-40.

Smaointe*

Tógaim anois an peann chun beagán do scríobh i nGaeilge don *Éireannach*, ach anois nuair suím síos, an peann im láimh agus an páipéar romham, níl mé cinnte cén áit is fearr dom do thosú, nuair a bhfuil an oiread sin is maith liom cur síos a rith tríom cheann. Agus insan gcéad áit tá mé dul gearán a dhéanamh i dtimpeall báis na teangan seo ina bhfuil mé féin a' scríobhadh, agus i dtimpeall na gcoiscéimeann áibhéil-luath leis a bhfuil sé teacht gach lá níos foigse agus níos foigse don uaigh — uaigh na dichuimhne.

Má dheirim leat, 'Nach trua é' freagróidh tú féin, a Dháthí, agus tusa, a Thuigim-go-Maith, agus freagróidh Ó Flannaoile, Ó Cochláin, An Carbadóir, Failbhe Fionn, agus beagán daoine eile, 'Is trua.' Ach má chuirim an cheist leis an bhfear coiteann, is é an freagairt gheabhfaidh mé uaidh, 'B'fhéidir', nó freagairt níos fuaire, níos measa, an freagairt náireach 'Is cuma liom.' Déarfaidh an duine coiteann ainbhiosach, sin. Ach an fear múinte, a bhfuil eolas ar Sheanchas agus ar theangthaibh eile aige, déarfaidh seisean go soiléir leat, 'Is maith liom.' Agus má leanann tú don chomrá agus má fhiafraíonn tú uaidh, cad chuige is maith leis teanga a thíre sa riocht so, a laghdú gach lá, freagróidh sé (muna bhfreagrann sé 'gur cuma leis an tír seo, agur gur maith leis gach cuimhne a bhfuil ceangailte leis an dteangain, bheith dul ar gcúl', mar adeir, faraoir, cuid mhór den lucht múinte, agus go háirithe más ó Choláiste na Trionóide thagann siad), freagróidh sé, deirim leat, 'gur teanga bocht lag an Ghaeilge, nach bhfuil rud ar bith fiú léamh inti, agus nach bhfuil sé nádúrtha teanga dona mar í do choinneáil a háite in aghaidh teangan iomláine breátha saibhre mar an mBéarla; déarfaidh sé sin agus mórán eile den tsórt. Ach mo fhreagra ar an bhfear sin (mar a dhéarfadh ár sean-Heroditus féin, an Céitinn macánta), mo fhreagra ar an bhfear sin, nach bhfuil ceart ar bith aige rá gur cóir dúinn an Ghaeilge ligint bás fháil, mar gheall ar í bheith gan dada fiú léamh, sul tá sé fíor-chinnte ar dtús nach dtiocfadh linn cuid mhaith fiú léamh do chumadh agus do scríobhadh, dá bhfaigheadh scríbhneoirí Gaeilge an brostú céanna agus an cúnamh céanna atá le fáil ag ár scríbhneoirí i mBéarla. Agus dhéarfainn leis, go bhfuil sé féin agus a shórt ciontach den staid ina bhfuil ár dteanga anois, mar gheall ar a leisce féin, agus mar gheall ar an gcúram beag do bhí acu ina timpeall.

* *The Irishman*, October 1880. See p. 34. The orthography of the text, apart from the Editor — Dáithí Ó Coimín's — footnote, and extracts from *Lucerna Fidelium* and from 'Justin's' letter, has been, in general, modernised.

Thoughts

EDITOR'S TRANSLATION

I now take the pen to write a little in Irish for *The Irishman*, but now when I sit down, the pen in my hand and the paper before me, I am unsure where best to begin, when so much of what I wish to put down is running through my head. And, in the first place, I am going to complain about the demise of this language in which I am writing, and about the extremely rapid steps with which it is approaching every day nearer and nearer to the grave — the grave of forgetfulness.

If I say to you 'Isn't it a pity', you yourself, Dáthí (David), will answer, and you, Tuigim-go-Maith (I Understand Well) and Ó Flannaoile (Flannery) Ó Cochláin (Coughlan), An Carbadóir (The Charioteer), Failbhe Fionn (Fair Falvey) and a few others will answer, 'It is a pity.' But if I put the question to the average man, the answer I will get from him is 'Perhaps', or a colder, worse answer, the shameful answer 'I don't care'. The average untutored person will say that. But the educated man, who has knowledge of History (Literature) and other languages, he will clearly say to you, 'I am pleased'. And should you continue the conversation and ask him why does it please him that the language of his country is in this condition, weakening every day, he will reply (provided his response is not that 'this country doesn't matter to him, and that it would please him that every memory connected with the language should recede', as many, alas, of the educated, especially those from Trinity College, say) he will reply, I say to you, 'that Irish is a poor weak language, that there is nothing worth reading in it, and that it is not natural that a wretched language like it should hold its own against a full fine rich language like English; he will say that, and much else of the sort. But my answer to that man (as our own ancient Heroditas, honest Céitinn (Keating), would say), my answer to that man (would be) that he has no right to say that we should let Irish die because of there being nothing worth reading in it, before he is fully certain firstly that we would be unable to compose and to write a good deal worth reading if writers in Irish got the same encouragement and the same assistance that our writers in English receive. And I would say also, that himself and his kind are responsible for the condition in which our language is at present, because of their own laziness and because of the scant attention they have paid to it.

Agus go cinnte, is iad féin atá ciontach. Níl mé rá go n-éirigh le céad bliain aon scríbhneoir Gaeilge bhí fiú mórán; ach ní thig le duine ar bith insint cé an méid oibreacha breá do bhíodh againn anois 'nár dteangain féin, dá mbeadh an brostú ceart dá thaispeáint di ó dhaoinibh uaisle na tíre seo. Ba chóir dóibhsan os cionn gach droinge eile, na baird agus aos ceoil agus na stairí agus gach aon duine do bhí cosúil rud éigin measúil do chumadh, do ghlacadh faoina gcúram.

Is é sin an cineál daoine is coitinne i measc muintire an oileáin so; ar chaoi ar bith de réir m'eolais-se casfar an sórt sin ort níos minice ná aon sórt eile. Ach tá fós árgúin an-choiteann i measc na ndaoine sin féin ler mhaith leas Éireann. Is é sin, go mbeidh ár ndaoine níos eolaí, níos saoire, agus níos ábalta dá gcleachtfadh siad Béarla amháin, deir siad nach mbeadh siad scoilte ansin eatarthu féin, agus go bhfuil sé chomh maith anois nuair a bhfuil ár dteanga caillte i measc trí ceathrún na ndaoine, í bheith imithe go hiomlán, agus amach 's amach.

Sílim gurab droch-árgúin é sin, mar ní raibh ár ndaoine ariamh níos teo i gcúis na hÉireann ná bhí siad go díreach ins na háitibh sin ina raibh a dteanga féin acu go fóill. Och, céad míle mallacht! tá sé chomh soiléir leis an ngréin. Bhfuil aon áit in Éirinn ina bhfuil tír-ghrá níos fearr ná sa gContae Mhaighe-Eó agus Gaillimhe. Féach Roscomáin agus Liathdroim agus cuir i gcomparáid leo-san iad, agus feicfidh tú chomh láidir is atá an cúnamh a bheireas teanga sinsearach do thír-ghrá. Atá an rud céanna fírinneach i dtimpeall Contae Chorcaí agus i dtaoibh áit eile. D'ainneoin sin is ait agus is aisteach an rud é nach bhfuil i measc na ndaoine i gConnacht aon amhrán coiteann in aghaidh na Sacsanach, agus sa gCúige Mumhan bhí na hamhráin do chum baird na cúige sin chomh folaithe le foclaibh arda thuighthe (*sic*) agus chomh lán de bhréag-anmannaibh[1] (*sic*), nach raibh siad ariamh simplí go leor le maireann ar bhéal na ndaoine tíre. An méid acu do tháinig síos chugainn féin, ba i lámhscríbhinnibh do sábháladh dúinn iad.

Caithfidh gach líne agus gach focal in amhrán bheith coiteann agus aithnithe, más maith leat an t-amhrán féin a bheith coiteann. Agus ligfidh tú dom anso a rá, go bhfuil sé deacair agus crua go leor do thuigsint an chuid is mó den prós Gaeilge, gan trácht ar na dántaibh. Agus sílim go mba chóir do gach duine atá ag scríobh Gaeilge, úsáid do dhéanamh do na foclaibh is simplí, agus gan toghadh amach uile crua-focal is féidir leis. Tá sampla an duine uasail Ó Néill Ruiséal le leanúin insa bponc sin, agus caithfidh mé an rud céanna rá i dtaoibh T. Uí Flannaoile; ba lúcháir fíor-aoibhinn a litreacha do léamh. Táimid i gcónaí ag glaoch amach go mba chóir do na daoinibh-tíre Gaeilge d'fhoghlaim, agus í do léamh; ach táimid 'nár n-amadánaibh má tá súil againn go dtiontóidh siad ariamh ó Bhéarla crua go Gaeilge níos crua fós.

Is breá an leabhar *Seanmóra Uí Ghallchóir*, agus dúirt seisean uile

---

1 = ainmneacha.

And for certain, it is they themselves who are responsible. I am not saying that within the last hundred years a worthwhile Irish writer has appeared, but nobody can say how many fine works we would now have in our own language if the right encouragement had been shown it by the well-off people of this country. They, above every other group, ought to take under their patronage the poets, musicians, the writers and every person who shows creative potential.

That is the most prevalent type of individuals among the people of this island; in any case, to my knowledge, that is the type you encounter more often than any other sort. There is another argument very common among those people who wish Ireland well. It is this, that our people will be more knowledgeable, more free and more able, should they use English only; they say that they would not then be divided among themselves, and that it is just as well now when our language is lost from among three quarters of the population that it be gone completely and for good.

I think that is a bad argument, because our people were never so warm in the cause of Ireland than they were specifically in those places where they still retain their own language. Oh, a hundred thousand maledictions! it is as clear as the sun. Is there any place in Ireland with more genuine patriotism than Counties Mayo and Galway. Look at Roscommon and Leitrim and compare those with them, and you will see how strong the support that an ancestral language gives to patriotism. The same holds true regarding County Cork and other places. Notwithstanding that, it is a strange and peculiar thing that among the people in Connacht there is no general anti-English song, and in Munster the songs composed by that province's poets were so covered with elevated vocabulary and so full of pseudonyms that they were never simple enough to live on the mouths of the country people. Those of them which have come down to us have been preserved for us in manuscripts. Every line and every word in a song must be ordinary and recognisable if your desire the song itself to be popular. And you will allow me to say here, that it is difficult and hard enough to understand most of the Irish prose, not to mention the poems. And I think that everyone writing Irish ought to use the simplest of words, and not selecting every hard word that he can. The example of Mr O'Neill Russell is to be followed on that point, and I have to say the same regarding T. Flannery; it is a great pleasure to read their letters. We are forever calling out that the people of the country should learn Irish, and read it; but we are idiots if we expect that they will ever turn from difficult English to Irish that is more difficult still.

Gallagher's *Sermons* is a fine book, and he said everything he wished rud ba mhian leis, gan focla gallda do tharraing isteach. Féach anois difear idir an fáilte do cuireadh roimh an leabhar sin, agur roimh an *Lucerna Fidelium* le Ó Maolmhuaidh. Níl sé níos mó ná céad agus dá fichead bliain ó cuireadh leabhar na Seanmóir sin amach, agus cuireadh amach fichead uair ón am sin iad gus anois. Agus cad chuige? Ní hé go raibh an méid bhí ann níos fearr ná a bhfuil san leabhar eile. Ní cuireadh amach leabhar Ó Maolmhuaidh ón bhliain 1676.

Ní raibh spéis ag an slua ann. Agus bhí ceart maith acu; is é a ghearán ins an réamhscéal nó díonbhrollach don Léitheoir, nach dtig leis seanfhocla crua scríobh as na seanleabhraibh, mar bhí sé féin chomh fada sin imithe as Éirinn. Ba dheas an t-ábhar gearáin, go deimhin, é!

Cad é an gnóthach do bhí aige leis an seanfhoclaibh nuair bhí na focla úra aige? Cad é an gnóthach bhí aige leis na seanleabhraibh, nuair bhí seisean dul leabhar nua le haghaidh daoine an lae sin, do dhéanamh? Ach béarfaidh mé a bhriathra féin dhaoibh. Deir sé 'air son iomorro nach bhfuil acfainn nó iomadamhlacht san Gaoidhilig againn ó nach mó atámoid, ó aois mhic-fhoghlama anuas, a ngar do na leabhruibh acht imchian uatha, le brollach dá fhithchiod bliadhain tar leat, agus a bhfad o'n aois ealadhna, ó bhfuighfimis ár sáith do chomhraidhthibh agus do sean-fhoclaibh snasda bríoghmhara do badh tairbheach, agus ó a mbeith an teanga saidhbhir soghabhála air neithibh maithe atá sna teangthaibh eile, agus ó a mbeith an labhairt liomhtha. Air a shon sin má thig linn amháin an meud atá romhainn maille le conghnamh Dé do chur síos go soiléir sothuigse, ge go rachfamaois air uairibh air seachrán san bhfoirchiodal nó a ndísleacht na mbriathar, saoilmid gur cóir ár leithsgeul do gabháil tré fhad ar ccuairt ameasg coiccríocha agus achdrann, agus go ma lia do dhaoinibh deaghaithneacha deisgrédeacha ghuidhfeas orainn air son ár ndidhchill agus ár nduthrachta, iná bhias ar iarraidh toibhéime do tabhairt d'ár saothar air son a isleadh agus a shimplidheachta, óir dá madh a ndubhaigéin Gaoidheilge do chuirfinn síos an t-iomlán so, budh lughaide an tarbhadh dhéanainn don phobal coitchionn, neimhgheurchúiseach.' Más ea is rith don dubh-aigéin, mar ghlaos Ó Maolmhuaidh go ceart críonna é, d'fhág ár scríbhneoireacht chomh dorcha míthaitneamhach is atá sí. Tharraing mé an píosa sin ó *Lóchran na gCreidmheach* mar is sampla deas a scríbhneoireachta féin é, agus chomh fiú léamh is aon leathanach eile san leabhar. Is fiú breathnú, sílim, ar foirm na dtrí bhfocal so do scríobh sé, .i. fad = faide; isleadh = isleacht, agus tarbhadh = tairbhe. D'athraigh an teanga beagán ó shin mar ní fheicimid anois na foirme sin. Ach is fada sul scríobhfadh Ó Gallchóir focla cosúil le 'neimhgheurchúiseach', 'deisgrédeacha', 'soghabhála' agus focla eile neamh-ghnácha atá ins gach líne aige, mar dhea = sean $_7$ rl. Ba mhaith an rud go deimhin do chuir sé roimhe, ach amháin is é an trua nár lean sé é. Is deas an píosa scríbhneoireachta dar ndóigh é, ach le haghaidh na cúise is cóir dúinne choinneáil faoi ár súilibh feasta, .i. leathnú ár dteangan i measc na ndaoine, is gan bhrí without bringing in foreign (strange) words. Note now the difference between the welcome accorded that book, and that accorded *Lucerna Fidelium* by O'Molloy. It isn't more than one hundred and forty years since that book of Sermons was issued, and since then they have been published twenty times up to the present. And why is that? It isn't on account of what was in it being superior to what is in the other book. O'Molloy's book has not been issued since the year 1676. The people were not interested in it. And they had a good reason; it is his complaint, in the preface or introduction to the Reader, that he cannot write ancient hard words from the old books, because he himself had been so long gone from Ireland. That was a nice cause for complaint, surely!

What business had he with the old words when he had modern ones (at his disposal)? What business had he with the old books, when he was about to produce a new book for the people of that era? But I will give you his own words. He says 'because moreover we have not resources nor abundance in Irish on account of our not being more adjacent to the books, ever since our student days, but far distant from them for approaching 40 years overseas, and far away from the learned classes from whom we would obtain sufficient phrases (conversations) and polished vigorous sayings which would be advantageous, and from which the language would be rich and adaptable to good things in the other languages, and from which the vocabularly (speech) would be fluent. Nonetheless, even should we succeed in putting down, with God's help, clearly and intelligibly what is before us, though we should sometimes err (stray) in precept or in verbal propriety, we feel that we ought to excuse ourselves on account of the length of our sojourn among strangers and foreigners, and may the agreeable and prudent people who will pray for us on account of our earnestness and zeal be more numerous than those who will attempt to reproach our work because of its lowliness and its simplicity, for if I should put down all this in obstruse Irish I would be doing less benefit to the general undiscerning public.'

Thus, it is pursuit of obstruseness, as O'Molloy correctly and wisely terms it, which has left our writing as obscure (dark) and unattractive as it is. I took that piece from *Lóchran na gCreidmheach* as it is a nice example of his own writing, and as worth reading as any other page in the book. It is worth scrutinising, I think, the form of these three words he wrote, i.e. fad = faide; isleadh = isleacht, and tarbhadh = tairbhe. The language has changed a little since, as now we do not see these forms. It would be a long time before Gallagher would write words such as 'neimhgheurchúiseach', 'deisgrédeacha', 'soghabhála' and other unusual words which he has in every line, as being supposedly old. It was surely a worthwhile object (good thing) he put before him, but it is a pity he did not pursue it. It is of course a nice piece of writing, but for the cause which henceforth we ought to keep in front of us i.e.

206   *MOST REV. DR. GALLAGHER.*

n-grasa anns an t-saoġal so, agus an ġlóir śioruiḋ anns an t-saġal eile : Niḋ ta mise 'g iarraiḋ ḋaoiḃ-se an Ainm an Aṫar agus an Ṁic agus an Spioraiḋ Naoiṁ.—Aṁén.

AN DEIĊṀAḊ SEANMOIR.

AIR TAIRḂE AGUS AIR ĊOINGIALLAIḂ NA AITRIGE.

Bona est oratio magis quam thesauros auri recondere.

Ni ḃ-fuil óirċiste air bit is tairḃiġe 'ná an Urnaiġe,— Briaṫra an Spioraiḋ Naoiṁ aig Tobias anns an t-octṁaḋ rann de 'n ḋoṁaḋ caibidil deug.

Do sgríoḃ an File eagnaċ, Cicero, air na suḃailcidiḃ go ḃ-fuil siad ċo sciaṁaċ sin annta fein, air ṁoḋ da m-b' feidir lé duine a ḃ-feicsint le n-a śúiliḃ corporḋa, go líonfaḋ se lán d'a ngraḋ, agus naċ ḃ-fuil niḋ air bit naċ n-deanfaḋ mar ġeall air a m-beiṫ aige. Is féidir liomsa 'n diu an niḋ ceaḋna a raḋ leis an urnaiġe, go ḃ-fuil si ċo aluin, maiseaċ sin annti fein, air ṁoḋ naċ ḃ-fuil duine air bit tuigfeaḋ a tairḃe agus a milseaċt naċ líonfaḋ d'a graḋ, agus naċ raċfaḋ sgiṫ air ċoidċe aċt aig urcaiġe.

Do ḃi an Naoṁ oirḋeirc San Antoine a ngraḋ ċo mór sin leis an urnaiġe, gur ṫuig se a milseaċt agus a tairḃe ċo maiṫ sin, air ṁoḋ go m-buḋ ġearr leis an oiḋċe b' faide aig molaḋ agus aig guiḋe De. Ann ait luaṫġáire beiṫ air faoi éiriuġaḋ na gréine ḃi se dólásaċ, torsaċ, faoi sgaraḋ le uaigneas na óiḋċe ; agus giḋ gur lonraċ, soilseaċ, an niḋ an grian, agus go sáruiġeann sí gaċ créatúr oile a sgeiṁ agus a n-deise, ṁeas San Antoine gur mó an solus, an ailne, agus an ṁaise, ḃi aṅns an urnaiġe 'na únntí féin agus a g-créatúir an t-saoġail uile.—*Quid me impedis, o sol*

Canon Bourke's edition of Gallagher's Sermons

LVCERNA
FIDELIVM,
SEV
FASCICVLVS DECERPTVS
ab Authoribus magis verfatis,
qui tractarunt
DE
DOCTRINA CHRISTIANA:

DIVISVS IN TRES PARTES,

Prima, Continet Articulos Chriftiano credendos;
Secunda, Senfus Articulorum apud Catholicam
Romanam Ecclefiam;
Tertia, Methodum, qua efficaciter apparet veritas
credendorum, & falfitas errorum Orthodoxiæ
contradicentium.

AVTHORE
FR. FRANCISCO MOLLOY
HIBERNO MEDENSI

Ordinis Minorum Strictioris Obferuantiæ S. Theologiæ
in Collegio Sancti Ifidori de Vrbe Primario
Profeffore, & Lectore Iubilato.

ROMÆ,
Typis Sacræ Congreg. de Propagandæ Fide,
MDCLXXVI.

Lucerna Fidelium

agus gan úsáid é. Níl aon ábhar is féidir liomsa fheicsint ag coinneáil na Gaeilge Albanaí suas ach go scríobhann a muintir uile leabhar agus uile rann i dteanga na ndaoine. Níl aon 'dubhaigéin' acu le dul ag iarraidh crua-fhocal as sean lámhscríbhinní meirgeacha. Agus tá fáth eile go bhfuil siadsan os ár gcionn. Scríobhann siad na focla mar labhrann siad féin, agus ní mar fuair siad rompu i seanleabhraibh iad.*

Fuair mé páipéar Americeánach scaitheamh maith ó shin, ina raibh litir ó 'Saorbhreathach' éigin; mo bheannacht air mar gheall ar a ghrá dár dteangain, ach mo mhallacht dá chaoi-scríobhadh. Caithfidh mé píosa de chur romhat. Dúirt sé i measc rud eile 'gidheadh is mór an meas bo chóir a chur air na cliartha cleas-uilte tá tabhairt eoluis gan dighealuidheacht' (cad é sin, níl fhios agam) 'dúinn, agus ag cur teanga tagarach na sean-tíre a bhfuirm a's a gclódh ughdarásach dúinn, ó nach tarcuisneach an nidh le casa linne, "Fearra Fáil; sinne tá do shíor dá reic gur míle feárr sinn 'ná an Sacsanach, nach uathbhásach an fhuaim a gcluis don fuar-spairt atá gan spré do thine na tíre ór — ab — as — é, na chroidhe na chreatalach. Nach cáinteach an casachán don té tá ag iomlat a ngustal an tsaoghail so. . . . Is aithreach liom a chairde, nach bhfuil an sprioch nó an t-imshniomh cóir ionnann a ngeall le mórán neithibh eile — a n-eagmhuis na Gaoidhilige — a teacht gnáthach faoi ár súilibh. Ó dá mbeadh aireamhsinnsir nó craobh-gheiniolach ag 'tar-lear-sibh' eile co hárd co hársuidh, co cian-tseabhach a's atá ag Clann na nGaedheal, bo mhór le muidheamh é air feadh na hÓirpe agus leathan-chríocha Cholumbia uile.'

Súd chugat an fhoghlaim! Súd an scríbhneoireacht! Ach, ná bí feargach liom, nach dtiocfadh leis an méid sin uile so chur síos beagán níos simplí, beagán níos soiléire, níos plánálta (más ceadaitheach dom, agus dlistineach, focal teacht ón mBéarla mar 'plánálta' do scríobh), nach dtiocfadh leis a smaointe maithe tírghrácha do chur síos san gcaoi do thuigfeadh gach uile dhuine iad. Dá ndéarfadh duine ar bith liomsa 'an dtuigeann tú Gaeilge' déarfainn leis go dtuigim, agus dá thaispeánfadh sé an litir sin dom tá faitíos orm nach dtiocfadh liom a míniú dhó; cé nach bhfuil ach an chiall is folláine inti, chomh fad is tuigim í. Is annamh casfar focal dothuigthe ort i gCéitinn, cé do scríobh seisean chomh fad ó shin, agus ins an aimsir do bhí Gaeilge faoi bhláth, agus dá cleachtadh ins gach áit den oileán. Agus an é sin le rá go gcleachtóimidne, nuair a bhfuil an Ghaeilge beagnach imithe ónár measc, focla níos airde agus níos doimhne ná Céitinn féin. Nuair a deirim gur furas Céitinn do thuigsint, tá mé ag caint i dtimpeall a Staire, agus ní i dtimpeall a leabhar luachmhar eile, mar atá cuid mhaith iontu-san nach

---

* Agus b'fhéidir go bhfuil ádhbhar eile fós ann; iodhan, go gcleachtann siad na litre deighneacha Rómhánacha, mar mhór-chuid na hEorpa: agus, mar sin, tá a dteanga réidh do phobal na Gaedhealtachta a leigheadh agus a scríobhadh;gan a congmháil air leith a bhfolach le beagán do shaoithibh agus d'ollamhnaibh. — Dáthi.

the extension of our language among the people, it is meaningless and useless. There is no reason which I can see that is keeping Scottish Gaelic in existence except that its people write every book and every verse in the language of the community. They have no 'obstruseness' to go seeking hard words out of ancient withered manuscripts. And there is another reason why they are more successful than (over) us. They write the words as they speak them, and not as they found them (written) in old books.*

I got an American paper some good while ago, in which was a letter from someone called 'Justin'; my blessing on him on account of his love for our language, but my malediction on his method of writing. I must place a piece of it before you. He said, among other things '(extract from verbose letter)'

. . .

There's learning for you! There's writing! But, don't be angry with me, could he not express all that in a slightly simpler way, slightly more clearly, more plainly (if I am permitted, and it is legitimate, to write a word coming from English like 'plánálta'), could he not express his good patriotic sentiments in a way so that everybody could understand them. If anyone should ask me 'Do you understand Irish?', I would say that I do, and if he should show me that letter I am afraid that I could not explain it to him, although it contains only sound sense, as far as I understand it. You rarely encounter an unintelligible word in Keating, although he wrote so long ago, and in the time when Irish was flourishing, and spoken everywhere on the island. And is that to say that we will use, when Irish is almost gone from among us, words more elevated and deeper than Keating himself. When I say that Keating is easy to understand I am speaking about his History and not about his other valuable books, as there is a good deal in those which is not clear, especially in *Trí Biorghaoithe*

---

*And perhaps there is yet another reason, i.e. that they practise the modern Roman letter as do most of Europe: and therefore, their language is prepared for reading and writing (of it) by the Irish-speaking community; (and) not being kept aside in secrecy by a small group of sages and professors. — Dáthí.

bhfuil soiléir, go háirithe ins na *Trí Biorghaoithe an Bháis*. Ach ní thig le duine ar bith insint an mhéid do gortaítear misneach na ndaoine tá ag foghlaim na Gaeilge inniu, trí aon líne agus focal crua nach dtig leo fháil san bhfoclóir, agus nár chuala siad i gcomhrá ariamh. Chaithfeadh an litir sin san bpáipéar Americeánach duine ar bith ar ais, agus bhainfeadh sé an misneach go hiomlán ón té bhí ag staidéaracht ár dteangan. Nuair thagann an t-am ina mbeidh meas uirthi, ag beag is ag mór (má thagann an t-am sin a choíche), ansin ní ligfimid na seanfhoirme agus na seanfhocla dul i ndearmad, agus tiocfaidh linne an rud céanna a rá i ndá nó i dtrí chaoi, gan bheith ag tabhairt taobh le aon cheann amháin, chomh maith agus i dteangaibh eile. Ach ní hé an fheoil láidir sin atá a' teastáil uainn inniu, ach bainne bog. Táimid ró-lag fós le bheith 'gár mbeathú ar bhia mar sin. Is é an simplíocht atá teastáil anois, agus nuair a bhfuil eolas againn air sin, rachaimid níos faide le cúnamh Dé.

Níl ach aon rud eile le rá agam. Nach fallsa atá na 'Gaeilgeoirí'[2] a léas an Ghaeilge san *Éireannach*? Léann siad go socair, sásta, an mhéid bheag a scríobhtar ann, gach seachtain, leis an droing bhig a scríobhas, ach ní chuirfidh siad an trioblóid orthu féin rud ar bith do scríobh nó do chumadh. Níl sé sin ceart. Tá siad ag cur leatroim orainne a scríobhas. Ní thig le duine ar bith, ach an duine le Gaeilge, tuigsint an lúcháir leis a léimid gach Satharn an méid thigeas ód láimh, a Dháthí, mar dúirt 'Tuigim-go-maith'. Ar an ábhar sin éirígí! sibhse a dhrong fhallsa, nach bhfuil ag tabhairt cúnamh don chúis le guth nó le peann. Ná caith an t-ualach ar Ó Néill Ruiséal, ar Ó Flannaoile, ar 'C.D.C.', agus ar mhuintir onóraigh eile tá ag déanamh a ndíchill ár dteanga do leathnú, le scríobh inti. Ní fheicim anois anmanna[3] an Charbadóra, fear an bhéil bhinn, nó Ó Loinseadh, nó Failbhe Fionn. Bhfuil siad sin 'na gcodladh? Ba chóir a ndúisiú. Agus bíodh onóir (mar atá buíochas) do na daoinibh do chomhairthigh mé. Rinne siad obair mhaith, agus thug siad mórán cúnamh do theangain a dtíre i bprós agus i ndán, 'ag taispeáint í bheith beo' mar dúirt an bard; muna mbeadh a n-oibreachasan b'fhéidir go mbeadh amhras orainn an raibh sí beo nó marbh.

Do shearbhónta umhal,

An Chraoibhín Aoibhinn.

---

2 'Gaedheilgtheóiridhe' ag de hÍde.
3 = ainmneacha.

an Bháis (The Three Shafts of Death). Nobody can tell just how much the courage of those who are learning Irish today is injured by any difficult line and word which they cannot find in the dictionary, and which they never heard in conversation. That letter in the American paper would throw anyone back, and would completely discourage the person studying our language. When the time comes when it is respected by small and great (should that time ever arrive) then we will not allow the old forms and the old sayings to be forgotten, and we will be able to say the same thing in two or three ways, without siding with any particular one, similar to other languages. But that strong meat is not what we need to-day, but lukewarm milk. We are still too weak to be feeding ourselves on such food. Simplicity is what we want now, and when we have knowledge of that we will proceed further, with God's help.

I have only one more thing to say. Aren't the Irish speakers who read Irish in *The Irishman* lazy. They calmly, contentedly read the little amount which is written there every week by the small group who write, but they will not bother themselves to write or compose anything. That is not right. They are putting a(n unfair) burden on us who do write. Nobody, except the person who understands Irish, can understand the joy with which we read every Saturday the amount which comes from your hand, Dáthí, as 'Tuigim-go-maith' said. Therefore, rise up! you, the lazy ones, who are not assisting the cause with voice nor pen. Do not throw the burden on O'Neill Russell, on Flannery, on 'C.D.C.' and on the other honourable people who are doing their utmost to spread the language, by writing in it. I do not see now the names of An Carbadóir, the sweet voiced one, or Lynch, or Failbhe Fionn. Are they asleep. They ought to be awakened. And let there be honour (as there is gratitude) to the people I have enumerated. They did good work, and they gave much help to their country's language in prose and poetry, 'showing it to be alive' as the poet said; were it not for their works we might perhaps doubt whether it was alive or dead.

Your humble servant,

An Chraoibhín Aoibhinn.

The Unpublished Songs of Ireland[*]

The sympathetic letter of Mr Justin Huntly McCarthy on the subject of the Irish language and literature, in the August number of this *Review*, gives encouragement to draw attention to another and humbler field of our literature which few have thought worthy of being laboured in, but which nevertheless is generally interesting, and always instructive enough to repay any trouble spent on it. This field consists of the songs and folk-lore of our peasantry as preserved in the Gaedheilg tongue, which form a kind of literature in themselves, none the less real for never having been committed to writing, and which, owing to the inextricable connexion between thought and language, will last exactly as long as the tongue of Oisin lasts, and will die when it dies. After gleaning for several summers in central Connacht, round the haunts of Turlough O'Carolan, the last of the Irish bards, and collecting such scraps of old songs, ballads, proverbs, and stories as chance threw in his way, the writer thought that to contemplate the result from a literary point of view might possibly be of interest to some of those (he thinks, an increasing class) who take an interest in this oldest surviving branch of Aryan languages, which a hundred years ago was spoken throughout the length and breadth of our country, even up to the walls of Dublin.

There are considerable difficulties in the way of collecting old songs and legends, especially if the collector cares to be accurate, and to take down things *verbatim*, for we fancy that all pursuers of folk-lore have found how the appearance of a paper and pencil acts immediately as a species of wet blanket which overawes the reciter and helps to damp his enthusiasm and spoil his memory. He hates, moreover, to be questioned about words or phrases, and probably ends by becoming irritable if you insist on the explanation of some archaism which you do not understand, and to which he possibly had never attached any meaning.

Of course as it is impossible to trust one's memory to retain a song of any length, and as the time at which one first hears it is generally no time for taking it down, one must only be content to make a mental note of how many verses were sung, and comfort oneself with the hope of getting them at some future time — a quest in which the wily

---

[*] *Dublin University Review*, October 1885. See pp. 35, 37. In the Irish texts orthography has been, in general, modernised, and the Roman typeface replaces the 'Gaelic'.

antiquarian will find his hands enormously strengthened (in Connacht at least) by a judicious application of the cup which both cheers and inebriates, an ally which however requires skill in its manipulation.

We all remember the exquisite lines in which Wordsworth expresses himself on hearing a young girl singing a Gaelic[1] song in the harvest-field, the lines which convey to Swinburne's ear so subtle a charm —

> Can no one tell me what she sings?
> Perhaps the plaintive numbers flow
> For old, unhappy, far-off things,
> Or battles long ago.

This paper is written partly for the purpose of telling what she does sing about, or at least what songs are on the lips of her sister in the Connacht Highlands. However, it is generally from the old men and old women in the chimney-corner that one draws the best things. Sitting over the smoke of a turf fire, and discussing a piece of twist tobacco, which you share with the *ban a' tee*, you can pretty easily sound her as to her knowledge about the Fianna Éireann, and as to the songs and 'bubberos' (spinning-wheel songs) which she used to sing as a girl; and often she will feel rather flattered than otherwise at your noting down her verses.

As to the verses themselves they are generally full of simplicity and naïveté, and as such they form the most extreme contrast to the poems of the regular bards, which are refined and polished away to a ruinous extent, making, in too many instances, the sense subservient to the sound; for the regular versifiers have far too often preferred a luscious sweetness and a delicious softness in numbers and rhythm to sound sense and striking thoughts. The poems by the Munster bards printed by O'Daly, in two volumes, and the two large volumes of Hardiman (unfortunately long out of print), afford the student a very good idea of what Irish poetry is really like; but most pieces contained in those publications are drawn from MSS., and few from the mouths of the peasantry. It has always been the bane of Irish song that the bards lavished upon the form that attention which ought to have been bestowed upon the matter; and while the structure of their verse in melody and smoothness, as well as variety of rhythmic measure, exceeds anything of which an Englishman could form a conception, surpassing by far what we meet with in most modern literature, the poverty of the matter is unhappily often such as to render pitiable any attempt at translation, which, if at all literal, must only produce a smile of contempt. In this respect they resemble a good deal the collections which we meet in any Italian

---

1 It seems better to retain the old form 'Gaelic' when we speak of the language of the Scotch Highlanders; and when we speak of Irish to use the Irish form 'Gaedheilg,' which, however, has nearly the same sound.

canzoniere — delicious to sing, and haunting the brain with their melody

> But if in pursuit you go deeper,
> Allured by the beam that shone.

You generally find that, as in Moore's Lagenian mine, the sparkle has been merely on the surface. But with the Arcadian verses that live amongst the peasantry, verses generated from the locality and the issue of direct emotions and natural spontaneous feeling, it is quite otherwise. They are melodious, it is true, and rhythmical enough, but still there is a directness and force about them which we miss in the more educated productions of the last century. Some of them are love-songs, some drinking songs, some *caoines*, some dialogues, but the most noticeable feature about them is the entire absence of that narrative, orderly, faculty which so greatly distinguishes the poetry of Teutonic nations. The Celtic poetic genius is an essentially lyrical one, and has never subjected itself willingly to the methodic and deliberate ballad style. One might search long enough through collections of Irish poetry, both printed and in MS., before one could come across a single poem recording a series of events, either fictitious or real, such as the ballads of Scotland, England, and Germany delight to do. We possess nothing at all of the character of Sir Patrick Spens, or Barbara Allen, or Die Schöne Agnese. Even in the ordinary street ballads, which are written in English and sung at all our fairs and markets, we may observe something of the same inability to arrange events in an orderly manner in verse — in a word, so as *to tell a story*. Indeed where such an attempt *does* happen to be made, we may notice that it is nearly invariably through the medium of a series of reflections put into the mouth of the speaker, who, by giving utterance to his own feelings upon his state and circumstances, generally contrives to convey to us a little of his story also. This predilection for lyrical outpouring in the first person is sometimes productive of rather amusing examples of what Dr Johnson paraphrased as 'habits of speech known in Hibernian land: for example, in the celebrated 'Tá mé mo hulla' (to the tune of which Moore wrote his exquisite 'Like the bright Lamp that shone in Kildare's holy Fane'), the first lines of which contain the reflections of a doomed man in prison, waiting to be sent out of the world the next morning, we find several times,

> Tá mé mo chodladh is mo chúis dá plé
> Tá mé mo chodladh is ná dúisigh mé.

that is,

> I am asleep while my cause is pleading—
> I am asleep and don't waken me.

So too in the English poem on the death of Napoleon I, which is, or used to be, popular all over Connacht, and is couched in a higher tone than such productions generally are, that despot himself is introduced in the first person —

> I am Napoleon Bonaparte, the conqueror of nations;
> I banished German legions, and drove kings from their thrones;
> I trampled dukes and earls, and splendid congregations,
> Till they had me transported to St Helena's shore.[2]

Further on, however, the conqueror of nations, with something like an appeal *ad misericordiam*, bewails himself as lying in his lonesome grave.

It is curious that there exist (that is in the mouths of the people) so few war songs and patriotic chants, and that very little hatred of the Sassanach is displayed in them. The very name of the colour green is not understood as having any political significance, and an Irishman who knew no English would not understand what was meant, if informed that the Green had triumphed over the Red. Almost the only verses in which the writer could discover a political or warlike character were some to the tune of the 'Shan Van Vocht,' which he came across in somewhat a curious manner. When out shooting on a bog, by the shore of a lake, he noticed a smoke rising from the heather, and upon going forward his foot slipped down between two planks covered with heath, which turned out to be the roof of a stillhouse carefully excavated in a turf-bank, in which half a dozen or a dozen worthies were congregated round an enormous pot, waiting for the 'doubling' of the poteen, which was running in single bright drops from a straw stuck in the top of the 'worm'. He was greeted with the hospitable cry of 'dhá dheoch do fhear na gaoithe,' literally, 'two drinks to the man of the wind,' which, in the highly figurative language of the Gaedheal, means that the chance comer who is *blown in*, as it were, upon the company, should get a double bumper; and immediately a 'noggin' of the raw drink was applied to his lips in a delf cup of amazing thickness which seemed to have already gone the rounds of the company more than once. Immediately afterwards an old man began to sing —

> Mo léan gan tú i mB'láthluain agam,
>   Ars an tSean Bhean Bhocht,
> Mo léan gan tú i mB'láthluain agam,
> Is Cúig Uladh mar dhúiche agam,
> Agus dhéanfainn ruaille-buaille
>   Leis an tSean Bhean Bhocht.

---

[2] The rhyme between 'thrones' and 'shore' is quite sufficient to content an Irish peasant, who, following the analogy of the Gaedheilg language, requires only a vowel rhyme or assonance even when speaking English. Whoever would care for an example let him buy a sheet of ballads from the next ballad-singer he meets, and examine them.

that is —

> I would you were in Athlone with me,
> And Ulster, for an estate with me,
> And I'd make a roolya-boolya,[3]
> With my Shan Van Vocht.

and then followed the next verses in English, barbarous enough in all conscience —

> And I'll go to Clover Hill,
>   Said me Shan Van Vocht;
> And I'll go to Clover Hill,
> Till I drink a glass of gin,
> And I'll jine the Ribbon min,
>   Says me Shan Van Vocht.

Other verses, mostly allegorical, followed in alternate English and Irish, equally rude and more blood-thirsty.

But of all the verses in which the peasantry delight, the love songs are by far the best. Many of them are genuinely pathetic, and speak the very excess of passion in nearly all its phases — generally its most despairing ones. A few verses are jotted down here, nearly at random, from these unknown and unpublished songs, and the wish to preserve what a score or so of years will find disappeared off the face of the earth must serve as an excuse for reproducing the *ipsissima verba*, for slowly but surely those who know them are disappearing; those who sung them are passing away; and soon, very soon, the place that knew them shall know them no more. Here is a song in which a lover, having opened all his mind to his mistress for the first time, and apparently meeting with a favourable answer, becomes suddenly enraptured with the beauty of everything round him, and exclaims twice —

> Tá na ba ag géimnigh
>   Agus na gamhna dá ndiúl;
> Agus a chuisle gheal mo chléibhe,
>   'S leat a leig mé mo rún.

> Oh, the kine they are lowing,
>   And the calves are at play,
> And you, white pulse of my bosom,
>   You have had my secret to-day.

In another poem the lover seems to have been less successful, for he cries in agony—

> Is mar sin atá mo chroí-se déanamh píosaí in mo lár,
> Mar bheadh crann i lár sléibhe is é gan fréamha nó croí slán.

---

3 *Anglicé*, 'terrific confusion.'

> Oh! my heart is breaking slowly, breaking in the midst of me,
> As the roots on some wild mountain give beneath the lonely tree.

And again, he exclaims, that though he were nailed down, and lying for three months in the grave, yet his love could never leave him —

> Go ndéantar comhra clár dom 's go dté na tairní inti go dlúth,
> Ní scarfaidh mo ghrá go bráth liom, dá mbeinn-se ráithe san uaigh.

Another song sings the beauty of some 'ainnir na naoi n-ór-fholt,' or 'Girl of the nine Gold Tresses,' of whom her admirer cries with more than Celtic hyperbole—

> Nach raibh a Solas scéimhe
> I ngleann na Réaltan
> Agus lasadh céad i mbarr gach dlaoi.

that there existed not

> In the valley of starlight
> Such splendour of beauty:
> There shines light for a hundred from each gold hair.

The somewhat archaic *Reultan*, for the ordinary *Reult*, adds beauty and effect to the original of this verse.

In another long poem, in which a lover urges his mistress to fly with him to Dúiche uí Bhriain, 'O'Brien's Country,' where no one shall be able to follow them, he assures her —

> Beidh mé féin mar sciath
> Cosanta, id dhiaidh,
>   A lile agus a ghrian ag éirí;
> Mharfainn duit mar bhia
> An torc-alla agus an fia,
>   Agus dhéanfainn carthanas den iar-chraoibhe.

> Oh! I shall be her shield,
> And nevermore shall yield
>   My lily and my love since I've found her;
> I'll slay the wild boar here,
> And chase for her the deer,
>   And teach the weasels near to play round her.

This poem, alluding as it does to the pursuit of wild boars and deer, and to shields, must have come down from great antiquity. The curious word *iar-chraoibhe* the reciter explained as easóg, weasel.

Here is another verse from a lovely song, the 'Drinawn Donn,' in which a peasant-girl regrets having set her affections on an object too high for her. In the original it is very affecting—

> Is fear gan chéill a rachadh i dréim leis an gclaí bheadh ard,
> Is claí íseal lena thaobh ar a leagfadh sé a lámh,
> Cé gur ard é an crann caorthainn, bíonn sé searbh as a bharr,
> 'S fásann sméara 'gus sú-chraoibhe ar an gcrann is ísle bláth.
>
> He is foolish, he who attempts the first high wall he sees,
> When a low wall stands beside he could vault across at ease;
> The rowan-tree clusters be bitter, though stately the tree, and tall,
> Oh, the low-bush berries beside it are sweeter after all.

Tears actually stood in the eyes of the old woman from whom this was taken down as she sang the words.

The following quatrain is an excellent example of the versatility of the Irish language. It was spoken once by a young girl who had two aspirants for her hand; one of whom, though he used to come and see her continually, and enjoyed the countenance of her people, was not liked by the girl herself; the other only came occasionally, but during his short visits he made such good running, that, contrary to the wishes of her family, the girl determined to marry him. On the occasion of some popular feast her father desired her to drink the health of her first lover, which she did in these words—

> Ólaim do shláinte a Mhinic-a-thig,
>   Faoi thuairim sláinte, a mhinic-nach-dtig,
> Is trua é, nach Minic-nach-dtig
>   A thigeas chomh minic le Minic-a-thig.

Which may be thus inadequately translated:

> I drink the good health of Often-who-came,
>   Who-often-comes-not I also must name;
> Who-often-comes-not I often must blame,
>   That he comes not as often as Often-who-came.

We have already taken up so much space that we have no room left for noticing the various convivial songs, 'caoines', and dialogues which, together with his love songs, appeal most powerfully to the aesthetic taste of the Irish peasant. Throughout the whole of them there exists something adventurous and unrealistic, and this tone of theirs, together with their general morality and stainlessness of sentiment, make them the very antipodes of the vulgar effusions which find such favour with his brother Hodge in England. Every separate locality has its own favourite traditions, songs, and stories, often descending to us from the dim twilight of antiquity; and whoever will take the pains to examine them will find them remarkable for a generosity of sentiment and an absence of vulgarity, which have done much to leave their impress upon the character of our nation. But, alas! all these traditions are so inextricably bound up with the tongue in which they are preserved, that as our language wanes and dies, the golden legends of the far-off centuries fade and pass away. No one sees their influence upon culture; no one sees their educational power; no one puts out a hand to arrest them ere they depart for ever.

A Plea for the Irish Language[*]

In the June number of this *Review* there were published some editorial remarks to the effect that it would be wholly undesirable to make use of the Irish language any longer, either in newspapers or conversation, and it is apparently the wish of the writer that we should cease to employ it for the future as a means of communicating our thoughts either in speech or writing. This was coupled with a complaint, perhaps a just one, of the indefiniteness of the aims of those who wish to preserve the language.

Rousseau at the beginning of his Emile lays it down as a rule that the first question a young child should be taught to ask about what it does not understand, is '*à quoi cela est-il bon?*' and in truth every one, as the world runs now-a-days, must be prepared with an answer to this horrible *cui bono*. And yet it is frequently more easy to ask the question than to answer it. When in a restless mood one flings oneself down at the piano and runs his fingers over the keys, it is easy to ask him *cui bono*, it is hard to answer it. He feels his whole soul go out to the music, he cannot leave off, it satisfies him. And yet even he if forced to put his feelings into words would be able, though it would be irksome to him, to explain why he did it. And so too we, when we are asked why it is we sing Irish songs, write Irish verses, or speak the Irish language, find ourselves compelled, though unwillingly, to give cold categorical reasons for that which we had considered merely natural, and hence it is that I cannot avoid saying a few words in depreciation of the editorial censure, and explaining why it is I do not share the wish to see my language dead and decently buried — to 'leave it to the universities,' as they call it. We know what that means. We have seen our very numerous, very ancient and very interesting MSS. handed over to the safe keeping of the colleges already. There they lie in their companies:

> No one wakes them, they are keeping
> Royal state and semblance still,

the mildew on their pages, the dust upon their covers, in the utmost repose and dignity, where we are requested to leave them, 'to the universities,' — where their placid rest may be disturbed only once or twice in a generation.

[*] *Dublin University Review*, August 1886. See pp. 35, 37.

Now if we allow our living language to die out, it is almost a certainty that we condemn our literary records to remain in obscurity. All our great scholars, nearly all those who have done anything for the elucidation of our MSS.. O'Connor of Ballingar, O'Donovan, O'Curry, Petrie, Hennessy, all these spoke the language naturally from their cradle, and had it not been so they would never have been able to accomplish the work they did, a work which first made is possible for a Jubainville or a Windisch to prosecute their Celtic studies with any success.

There is no use in arguing the advantage of making Irish the language of our newspapers and clubs, because that is and ever shall be an impossibility; but for several reasons we wish to arrest the language in its downward path, and if we cannot spread it (as I do not believe we very much can), we will at least prevent it from dying out, and make sure that those who speak it now, will also transmit it unmodified to their descendants.

Here again in you materialistic *cui bono*, and I must candidly and honestly confess, that what I advocate brings with it no substantial or material advantages at all. It will neither make money nor help to make money; but I hope that this confession will not put us out of court with an Irish audience, as I know it would with an Anglo-Saxon one. It is not particularly easy to state my case, but my first feeling is like this.

To be told that the language which I spoke from my cradle, the language my father and grandfather and all my ancestors in an unbroken line leading up into the remote twilight of antiquity have spoken, the language which has entwined itself with every fibre of my being, helped to mould my habits of conduct and forms of thought, to be calmly told by an Irish journal that the sooner I give up this language the better, that the sooner I 'leave it to the universities' the better, that we will improve our English speaking by giving up our Irish, to be told this by a representative Irish journal is naturally and justly painful.

I do not think the Saxon language has greater claims upon the western peasantry or on myself, than the Irish language has, or that we should be told to give up the tongue of our fathers that we may better speak the language of strangers. I — and there are hundreds of thousands of Irishmen who feel on this subject as I do — have always liked my Celtic countrymen and disliked the English nation; it is a national trait of character and I cannot well help it; am I then to quietly fall in with the wishes of those milk-and-water, would-be cosmopolitan, pseudo-international patriots who would make out of our country a lesser England lying to the west of Great Britain? I should be sorry to see them succeed. Englishmen have very noble and excellent qualities which I should like to see imitated here, but I should not like to imitate them in everything. I like our own habits and character better, they are more consonant to my nature; I like our own turn of thought, our own characteristics, and above all I like our own language and do not wish to see the effacing hand of cosmopolitanism prevail against it. I cannot conceive a more acute pain in the power of sentiment to inflict than that which I should feel if, after a life passed in England or the Colonies or India, I were to come back to my native mountains and find that the indifference or the actual discouragement of our leaders had succeeded in destroying the language of my childhood, and with it the tales, the traditions, the legends, the imaginations, with which my cradle had been surrounded.

I do not think it would be for the advantage of our race to let our language die. I have had some experience of my Celtic countrymen, and I most unhesitatingly affirm that those who continue to speak their own language are in every way the intellectual and generally the moral superiors of those who have allowed it to die out. When a locality allows Irish to die out of it the people lose nearly all those distinctive characteristics which make them so lovable and so courteous. I have verified this over and over again, and feel sure I am asserting the truth. The reason of it is transparently obvious. When they lose the language they lose also the traditional unwritten literature which, inculcating and eulogising what is courteous, high-minded, and noble, supplied continuously an incentive to the practice of those qualities.

The saying is fathered upon old Fletcher of Saltoun, 'Give me the making of the ballads and let who will make the laws.' It is a foolish saying, but there lies at the bottom of it a germ of truth; it means that no laws can quite stamp out the spirit of liberty, while ballads of freedom are on every tongue —

> For these keep a record of those the true hearted
>   Who fell with the cause they had vowed to maintain:
> They show us bright shadows of glories departed,
>   Of the love that grew cold and the hope that was vain.
> The page may be lost and the pen long forsaken,
>   And the weeds may grow wild o'er the brave heart and hand,
> By ye are still left, when all else has been taken,
>   Like streams in the desert, sweet songs of our land.

It is exactly so with us. When Irish is the vernacular language of the peasantry there live enshrined in it memories and imaginations, deeds of daring and tragic catastrophy, an heroic cycle of legend and poem, a vast and varied store of apothegms, sententious proverbs, and weighty sentences, which contain the very best and truest thoughts, not of the rude forefathers of the hamlet, but of the kings, sages, bards, and shanachies of the bygone ages. Such a stream of collected thought as is everywhere found where the Irish language remains spoken, must exercise an influence on those who come into contact with it, as all the peasantry do, and such an influence must be an advantageous one. I, for one would be very slow to barter away this great and certain advantage for the hypothetical gain which it is alleged would then accrue to the 'free circulation of thought,'

> Shooting in pulses of fire, ceaseless, to vivify all.

I, for one, do not believe that the Third National reading-book, or the perusal of the *Weekly News*, which is amongst four-fifths of our peasantry what the 'free circulation of thought' amounts to, are at all an inadequate compensation for what we lose by laying aside our language. If by ceasing to speak Irish our peasantry could learn to appreciate Shakespeare and Milton, to study Wordsworth or Tennyson, then I would certainly say adieu to it. But this is not the case. They lay aside a language which for all ordinary purposes of every day life is much more forcible than any with which I am acquainted, and they replace it by another which they learn badly and speak with an atrocious accent, interlarding it with barbarisms and vulgarity.

The language of the western Gael is the language best suited to his surroundings. It corresponds best to his topography, his nomenclature and his organs of speech, and the use of it guarantees the remembrance of his own weird and beautiful traditions. Around the blazing bog fire of a winter's night Dermot O'Duibhne of the love spot, Finn with his coat of hairy skin, Conán the Thersites of the Fenians, the old blinded giant Esheen (Ossian), the speckled bull with the moveable horn, the enchanted cat of Rathcroghan, and all the other wild and poetic offspring of the bardic imagination pass in review before us. Every hill, every *lios*, ever crag and gnarled tree and lonely valley has its own strange and graceful legend attached to it, the product of the Hibernian Celt in its truest and purest type, not to be improved upon by change, and of infinite worth in moulding the race type, of immeasurable value in forming its character.

The native Irish deal in sententious proverbs perhaps more than any other nation in Europe; their repertoire of apothegms is enormous. It is a characteristic which is lost with their change of language and consequently has not been observed or noticed. Let their language die and not one of their proverbs will remain. Of the hundreds of stereotyped sayings and acute aphorisms which I have heard aptly introduced upon occasions where Irish was spoken, I cannot say that I have heard five survive in an English dress when the language has been lost. And if this is the case with aphorisms and sayings, much more does it hold good of the songs, the legends and the heroic cycle of stories. I believe for example that the character of the people has deteriorated in the east of the County Leitrim and in the County Longford, where Irish died out a generation or two ago. There Dermod of the love spot is unknown, Finn MacCool is barely remembered as 'a giant', Ossian is never heard of, the ancient memories have ceased to cling to the various objects of nature; the halo of romance, the exquisite and dreamy film which hangs over the Mayo mountains has been blown away by the brutal blast of the most realistic materialism, and people when they gather into one another's houses in the evening for a *cailee* (céilidhe — a night visit) can talk of nothing but the latest scandal or the price Tim Rooney got for his calf, or the calving of Paddy Sweeney's cow.

I have no doubt whatever that when a language like the Irish, Welsh or Breton, is replaced by another whose whole spirit and tone is at variance with, and hostile to, its departed rival, the race whose language is thus taken from them does not recover the change for at least a hundred years. I have found a much nearer re-approchment between the natives of Western Leinster where Irish has not been spoken for a great while, and the natives of Mayo, than between the natives of Mayo and their neighbours 80 miles away where Irish has only recently died out.

Those who have not experienced it can have no conception of the way in which the death of the native language acts on the thoughts and habits of the people, and though Dublin philosophers and international doctrinaires may talk grandiloquently about the impossibility of the ordinary peasant or artisan speaking two languages equally correctly, and though they may preach to us the benefit it would be to humanity and to the Irish themselves were they to consent to lay their language on the shelf, and to adopt a new one, we whose misfortune or fortune it is to live amongst the western or inland mountains refuse to be won over by such persuasive plausibilities or to believe, contrary to the evidence of our senses that the race has improved in any one way, morally, intellectually or socially by dropping its old tongue.

We are told that the keeping alive a language spoken by so small a number of the community is a barrier to progress and to the free play of thought, but for one idea, probably a vulgar Philistine idea, which would permeate us were we to adopt English exclusively, we would, as I have shown, lose multitudes of memories endeared to us by the traditions of five hundred years, lose all that beautifies humanity, all that makes us love our race, all that makes our life most worth living.

I believe it is at bottom some such thought that prompts gentlemen to attempt the preservation of the Irish, Welsh and Scoto-gaelic languages. I should be sorry were they not to succeed, and sorry for the reasons I have stated. I do not wish that those who take a patriotic interest in our language should be accused of being prejudiced visionaries who in the teeth of existing circumstances would attempt to force upon the people an impossible *status quo*.

I do not believe in resuscitating a great national language by twopenny-halfpenny bounties. If the Irish people are resolved to let the national language die, by all means let them; I believe the instinct of a nation is always juster than that of an individual. But this at least no one can deny, that hitherto the Irish nation has had no choice in the matter.

What between the Anglo-Irish gentry who came upon us in a flood after the confiscations of 1648, and again after 1691, whose great object it was to stamp out both the language and institutions of the nation, with their bards and shanachies and ollamhs and professors; what with the brutalized sensual unsympathetic gentry of the last century, the racing blasting drunkard squireens who usurped the places of the O'Connors, the O'Briens, the O'Donnells, the O'Cahans, and the MacCarthys, our old and truly cultured national nobility who cherished hereditary poets and historians; what with the purblind cringing pedagogues of the present century whose habit it was to beat and threaten their pupils for talking Irish; what with the high-handed action of the authorities who with a cool contempt of existing circumstances surely unequalled in an European country, continued to appoint English-speaking magistrates, petty session clerks and local officials among a people to whom they cannot make themselves intelligible; what with the hostility of the Board of Education who do not recognize the language of those baronies where no English is spoken even to the extent of publishing school books in it; what with all this and our long slavery as a nation, we assert that the Irish language has had no chance of showing its capabilities, or those who speak it of taking their own part and making their voice heard.

Our emancipation as a nation is at hand, a few short years will surely see the dreams of centuries fulfilled, and then it will be the duty — can any one deny it? — of our rulers to see that our language is treated as the language of any other country of Europe would be treated in like circumstances; to see that those who learn no other language shall be taught to read the one they do know, and that as much encouragement be given to it by the Government as is given to English.

I believe there is a very strong and real feeling against leaving our national language 'to the Universities'; artificial restraints have prevented if from growing here, but in America at least it is very powerful. A great part of the integrity of Irish nationality in the new world is due to the cultivation of Ireland's old language, which, proh pudor! has found a more congenial soil in the squares of New York than in the streets of Dublin.

So strong is the feeling in America in favour of an attempt to preserve what many people there feel to be the purest and most seductive thing that Irish nationality can present them with, that even the *New York Herald* the leading newspaper in America, opened its columns the other day to a portion of a speech spoken in Irish by some prominent patriot in New York, which it not only printed in Irish as delivered, but also in the native type. Have we lived to see it? Are they less materialistic over there beyond the seas than we are at home? Does the *New York Herald* actually do for us what *United Ireland* obstinately refuses to do?

There is just one other objection to be noticed, we are told that in learning English we are learning a superior language to that we are invited to leave off. It is so; but unless we learn it in a superior way we get no good by the change. My settled opinion is that the Western and Southern peasantry have a far better clearer and more flexible medium for expressing their thoughts than the Leinster and Ulster men have. For all the ordinary purposes of everyday peasant life Irish is I believe enormously superior to English, at least to the English spoken in Ireland.

When we see the Dutch for the benefit of humanity at large consent to merge their language in the German, when we see the Belgians throw aside their own and adopt French, when the Welsh are found willing to lay aside their Cymraig and become anglicised, then we, though we have a language which in the antiquity and extent of its written records is vastly superior to any of these, may also consent to fall in with the kind suggestions of our friends and to leave aside our Gaedheilg for ever.

In conclusion we may say this, that while our social and commercial relations make it a necessity for every man woman and child in this kingdom to learn English sooner or later, reverence for our past history, regard for the memory of our ancestors, our national honour, and the fear of becoming materialized and losing our best and highest characteristics call upon us imperatively to assist the Irish speaking population at the present crisis and to establish for all time a bi-lingual population in those parts of Ireland where Irish is now spoken, from whom all those who in the distant future may wish to investigate the history or the antiquities of our nation, may draw as from a fountain that vernacular knowledge which for such purpose is indispensably necessary.

Some Words about Unpublished Literature*

'Unpublished Literature!' you say. 'That must surely mean unprinted MSS.' Well yes, I confess it may mean that also, and so the title of my article may be a little misleading, for the literature of which I intend to speak has nothing at all to do with white paper or blotted foolscap, never was drawn from an inkstand, and never ran out of the end of a patent steel pen or goose's quill. No, the literature I mean to glance at is a literature not only unpublished, but also unwritten, little known, and never appreciated by those fastidious denizens of the 'Great Republic of Letters.'

'Is it well then,' you will probably ask, 'to designate that by the title of literature which has never been committed to writing?' Yes; I think, unquestionably, that the unwritten tales, poems, and aphorisms of a nation are, in every respect, as truly literature as the deathless lays of that 'blind old man of Scio's rocky isle,' which were for ages chanted traditionally before they were acknowledged as the glory of the Greeks, the heritage of the nations, and the first epic poem of the world, before ever they worked their way through a thousand editions, a thousand thousand copies, or called into existence a tribe of studious and deadly-dull commentators, beyond number or reckoning. Nay, the great epic of the German race the Nibelungenlied filling for it (and not so scantily either) the place of Iliad and Oddysey in one, was itself also the product of semi-barbarous and probably untutored lips, but lips touched with the true Promethian fire. Why, is it not only the other day, so to speak, that a piece of literature was found among a peasantry where least expected, taken down from oral recitation, rescued from obscurity, committed to writing, and laid before the world in a manner to merit its universal applause, and to extract from Max Müller himself the confession that the Kalewala of the Finns was the fifth epic poem of the world!

Having now said so much by way of preface, and merely with the desire of showing that to exist in black and white is not always a necessary concomitant of literature, I would willingly go on to give some description of that store of poems, epigrams, and stories, which, instead of being enshrined between the leaves of a dead book, are inscribed upon the living page of the hearts of the Irish people, and consequently,

---

* *The Gael,* 7 January 1888.

wherever Scions of our race are found, be it at home or in the new world, should possess an interest relatively greater than that of anything foreign.

But here I am met by a difficulty which I find insurmountable, for the language in which the unwritten treasures of the golden bygone ages are enshrined, is itself in a dying condition, and the great traditions of the past of necessity must fade away with the framework in which they have been set. I cannot, consequently, venture to produce any of them here; few of the readers of the *Gael* would (I regret infinitely to say) understand them, and any attempt at translation so as to give the tone or keep the spirit of the original, would be at once disheartening and impossible.

Putting aside then, for the present, any examination of the unpublished literature contained in the Irish language, as far as research amongst the peasantry has brought it under my notice, I shall confine myself here to calling attention to some of what I thought a pity not to collect along with it, some of those few folk-songs composed in English, which have spontaneously sprang up and taken root amongst the peasantry — poor and scanty successors of the noble army of those which they are displacing or have displaced.

Now it is not generally understood, or at all sufficiently realised, that it is in fact quite recently that the English language has superseded the Irish over this island. In a curious old production, published about the middle of the last century, and entitled the *Ulster Miscellany*, there is a dramatic piece in which a couple of Dublin nightwatchmen are introduced, and these worthies are made by the author to talk in Irish, their sentences being given in real Gaelic, phonetically spelt, from which it would appear both that the lower classes in Dublin in the middle and the last century spoke Irish, and also that the language was so generally understood, that several sentences could, without impropriety, be inserted in a piece meant for dramatic representation. We must remember too, that Eugene O'Curry found people within twenty miles of Dublin who in their youth had never heard English spoken, except by the car-drivers from the city, and I have myself met old people equally close to the great town who, when young, used to repeat the Rosary in Irish. In 1820 it was calculated that fourteen out of fifteen spoke the language in Connaught and Munster, and it was at that time nearly universal in such counties as Cavan (which in the last century produced many native poets), Meath (the birth-place of O'Carolan), and Louth, where old men, labourers from Mayo, who could talk no English, assured me that sixty years ago, when they used to take shipping at Drogheda to reap the harvest in England, Irish was universally spoken even amongst the townspeople.

Bearing all these facts in mind it will not be at all surprising if we are to expect very little from those English productions which have succeeded in supplanting the old folk-literature. We must be careful in judging them to remember that they are the merest mushroom growth of a late day, and that the language in which they are composed being not native to the people, has had scarcely time enough as yet to absorb, as it were, the proper nutriment from the soil; it is as though its own bark had rudely been stripped off the Irish tree, and a new artificial covering wrapped around it, and it is now only that is beginning to absorb the sap and to cling to the trunk like something natural.

We must not, then, wonder if such songs as have found a place for themselves in the hearts of the people are rude in the extreme; many of them are half Irish, half English, in districts where both languages are spoken, and many again are merely course translations from the Irish, such as the well known *Drinawn Donn* (the Brown Blackthorn); or 'The Colleen deas crootha na mbo' (the pretty girl milking the cow). Many again are English, with Irish choruses, which choruses have not unfrequently survived even where the language has died out. Some of the combinations are amusing, as in the *Drimeen Dubh*.

> I would rather lose *Paudyeen* my wan *bohal beg*,
> Than lose you my *Drimeen Dubh* now you are dead.'

The lower Irish are born songsters, they make songs upon anything and on the slightest occasion, and no sooner do they lay aside their own language than they attempt versification in English. I knew intimately a man who, when he was young, never spoke English, and to the last persisted in talking of the *proker* and tongs, and the grouse coming to the *oatses*, who in his old age was driven, nevertheless, to versify in that language, badly as he spoke it. I remember one verse at least of a song in which he attempted to punish a woman who robbed him of the price of a little black pig he had sold in the fair some ten years ago. It has some little rythm about it and is a fair example of how songs become spontaneously generated as it were, from amongst the people themselves; what I remember of it ran thus:

> I went to the fair like a sporting young buck,
> And I met with a dame,
> Who belonged to the game,
> And up to me came
> > To be sure of her luck.
>
> She tipped me a wink,
> And we went into drink,
> We danced a few reels,
> > And wan double jig.
>
> But in the phweel round
> She slip her hand down,
> And robbed me quite bare of
> > The price of me pig.

This ditty he taught his seven-year-old grand-nephew to sing for him, and used to chuckle inwardly over the terrible revenge he had taken upon the treacherous female who defrauded him.

In the so-called *Búbbero* songs which women and girls used to sing in a kind of measured time to the music of the spinning wheel, composing often as they went along, some of the lines used occasionally to be in English, but this depended upon the will of the girl herself. I have rescued a few as I heard them, in all their exceeding rudeness, and chiefly for the sake of illustrating how one language glides into another, and how well the Irish love to rhyme even with the scantiest materials. In these Bubbero songs two lines are always invariable, they are *Eena beena bubbero — is ora veela grau,* the first line being unmeaning and merely meant to correspond in sound to the whirr of the wheel, the second meaning, 'and oh, my thousand loves' (*recte,* ó a mhíle grádh). The measured singing or droning of these two lines gave time to remember or compose two others to rhyme with them. I give a specimen or two here, but it must be remembered that the girls spoke English badly and vulgarly, while as a rule, they spoke Irish where they spoke it at all, with grace and propriety:

> And after you what will I do,
> Or will I live at all,
> Eena beena bubbero,
> Is ora veela grau.
> The night is young, the boys may come,
> And the girls may get a call, Eena beena, etc.,
> It's all I had agin me lou (love).
> His mother was a barge, Eena beena, etc.,
> It's all I had agin my lou.
> He was bracket in the jaw, Eena beena, etc.,
> Come to-day and go to-morrow
> Never was a grau (i.e. a love),
> Eena beena bubbero,
> Agus ora a veela grau.

And so on, *ad infinitum,* sometimes for a whole night.

But the longer songs and ballads which have taken root, and descended for two or three generations, seem many of them to have worked their way down from the North, the only part of the Island where English has been universally spoken for over a hundred years, though there too, even in such counties as Antrim, many of the plantation people being Gaelic-speaking highlanders, the language lingered even among the settlers until recently. The following ballad which I learned when very young, I have, on more recent inquiry found to be known in many counties, and it may be worth giving, not so much for its own merits, but as a pretty fair specimen of an Anglo-Irish folk-song.

There was a rich farmer in Ulster did dwell,
He had a pretty daughter, and none could her excel,
He had a handsome daughter, and her fortune happened so,
That away to her service she was obliged to go.
        Lalli tare toora ny.

One day to her master and her mistress she did say—
'I cannot bear this usage, and I must go away,
Get for me my box, my wages, and my clothes,
For this is the very day that I am resolved to go.'
        Lalli tare toora ny.

So as she was a-walking adown the street,
Who but a tinker she chanced for to meet,
Says he, 'My purty girl, will you come along with me,
And I'll show you the high way across the countree.'
        Lalli tare toora ny.

Then as they were a-walking adown a narrow lane,
He turns right about and thus to her did say—
'Before that any longer you go with me,
First pay your passage and then you may go free.'
        Lalli tare toora ny.

'Where is the keys that does open your box?
Before with the pinstaff I break open the lock.
To me box and me clothes you may do what you please,
To me master and me mistress I have give up the keys.'
        Lalli tare toora ny.

So as he stooped down to break open the lock,
She up with the pinstaff and gave to him a knock,
Before he could recover she was to let him know
That she had the pinstaff ready for to give him another blow.
        Lalli tare toora ny.

Then she went along with the box on her head,
And she didn't go very far until she met a gentleman.
'My purty girl', says he, 'can you open this gate?'
'I am in such a hurry, sir, I have not time to wait.'
        Lalli tare toora ny.

'That box on your head to whom does it belong?
To your master or your mistress you have done some wrong,
To your master or your mistress you have done some ill,
For one moment from trembling you cannot stand still.'
        Lalli tare toora ny.

'This box on my head to myself it does belong,
To my master and my mistress I have done no wrong,
To my master and my mistress I have done no ill,
But to tell you the truth a tinker I did kill.'
   Lalli tare toora ny.

So they went along to where the tinker he lay dead,
And the strames of blood flowing down from his head,
The pools of blood from his head did flow,
And it was his bad intention that left him lying low.
   Lalli tare toora ny.

They went to his budget to see what they had got,
Two case of pistols full of powder and shot,
Two case more full of powder and ball,
And a loud, loud whistle his ruffians for to call.
   Lalli tare toora ny.

'My purty girl', says he, 'can you handle your gun;
And if any danger happens, and sure you won't run.'
'Kind sir', says she, 'I have a valiant heart,
And if any danger happens I can play my own part.'
   Lalli tare toora ny.

He put the whistle to his lips, and he whistled loud and shrill,
And there appeared three swaggering vellans a-marching over the hill,
This maiden being nimble at the handling of her gun,
Shot the vellans as they came along.
   Lalli tare toora ny.

'My purty girl', says he, 'you have saved your own life,
And all for your valiancy I'll make you my wife,
For nothing but your courage and the action you have done,
For the handling of your pinstaff and the firing of your gun.'
   Lalli tare toora ny.

These verses are rude and irregular, and the song may suffer by my having, probably, forgotten some of them; but there is in it a touch of humour which makes it amusing, as where the gentleman gets huffed at the girl's refusing to open the gate, and changing his tone of voice (as the reciter always does) demands suspiciously what it is she has on her head, and again where the girl was to let him know that she had the pinstaff ready for to give him another blow. In Connaught, where the instinct of the peasantry apparently revolted (such a curious combination are we!) against the idea of a gentleman marrying a farmer's daughter, I have heard the addition made to the story in prose that the girl turned out after all to be a high up 'lady of honour', who waxed so indignant at the trial to which the gentleman had subjected her, that so far from accepting his handsome offer, she drew her pistol and 'put the contents of it' through him. Needless to say this is a most unauthorized and improbable *denouement*, probably the last in the world to occur to the stout Cromwellian or democratic Northern, with whom I suspect the ballad to have originated.

If Ulster was, as I imagine, the birthplace of the foregoing piece I thing there can be little doubt of its having given rise to this one also.

    Roger, the miller, came coorting of late,
    A rich farmer's daughter, called Katty by name.

    She has to her fortune goold, dimins and rings,
    She has to her fortune fifty-five things.

    She has to her fortune a large plot of ground,
    She has to her fortune five hundred pound.

    When dinner was over, and all things laid down,
    It was a nice sight to see five hundred pounds.

    The sight of the money and beauty likewise,
    Tickled his fancy and dazzled his eyes.

    And now, as your daughter is comely and fair,
    It's I that won't take her,
    It's I that won't have her
                Without the grey mare.

    Instantly the money was out of his sight,
    And so was Miss Katty, his own heart's delight.

    Roger, the miller, was kicked out the doore,
    And Roger was tould not to come there no more.

    Roger pulled down his long yalla hair,
    Saying, wishing I never,
    And wishing I never
                Spoke of the grey mare.

    It was in twelve months after, as happened about,
    That Roger, the miller, saw his own true love.

    Good morrow, fair maid, or do you know me?
    Good morrow, kind sir, I do well, says she.

    A man of your complexion, with long yalla hair,
    That wanst came a coorting,
    That wanst came a coorting,
                My father's grey mare.

It was not to coort the grey mare I came,
But a nice handsome girl, called Katty by name.

I thought that her father would never dispute,
In giving his daughter the grey mare to boot.

Before he would lose such a beautiful son,
It's then I was sorry,
It's now I am sorry,
      For what I have done.

As for your sorrow I do value not,
There is men in this town enough to be got,

If you had the grey mare you would marry me,
But now you have nayther the grey mare nor me.

The price of the grey mare was never so great,
So fare you well, Roger,
So fare you well, Roger,
      Go mourn for Kate.

I think there is the true Teutonic tone about this. The match-making and the calculation of chances indulged in by Roger is rather foreign to the Celtic nature, and all Irish love-songs deal in broken hearts, not in disappointed ambition.

The next ballad which I shall give I have also found pretty widely circulated in various versions, and I confess myself at a loss to conjecture its probable origin. It appears the work of an English rhymer, though how it became naturalized here is difficult to say. Some Irishman serving in the army or navy may have brought it home during the last century, and it is astonishing the rapidity with which songs diffuse themselves over a wide expanse of country. To give an instance; there was a doggrel in Irish about a cock who was represented as a fine gentleman walking down the street with his sword by his side, his watch in his fob, boots of Spanish leather, and fine lace hat, etc., but despite his pride and his magnificence, the women of Doire-leathan caught him and killed him and ate him, 'instead,' adds the poet indignantly, 'of clubbing their money together to by a *spoleyeen* (leg of mutton), which would have been decenter for them,' and not cause the poor hen to utter the lamentation which she did when

      The father of her children
        The partner of her youth,
    Was going into the pot,
      And a flag put over its mouth.

I had always imagined this song to have been an imaginary one, and the place, Doire-leathan, whose women were held up to ridicule, to have been fictitious, until to my great surprise, I met in Dublin an inhabitant of the very village, who assured me that the song had been made in his own youth, and had really been composed to punish the women of the aforesaid village for their greediness. Yet this doggrel seemed to have tickled the popular fancy so much that it had become well known in the place when I first heard it sixty or seventy miles away. So two verses which I know to have been composed in the County Cork, have worked their way upwards as far as Connaught, so as to become quite proverbial there. It will be seen that the ballad here given bears some resemblance to a well-known Scotch ballad three or four centuries old, and in no case do I think the author to have been of Irish extraction. I give the lines just as I heard them —

> Come all young maids that's fair and handsome,
>   While in Vanius (sic) the tears do flow,
> It's for me true lou I'm daily weeping,
>   He is my charming Willie O.
>
> My lou is gone abrooad a tinder,
>   Where to fine him I do not know;
> May kind Providence still protect him,
>   And send him home to his Molly O.
>
> If I had all the goold in the West Indies,
>   Or all the silver in Mexico,
> I'd freely give it to the King of England,
>   If he would grant me my Willie O.
>
> As Mary lay sleeping her lover came creeping,
>   And to her bed-chamber doore did go,
> Saying, rise up, rise up, lonely Mary,
>   For it's I'm your own true Willie O.
>
> As Mary rose and put on her clothes,
>   And to her bed-chamber doore did go,
> And it's there she saw her Willie standing,
>   And his face as white as snow.
>
> Oh! Willie, dear, where is those blushes,
>   That blush you wore some time ago?
> Oh! Mary, dear, the clay has changed them,
>   For it's I'm the ghost of your Willie O.
>
> It's seven long years I'm daily writing,
>   Unto the Bay of Biskay O.
> Till cruel death sent me no answer,
>   I looked for me charming Willie O.
>
> They spent that night in deep discoorsing,
>   Of love and coortship some time ago;
> They kissed, shook hands, and in sorrow parted,
>   Just as the cocks began to crow.

And though my body lies in the West Indies,
  My ghost shall guard you to and fro;
So Mary jewel, since we ever parted,
  For I'm no more your Willie O.

So when she saw his disappearance,
  Down her cheeks the tears do flow;
So farewell, dear, sweetheart and darlin'
  And weep no more for your Willie O.

This piece is, as we have said, of apparently non-Irish origin, and the same may be safely predicated about nearly all which are real ballads, that is, which relate a story concisely in verse, for of doing this the native Celt has little conception. His thought appears too excitable, and his poetic temperament too nimble and vivacious to endure the strain of keeping up a regular story in rhyme, for of all the Gaelic songs which I have collected I cannot say I have met three which could properly speaking be called ballads. There is plenty of imagination, fire and feeling about them, but of ordered thought and carefully arranged story there is next to none. They are essentially lyric, while the popular songs of England and Scotland are, as a rule, essentially of the ballad character, and this I believe to be the radical and unmistakeable difference between the poems of the two countries. Compare, for instance, with the songs already given, this other, which is evidently the product of a genuine Celt. The adjectives (rarely employed by the Teutons) the similies, the rather sudden transitions of thought are the pure and easily recognised tokens of the Gaelic mind. This song, such as it is, is also very popular :—

In the golden vales of Limerick, beside the Shannon strame,
The maiden dwells who houlds me heart and haunts me like a drame,
Her shining showers of golden hair so gently round her fall,
Her cheek would make red roses pale, she's my sweet Colleen Bawn.

Although I seldom spake to her, I think on her with pride,
For five long years I courted her, and hoped she'd be my bride,
Through dreary times of cold neglect, its all from her I've drawn,
For I am but a labouring boy, and she's the Colleen Bawn.

Her hands are whiter than the snow that falls on mountain side,
And softer than the cramy foam that sparkles on the tide;
Her eyes are brighter than the sun that shines upon the lawn,
The sunshine of my life is she, my darling Colleen Bawn.

And the women of Limerick take the sway, throughout all Erin's shore.
To fight upon the city walls as they have done of yore,
To keep away the enemy from midnight until dawn,
Most worthy of the title was my darling Colleen Bawn.

In many of these songs the pronunciation of English words and classical terms (which latter they affect as much as did the be-periwigged English poets of the last century, or the German poetasters of the *Zopfperiode*) is very trying, and in not a few instances so puzzling as to render any attempt at recognition absolutely hopeless. So, in the case of a poem upon the death of Napoleon I, which when young I picked up by ear, there occurs innumerable words which defy either explanation or amendation. To this day I sometimes wonder what it was the great Emperor meant when he boasted that —

> Although I am an *allijoke*,
> With fire and sword I made them smoke.

Or, what was running in the mind of the hero of the Colleen Bawn, where, in another verse of that song which I omitted on account of its untelligibility, he asserted that—

> I have seen some *oscreen* upon her footsteps fall.

By-the-bye, the opening verses of this poem upon Napoleon may be worth giving here for two purposes. First, as a fair sample of the hedge schoolmaster *sesquipedalian* style, teeming with classical names and allusions; and secondly, as an instance of how unintelligible words and names become when repeated from mouth to mouth by a people which does not understand them. I transcribe here the first few lines exactly as I picked them up myself. I did not then understand them any more than the old gardener from whom I picked them up, but man has something of the parrot about him, and imitates sound, leaving the intelligence torpid. At all events I have retained them in my memory ever since —

> I did visit that splendid citadil, the meterapolis called Paris,
>   Situated every morning by Sol's refulgent bames,
> Cojined by bright Arora advancing from the Arient
>   With raudiant light adorning and pure-shining rays,
> Commanding Cynthia to retire,
> The windies glance like fire,
> Which the Universe admires
>   Their merchandise in store.
>
> Where Flora spreads her frogarins,
> The fertile plain I'll decorate
> To illuminate the Royal Corsican
>   Agin on the French shore, &c., &c.

These few specimens of Anglo-Irish folk-songs may not be very pleasant to contemplate, when we compare them with the beautiful Irish lyrics, the 'Dark Rosaleen,' or the 'Silk of the Kine,' or a hundred others which they have so unworthily supplanted, we are tempted to exclaim with Hamlet, 'Oh, what a falling off was there.'

I have already attempted to account for their comparative vulgarity and coarseness by drawing attention to the sudden change of language which has taken place throughout the nation, with a facility and speediness actually unparalleled in the annals of Europe, and which if it has been, as asserted, pregnant of good results, has also, I fear, been in a way productive of many bad ones. The best we can hope for the future is that as the new language of the peasantry becomes more easy to manage, and begins to fit better the organs and mind of those who use it, the beautiful and pure lyrics of such masters as Moore, Mangan, Davis, and Griffin, as well as the songs from that golden repertoire *The Spirit of the Nation*, and other collections of a similar character, may gradually spring up with it, as it were, a natural growth in the hearts of the young generation, and quietly supersede the semi-barbarous productions which are as yet only too prevalent in the homes and round the hearths of the Irish nation.

Irish Folk-lore*

I feel that in attempting to interest you tonight in such a subject as that of folk-lore in general and Irish folk-lore in particular I am engaging on a difficult task, because it is so hard to make an educated body of men and women realise the conditions of life under which folk stories become possible.

Nevertheless it is absolutely certain that there existed in our midst until quite lately, and in spots even still exists a certain number of men and women like ourselves who when the twelve work-a-day hours are completed, seek like ourselves for mental recreation, and find it, in a domain to which few indeed of ~~ourselves~~ us have been privileged to enter.

When our work is over and we wish to unbend the mind, we fly to literature, perhaps to one of Mr Ashe King's admirable novels, to Robert Elsemere, or the latest '10 penny Awful', with a gorgeous murder on it's cover. But these people of whom I am speaking know nothing of the thrilling delights of dark passages, forged wills, ~~adulteries~~, daggers, ~~cruel~~ murders, and all the rest of the attractive paraphernalia of the modern sensational novel, and yet an unwritten literature of their own supplies them with every effect and emotion which the 19th century romance supplies to us. Fear, anger, anxiety and highly wrought feelings, are for them as really aroused by a spoken tale as they are for us by a printed yellow-back.

But between Mrs Ward's or Basil King's novel and the fairy-tale which with our Western peasantry is, or was till lately, its equivalent there is a great gulf fixed. The printed book is by an author whom we, or at least our contemporaries know. As we read its pages we can almost see our author erasing this, heightening that, and laying on such and such a touch for effect. His book is the work of his own mind, the product of the individual brain, and some of us have been present at its genesis.

But no man and no woman can tell us the genesis of the folk-tale, no one has been present at its inception, no has seen its growth. It is a mystery, a marvel, part of the flotsam and jetsom of the ages still beating against the shore of the 19th century, swallowed up in England after thousands of years existence by the waves of materialism, but still surviving unengulfed upon the West coast of Ireland, where I gathered together many bundles of it.

* Rathmines, December 1889. N.L.I. 17,297: 'Essay on Irish Folklore sgríobhtha Mí Nodlaig 1889, Baile Átha Cliath'. Some textual emendations shown. See p. 41.

But what is this mystery of which I speak. Why should the folk-tale be in any respect more marvellous than the stories which I invent out of my own head to amuse a child?

This is a natural question to put and I must answer it. If then Irish folk stories bore no resemblance to those of any other nation, if there were no indication upon the face of at least some of them that they were myths in disguise, then there would be nothing so very wonderful in the existence of a body of tales such as we might any of us invent to amuse children with. But if we find the same story that old Biddy Morrisroe tells me today in her little smoky bog hovel told tomorrow by an Eastern ayah to a white child in a palace at Calcutta or Hyderabad, and find from Russian sources that the same tale is ~~told~~ known amid the snows of Siberia — does not this suddenly invest the fairy tale with a hundred-fold interest and a ~~trebled~~ importance. Again if we can prove that some of these stories at least are the remains of myths invented by man in the earliest stages of the race, to explain the natural phenomena which encountered the gaze of young humanity, what a deep interest this gives us in the story. It actually constructs before our eyes the frame of mind with which prehistoric man long ages before our first notices of him looked upon nature and upon the world.

You may perhaps smile at the idea that the story which old Shawn-Mac-a-drury tells me as he burns his seaweed ~~beneath~~ at the base of the ~~stormy~~ wild wind-swept cliffs of Achill, that natural bastion of Europe as it has been named, can in any way reflect to me listening to it the notions of prehistoric man, and yet nothing can be more certain than that I find in it such traces, — but in order to make this intelligible to you, you must allow me to have access to other sources besides Celtic ones. On turning then to Greek mythology I find such a tale as this:

Kephalus (which means 'head', and in this instance must mean the sun's head) became enamoured of Procris the daughter of 'Ερση (but Hersé means dew) and she returned his love, which means that the dew drop reflects the sun-light. But 'Hως (which means the dawn) is also enamoured of Kephalus and she begs of Diana the spear which never misses its mark. (What is the spear that never misses its mark except the sunbeam?), and with this Kephalus slays Procris as she lies asleep in the middle of the forest — the very place where the last dew drop would linger.

Now this tale is a myth, a pure myth, and nothing but a myth, and the names Kephalus 'Hως and 'Ερση prove it, because they carry their own meanings on the face of them. And when I say that this story is a myth, I mean that it was invented either to account for, or at least in accordance with, a natural phenomenon that struck the minds of the early Greeks. Of this there can be no question and the ~~words~~ names as I say carry with them their own meaning. But there are other tales, numberless ones, which were also originally myths although the names have long lost all meaning. Thus the well-known story of Sisyphus being compelled to roll a great stone up a hill every day and just when he got it to the top being compelled to see it roll down the hill again, is only a sun-myth. The pre-historic Greeks saw the great ball, the sun, going up the sky, and they said 'the wise man is rolling the ball up the sky', and when they saw the sun past noon, they said, 'the ball is going down'. But in process of time the Greeks became more cultured, and looked upon nature with other eyes. The story was still told, but was not understood to apply to the sun, so a story was invented of Sisyphos (which probably means 'the wise man'), a king of Corinth, very wise and very wicked who was compelled as a punishment to roll a great stone up a hill every day, and not to be able to keep it there but to see it tumble down. So in the Hindoo story when we find Krishna espousing sixteen thousand one hundred maidens at the same time, we see that this is the Greek story over again of the sun and the dew drops, the sun shines upon all the dew drops at the same time.

Now in a very curious story which I heard from an old man, I meet an evident trace of this sun God. The hero of the story is a kind of Hercules, he is the strong man who can do anything that he is asked, even like Hercules go to hell and drive the spirits back to earth with his club. He is desired to drain a lake full of water. The lake is very steep on one side like a reservoir. He makes a hole in this, puts his mouth to the aperture, and sucks down all the water of the lake, with boats and fishes and everything it contained. Now this is manifestly the remnant of an Aryan sun-myth, and personifies the action of the warm sun drying up a lake and making it a marsh, killing the fishes, and leaving the boats stranded.

The question was never asked, how did the man hold all the water in the lake, wouldn't he burst before he had drunk more than his own size of it. The story was just told as it had been handed down for probably thousands and thousands of years, when our Aryan ancestors were in the same rude and mind-less condition in which the Australian blacks or the Digger Indians are to-day.

Again, in a well known Irish story there is a boat that can sail equally well over land or sea or in the air, and go straight to its mark at the word of command. But this same boat is to be met with in Norse story and in the old Greek poem we call Homer's Odyssey, and in the Norse story the boat is large enough to hold whole armies when they enter it, and when they leave it, it becomes so small as to be invisible. Now ships do not go over land and sky, but only upon the sea, nor do they grow large and small, nor go straight to their mark. It is evident then that here we have another nature myth, vastly old, invented first by prehistoric man, and that these ships are the clouds, that go over land and sea and in the air, are large enough to hold armies and small enough to be nearly invisible, and which go straight to their mark. The meaning of this story has been for countless ages forgotten but the story has survived.

And of all that we know, of all that reminds us of man and the human race, is there anything approaching the antiquity of these myth-stories told by a half-starving peasant in a smoky hovel. To those who understand this and gather folk-lore with intelligence, the study is indeed profound and marvellous.

But how did these myths come into existence at all? That is a question which has been very often put and very variously answered. It has exercised the brains of our greatest philosophers, etymologists and philologists, and the problems connected with myths and the origin of folk-stories seems as far as ever from solution. I must place before you some of the principal theories.

Mr Max Müller, the celebrated Oriental scholar and Oxford philologist, has propounded a theory which is to explain these myths through etymology — the science of words. According to him the human race passed through a time which he calls the dialectic period, that is the stage in which language was before such languages as Greek, Sanscrit or Gaelic broke off, as it were, and differentiated themselves. At this time there were according to Max Müller no myths. After this comes what he calls the mythopoeic or myth-making ages, half way between the dialectical period and the time when the human race diverged into different families and languages and nationalities. It was at this time that Max Müller thinks the myths sprang up, through words remaining on in the various newly-formed languages but their meaning becoming obscure. Here is an example which he gives. In the mythopaeic age some one says 'the shining one pursues the burning one', meaning 'the sun follows the dawn''. Suppose the word for shining one was the Aryan prototype of 'ηλιος and the word for the burning one the Aryan prototype of the Sanscrit Dahana (or dawn). Suppose the Aryan term for 'ηλιος (the Sun), camcame (*recte* became) confused with Apollo, and the word for 'burning one' became Daphne. Suppose too that Daphne was the name of a tree. Then when all these changes were forgotten the Greeks would find this in their language, Apollo pursues Daphne and to explain it they would make a myth, and Apollo being masculine and Daphne feminine they would invent a story of a young and handsome God pursuing a fair nymph who to escape him changes herself into a laurel tree. There would be, Max Müller thinks, at this transition period many words understood perhaps by the grandfather, familiar to the father, but strange to the son and misunderstood by the grandson, and thus he thinks originated the myth, through a disease of language.

This solution of the question does not in the least get rid of the difficulty as Mr Andrew Lang points out. For where do the savage silly senseless details of the Greek myths come from, the disgusting stories about Zeus, his taking the form of a bull, a cuckoo etc., and the vile and senseless tricks that he played. The Greeks once they had become a nation — at the time when Max Müller says the myths sprung into existence, would never have sunk so low as to make such inventions.

Mr Herbert Spencer puts forward a different theory. He thinks that the names of persons were derived from natural objects like those of the Indians of today, as, Sitting Bull, Sun-cloud etc., and that in process of time people got to think that they were descended from an ancestor who was a cloud or a bull, and that other myths sprang up in kindred ways.

Mr Andrew Lang has however given I think the true explanation. He has investigated the myths, folk-lore and superstitions of the various savage races of the earth, and he finds that no matter how different the race may be in Asia, Africa, Australia or America the beliefs of these rude men bear to one another the greatest resemblance. In this state of intellect the savage men scarcely distinguishes his own race from beasts and birds, which to him appear to be almost so many editions of himself, all animated with feeling and understanding. A spider has made the sun. A wolf is the creator of man. The moon was once a woman, and so on. Savage myths in fact are 'a jungle of foolish fancies, beasts and men and stars and ghosts all moving madly on a level of common personality and animation and all changing shapes at random as partners are changed in some fantastic witches revel.' This is the natural consequence of that 'nebulous and confused state of mind to which all things animate or inanimate, human animal, vegetable or inorganic seem on the same level of passion and reason'.

And now after we have carefully distinguished between those tales which may be scientifically interpreted as nature myths, we are confronted with a vast body of stories which cannot be so interpreted — and the more we investigate these stories, the more we find the mystery connected with them to grow and increase. I must try to explain now what this further problem is.

The brothers Grimm who during the first thirty years of this century were the first to collect and edit scientifically that ~~vast~~ delightful body of German tales with which the most of you are doubtless familiar, called attention to the fact that several of the stories they collected from the old women in Germany were identical with stories found in India and in Russia. Now the human mind has only a limited number of ideas and it is possible that some of these stories which bear to each other so close a likeness may have originated independently of each other — and this explanation satisfied people for a while.

But after this it began to be observed that though certain incidents of these stories might have ~~arisen~~ been invented independently of each other, yet that when we meet the same sequence of events in a German story and an Indian story, that this is proof positive that the two stories have either had the same origin or else that the one nation borrowed the story from the other. Again it was found that some of these stories were so remarkable that it was quite impossible that two peoples should have thought of them independently. Here for instance is an example of such a ~~story~~ tale.

A young man gets possession of a magical ring. This ring is stolen from him and recovered by the aid of certain grateful beasts, whom the young man has benefited. His enemy who has stolen the ring hides it away in his mouth, but the grateful mouse insinuates his tale (*recte* tail) into the nose of the thief, makes him sneeze, and out comes the magical ring.

Now this story is found in the Punjaub, among the Bretons, the Albanians, the modern Greeks and the Russians. But it is quite absurd to think that each of these peoples invented the story for themselves. The story was evidently invented by someone once for all. The Grimms of course saw this, and they started the theory that since the story — and many others like it — was found amongst the Celts, the Sanscrit-speaking Indians, the Greeks and the Slavs that it had its origin in the home of the Aryan race before these various Aryan-speaking peoples started from it, to populate India and Europe. The theory was that all these various nations carried this story with them from their original home near the Caucasus, — or in the North of Europe as modern writers seem inclined to believe.

Well this theory seemed the most natural thing in the world and found no one to gainsay it, until writers and travellers within the last twenty years began to collect and publish the folklore of various savage peoples, and then it was discovered that this tale, young man, ring, mouse, and all, was common not only to the Aryan-speaking races I have mentioned but to the Japanese(?), the Indians of California(?) and one or two other savage tribes as widely separated both racially and geographically as the world will allow of. How did these come by this story — to give only one specimen — or where did it come from first. That is the problem, and it is one that never yet has been solved. Various solutions of it have been attempted, to go into which would try your patience too severely, but to my mind it is one of the strongest ~~proo~~ corroborations I know of the Biblical tradition that all man-kind sprang originally from one couple, for any theory which makes these various nations borrow the tales from one another seems perfectly incredible.

I have now attempted to set before you as intelligibly as I could, a few of the weighty and deeply interesting problems connected with the study of folk-lore. But I have as yet hardly touched upon Irish folk-lore.

The fact is that no ~~body~~ Irish folk-lore has been given to the world, that is worth a rush for scientific purposes. John Sutherland Black for instance gives in the Encyclopaedia Britannica a list of about fifty books for the study of folk lore, and amongst them not a single Irish one. And no wonder, for none such exists. And yet, speaking à priori, it is precisely in Ireland that one would expect the most valuable and copious folk-lore of any country in Europe, and that for several reasons. In the first place we along the west coast of Ireland are of pure blood, we have been unmixed with other nations, we have been longest left alone, we have been the only nation unconquered by the Romans, we must have carried directly from our Aryan home a stock of more original folk lore than the Slavs, Teutons or Scandinavians whose migrations came after ours, civilisation has touched us less, and living undisturbed for a couple of thousand years or more among the mountains of the sea coast with no intercourse with strangers, it is precisely amongst ourselves that the most important and interesting stock of prehistoric stories should be found. Well, has it been the case? Our noble countrymen have acted in this case matter exactly as you would expect from them. As they have let their national language, their national games, their national literature, their national music die without a thought or a pang, so they have done by their traditional folk-lore. No one has ever put out a finger to collect it, and it is now thanks to railroads, English, and *United Ireland* and our patriots in general, all but too late to rescue something that would have been of importance to the whole scientific world.

Many of you may doubtless think that I have spoken too hardly of what has been done, that Crofton Croker, Lady Wilde, Carleton, Kennedy and Mr Leamy have preserved our folk-lore for us. Well, they have not! They tell us stories in which like Aeneas they bore a great part themselves. We have more of Crofton Croker and Lady Wilde than we have of anybody else, in fact we hear of no one else. They do not pretend to give the stories as they found them. They never tell us where they got them, or when, or from whom. Every one who has ever collected genuine folk lore and then turns to their books will see traces of the educated nineteenth century gentleman and lady in every second sentence.

But to return to the general subject of folk stories and romantic tales over the world. The German Von Hahn has classified these roughly, and out of the fourteen classifications given by him I have myself collected stories in which I find eight subjects treated of out of his fourteen. I shall give their heads here:

1. Slaughter of a monster.
2. Flight of a lady and her lover from giant or canibal father.
3. The youngest brother the successful adventurer.
4. Bride given to whoever will accomplish a difficult adventure.
5. The grateful beasts who aid a man in his distress.
6. Story of the strong man and his adventures.
7. Descent of the hero into Hades.
8. The bride who produces beast-children.

Now all these are of great antiquity, the slaughter of monsters and dragons reminds us that man once came in contact with beasts which we do not find now. The canibal father reminds us of a time when our Celtic ancestors must have come across and subdued canibal races on their migration westward. The victory of the youngest brother is a reminiscence of a state of society in which as is well known the youngest and not the eldest son succeeded to his father's property. The grateful beasts make us look to the time when our ancestors were in much the same intellectual state as the Australian blacks or Digger Indians are at present, and saw no great difference between man and beasts. The same thing holds good of the bride and beast children, and the story of the strong man and the descent into Hell appear to be ~~peculiar~~ common to most races. But besides these I meet with a great many suggestive allusions in these Irish stories which appear to me to throw light upon the past origin of the race. The 'sword of light' is one of these. I have constantly met with this in Irish stories but never once in Irish MSS, and this as well as other reasons makes me believe that the popular stories are ages and ages older than our oldest MSS. For what can this 'sword of light' which is generally in the possession of a king or a great giant ~~mean~~ be, but the earliest record of a race which used bronze weapons meeting with a race that had swords of polished steel, which were looked upon as the rarest and greatest trophies, the property only of a king or great man. This sword when it does not belong to a king belongs to a giant and the giant I take to be a member of some of the non-Aryan races that the Celts met with on their journey westwards. For the giants of these folk-tales are not the giants of Greece or Rome, monstrous beings that are nearly equal to the Gods themselves, but ~~men~~ savage men, generally dwelling in caves, somewhat larger than other men but not so large but that they can be conquered in wrestling or in fighting by common men.

Again where does the 'lion' which occurs in many of these stories come from? No lions have been been (*recte* seen) in Europe within historic times. And yet the lion, called *leómhan* in Irish, is often to be met with in folk tales, and it seems to me that this can only be a reminiscence of a time when our ancestors met with these animals on their journey from the east, and as a presumption — though no one has ever noticed it — that the new theory of the Aryan races having sprung from the North of Europe instead of from Asia, is incorrect. You see that folk-lore, despised as it is, if properly read can throw a light even upon such matters as these.

In another story a man follows a sweet-singing bird into a cave under the ground, and finds a country where he wanders for a year and a day, and finds a woman who shows him how to escape being killed down there and how to bring back the bird. At the end of the tale the narrator mentioned quite simply that it was his mother he had met. But this touch shows the land where he wandered to have been Hades the country of the dead underneath the ground that stamps the tale at once as pre-Christian. So much for the antiquity of these stories.

It is time however to say a little about the stories themselves and how I got them. They are as far as my researches have gone to be found only amongst the oldest and most neglected and poorest of this Irish-speaking population. The English-speaking population either do not know they at all, or else tell them in so bald and condenced a form as to be useless. All the men from whom I used to hear stories in Roscommon when I was young are now dead. I heard a great many stories then, but did not understand their value. Now when I go to look for them I cannot find them. They have died out and will never again be heard on the hill sides where they existed for two or three thousand years, never again as we say in Irish, while grass grows and water runs. Several of these stories I got from an old man on the border of the county Roscommon where it joins Mayo. He never spoke more than a few words of English till he was fifteen. He was taught by a hedge-school master from the South of Ireland out of Irish MSS. The teaching seemed to consist in making him learn ~~things~~ Irish poems by heart. The next school master put a ~~notch~~ piece of wood round his neck and pretended that it told him how often he had spoken Irish when he was at home. He was beaten whenever he was heard speaking a word of Irish, even though he could speak hardly a word of English. His son and daughter now speak Irish though not fluently, his grand-children do not even understand it. He had at one time as he expressed it the full of a sack of stories, but he had forgotten them. His grand-children stood by his knee while he told me one or two, but it was evident they did not understand a word. His son and daughter laughed at them as nonsense.

Afterwards I went farther west to the Island of Achill. There if anywhere one would imagine one could find folk-lore stories in their purity. But now they have built a bridge to the main-land and call it Davitt Bridge, and the youngsters speak English, read *United Ireland*, and hold Land League meetings where the language is English. A fine looking dark man of about forty-five who told me several stories and could repeat many of Ossian's poems, told me that now-a-days when he would go to a house of an evening and the old people would get him to recite, the boys would go out. 'They wouldn't understand me', said he, 'and when they wouldn't they'd sooner be listening to 'géimneach na mbó, the lowing of the cows'. This is the way at present all over the country from Donegal to Skibereen.

Now there is not the slightest necessity for this state of things. A few words from Michael Davitt or Tim Healy or any of our other patriots the next time they go to Achill would be quite sufficient to keep Irish alive there in saecula saeculorum, and with the Irish language to keep alive the old Aryan folk-lore, the poems of Ossian, and a thousand and one other interesting things that survive where Irish is spoken, and die when it dies. But either through their own gross materialism or else their own defective education, the men who have had the ear of the Irish race from O'Connell down, have neglected everything that is specially Celtic and racial and while protesting all the time against West Britainism have been themselves the very men to assimilate us to the English. And the people are not the better for this, for the man who can repeat Ossian's poems and tell Fenian stories is intellectually a higher and nobler type than the man who can just spell through an article in *United Ireland* (or the *Weekly News*) or perhaps not spell through it at all, but only listen to it.

I may mention here that it is a dreadfully difficult thing to collect folk-tales. I hear that such and such a man can tell stories. He is generally a very old man. When with difficulty I get as far as him he may (*recte* ~~may) have~~ has probably some work on hand. If it is harvest time I may say it is perfectly useless going to him at all, unless you are prepared to sit up by the fire all night, for his mind will be so distraught with his harvest operations that he can tell you nothing. If however it is the winter time and you are fortunate enough to find him unoccupied, it nevertheless requires a good deal of management to get him to tell his stories. I always start by half a glass of whiskey and a pipe of tobacco, and perhaps a story of my own. One must be careful to start with half a glass of whiskey only, I have several times after much trouble and long journies frustrated my own intent by giving them a whole glass which generally puts them off their heads, but half ~~a glass~~ that as a rule makes them go on famously.

Now if you start to take down the story verbatim with a pencil and paper, as an unwary collector will do you destroy everything. You will make the *shanachie* irritable, he will not wait for you to write down your sentence, and if you call out 'stop stop! wait till I get this down', he will forget what he was going to tell you, and you will not get a third of the story, though you may think you have it all.

What you have to do is to sit quietly smoking your pipe without the slightest interruption, not even when he comes to phrase or a word you do not understand. You must let him tell it to the end, praise him, have another smoke, and then say as if the thought suddenly struck you, budh mhaith liom sin a bheith agam air pháipéar, 'I'd like to have that on paper'. Then you can get it from him easily enough, and when he leaves out whole incidents, as he is sure to do, you having heard the story before will put him right and so get the whole from him. All the same it is by no means easy to write down these stories, for they are full of old words which neither your narrator nor yourself understand, and if you press him too much over the meaning of them he gets confused and irritable.

Altogether I have got some twenty or thirty stories, some of which

I published in Irish with copious notes and more of which I am going to publish in Irish and English. Many of these stories resemble the German tales of the brothers Grimm rather closely, so closely indeed that if anyone had published a collection of Gaelic stories thirty years ago it would hardly have been necessary for the great philologist Zeuss to spend fifteen years of his life in proving that the ~~Celts~~ Irish are Aryans.

I have now attempted to explain to you what the science of folk-lore is, what the problems connected with it are, and what is the interest attaching to it. I have showed you that interesting as the books of Irish tales which have hitherto been published are, they are quite useless for scientific purposes, because they are as much the invention of gentlemen and ladies as tales of the Aryan race handed down for indefinite ages, and I have perhaps gone out of my way to enlist your sympathies in behalf of the old Irish language with which these weird and graceful legends pregnant with historic value, are inseparably connected.

Had I told you a few of the stories themselves I should doubtless have made this essay more ~~amusing~~ interesting — certainly more amusing. But this was not my object.

The science of folk-lore has been shamefully misunderstood and neglected, and to show you that these stories are not old wives tales, but, if read aright are seen to mean more than meets the ear — that has been the object of this — I fear me, very uninteresting and intricate paper.

Gaelic Folk Songs*

PART I

Some time ago a gentleman of my acquaintance handed me a small collection of Irish songs which, in the course of his travels, he had taken down from the mouths of the peasantry in almost every county in Ireland where Irish is still spoken. Of such songs I had already myself made a large collection, and I scrutinised this new one with avidity. It convinced me of a fact of which I had been pretty certain before — namely, that the great classical songs of Ireland, if I may so call them, vary little in any locality, but that besides these there are countless little gems of music and feeling to be picked up like pearls on almost every mountainside, in almost every valley, in every county, barony, and even townland in Ireland — if only there were anyone to take the trouble to collect them.

But people, even the few-and-far-between people who are acquainted with Irish literature, may think that if that were so, the Irish being a born nation of scribes would have committed them to paper, and that they would now be extant in some one or other of those innumerable hosts of MSS. which circulated amongst the people in the last century and the beginning of this, and of which so large a number have been saved from the destruction to which that unsavoury thing called the advance of civilisation, but in reality the carelessness and discouragement of ourselves have been consigning them for the last sixty years. This, however, is not so. The pieces of which I speak, the 'wood-notes wild' of Irish hill and glen, the quaint and feeling verses which have been sung in the same locality ever since they were first composed, have never been deemed worthy of a place in his carefully written 'Bolg-an-tsoláthair' or Miscellany, even by the most miscellaneous-minded of hedge schoolmasters, even by him who runs with scarcely the break of a line the 'Tragical Fate of Conlaoch' into a sermon on the Trinity, and the sermon into the Cruiskeen Lawn, to be followed, it may be, by a poem of Ossian, or a hymn to the Virgin.

The real reason why these scribes, to whom we owe so much, have never taken the trouble to perpetuate these pieces, is partly, I imagine,

---

* *The Nation*, April-May 1890. See pp. 37, 43. In the Irish texts orthography has, in general, been modernised.

because they were unacquainted with many of them, but chiefly because they utterly despised them. They looked upon them with much the same contempt that Dr Johnson looked upon Percy's Ballads — because they were so simple, so natural, so unartifical — because they were not the work of bards or professed poets, because their rhymes were rude, and because they knew nothing of 'assonance,' 'union,' 'alliteration,' and the rest of the fetters which the bards forged for themselves with so much misused ingenuity.

Accordingly, scarcely one of the pieces which form the subject of this paper was ever written down, at the time when we had men amongst us who could do so, and now they never reach the ear of anyone who could transfer them to paper.

But before I proceed, I must explain what it is I mean by the songs which I have called 'classical.' By the classical songs of Ireland, I mean some twenty or thirty of those great songs which are not common to one locality or one county only, but which, with little variation, are known and sung all over Ireland from Donegal to Kinsale, and which, were such a thing possible, should go to form the staple and back-bone of an universal modern Irish literature. Most of these great classical songs of Ireland have, as a rule, struggled into print somehow or other, and many of them have been even translated into English. It will be sufficient to mention a few of the most prominent of these time-honoured lyrics, the 'Dark Rosaleen,' 'Drimeen Dhu Deelish,' 'Shawn O'Dwyer in Glanna,' the 'Cruiskeen Lawn,' the 'Collen Dhas Crootha nam Bo,' the 'Cooleen,' the 'Drinawn Donn,' the 'Clár Bog Déal,' 'Emun na Gcnoc,' or 'Ned of the Hills,' 'Eileen a Roon,'' &c; all these we may call classical. After them come a multitude of less known pieces, popular in a particular province or county, but not universally known; and, lastly, we meet innumerable gems of songs, isolated and unrecognised, which have lived on in particular localities, and which a careful searcher may even still find in tolerable abundance in almost every hole and corner where Irish is yet spoken. There are veritable

> — Children of the place
> That have no meaning half a mile away,

or which, at least, though they may have a meaning, seem to be quite unknown outside their own very narrow limits. But before we proceed to examine our specimens of this last class, let us cast a moment's glance at the state of Irish poetry for the last three centuries.

It is an irreparable loss that there has never arisen a poet in Ireland who might do for us what Burns has done for Scotland or Schiller for Germany, or Beranger for Paris — who might, in other words, form an intellectual bond of union between the upper and lower classes, and whose strains might be equally familiar to cabin and to drawing-room.

Ireland, unfortunately, has never produced anything of the kind. The reason is obvious. Three hundred years ago, when Ireland was still Gaelic and the Irish language universal, the bards, whose dialect was the literary and standard one, though they composed pieces which were widely read and understood by a certain class all over the island, yet never produced anything popular, they never produced anything which caught hold of the people's imagination and lived in their memories as did the Ossianic and heroic poems. The bards wrote a cultivated and artificial Gaelic, for, being attached to the great houses of chiefs and nobles, they composed for them and not for the populace, after a manner the most intricate, and following rules the most complex of probably any school of poetry that ever existed in the world. Strains like theirs, though they may have been able to win a shower of gold and jewels from the great chiefs, could never gain the ear of the populace, and a glance at that great collection of 16th and 17th century poems called the 'Contention of the Bards,' shows at once that it would have been as incongruous for an Irish peasant to recite such verses as for an English ploughman to whistle 'James Lee's Wife,' or a sonnet from the 'House of Life.'

Afterwards when the power of the bards was gone and the great families who supported them were broken up or had perished, there was for a moment a possibility of an Irish Burns arising, and in point of fact, a number of highly popular poets did immediately spring up, singing in new modes and metres and language, and catching the ear of whole provinces. But, unfortunately, with the old bards disappeared the consciousness of Gaelic unity, and men like Turloch O'Carolan of Connacht, or Aodh MacCurtin of Munster, lived and sang for their own provinces in their own dialects, and never became well known beyond their own immediate spheres. Irish dialectic differences, which appear to have been unknown amongst the bards, began to accentuate themselves the moment that Irish ceased to be the language of the schools, colleges, and law-courts, and thus it became impossible for any one poet to gain the ear of all the provinces. But what the rapidly developing dialectic differences commenced was continued and accentuated by the division of language which followed the plantation of Ulster, and which has from that day till this made it impossible for any song-writer to spring up who could be popular all over Ireland.

Even amongst the English-speaking portion of our race no one poet has as yet laid hold of the popular heart and the popular imagination, for Moore's brilliant but eminently artificial diction has never gained a hold upon the masses, though it is familiar enough to our drawing-rooms; and as to his great rival, Thomas Davis, though he has succeeded better amongst the people, yet we wonder in how many drawing-rooms in Merrion-square or Fitzwilliam-place would we find his poems — possibly in one out of twenty.

Now, however, that the force of circumstances, or to speak more truly the example of some of the leaders of the Irish race, have induced men to contemptuously throw aside Gaelic, and seeing that from the centre to the sea English will be the language of the rising generation, it may be possible that a poet may yet spring up amongst us who shall combine in a union of sympathy both the upper and lower classes, not of one province only, but of all Ireland. In the meantime, since every locality has its own particular favourite poet, or rather has, since the poet is generally forgotten, its own particular songs, it may not prove whole uninteresting to gather up some of these dispersed and unknown flowers of national poetry. We shall find that, though in their origin and diffusion they are purely local, yet in their essence they are wholly national, and, perhaps, more purely redolent of the race and soil than any of the real *literary* productions of the last few centuries.

Indeed, it is in these traditional verses, many of which have stood the test of centuries, that we best overhear, as it were, the breathings of the Celtic soul, that we surprise the Gaelic genius off its guard, pure and unvarnished, no longer locked up in the tight waistcoat of literature, nor tricked out in the pretentious professional trappings of the bards.

The local songs which we discover lurking in the most unexpected places are of very various dates, some probably two or three centuries old, some perhaps older, but most of them belonging to the last few generations. They are as various in their subject matter as they are in their versification and their dates. Many of them are occasional, many others allegorical, may are praises of particular localities or particular people, or humorous descriptions, or fairy visions or dialogues, but the two most numerous classes are probably the love poems and the drinking songs. Accordingly, putting aside for the present the more miscellaneous pieces; let us glance in this paper at those only which celebrate that world-worshipped pair — Cupid and Bacchus.

PART II

In the love songs we find almost every shade of passion delineated, from the confident to the despairing, from the endearing to the indignant, with a versatility something like that of a Heine. We find tenderness, pathos, anger, despair, longing, and all the other primary elements of love portrayed by the actors in a language simple and passionate, but without the least trace of vulgarity — the language neither of learning nor pedantry, but of the heart. The key-note is struck, and rightly, in these simple lines, apparently by a girl:

> Deir siad liom féin
>   Gur ní beag suarach an Grá,
> Ach is mairg ar a mbíonn sé
> Mí nó seachtain nó lá.

> They tell me that love is a small thing,
> It is petty and mean, they say,
> But, and oh! but it's woe for who feels it
> For a month, or a week, or a day.

Here, again, the natural cry of a heart forsaken: —

> Tá crann ins an ngarraí,
> Ar a bhfásann duilliúr is bláth buí,
> An uair a leagaim mo lámh air,
> Is láidir nach mbriseann mo chroí.

> There is growing a tree in the garden,
> With flowers of yellow that shake,
> I lay my cold hand on its branches,
> And feel that my heart must break.

That tree must surely have been the laburnum under which the girl and her lover had once exchanged their vows. Whether he died or proved false we cannot conjecture from the contents. The next is a complaint more direct and less sentimental: —

> Is trua a Bhríd nach bás do fuaras
> Sula thug mé grá chomh buan duit;
> D'fhág tú m'intinn brónach buaraithe
> Mar an crann creathain is an ghaoth dá luascadh.

> I would I had died without sorrow or pain
> Ere I gave you the love that you gave not again;
> But my heart has been troubled and moved for you,
> Like the leaves of the aspen the winds blow through.

In the following verses, again, we discover the plot of many a three-volume novel:

> Shíl mise a chéad searc
>   Go mbeadh aontíos idir mé is tú,
> Agus shíl mé 'na dhéidh sin
>   Go mbréagfá mo leanbh ar do ghlún.
> Mallacht rí neimhe ar an té sin,
>   Bhain dhíomsa mo chlú,
> Sin agus uile go léir lucht bréige,
>   Chuaigh idir mé 'gus tú.

> I thought, oh, my hundred affections,
>   That one house between us, love, would be,
> And I thought after that I should see, love,
>   You coaxing my child on your knee.
> But the curse of the high king of heaven
>   On my slanderer's head let it be;
> May it fall on them all, all together,
>   Who put in, love, between you and me.

These next verses, though they belong to another song, would seem to be a natural sequel to the foregoing. Lovers who have been married to other people meet only to acknowledge the hopelessness of their continued affection:

"A Nóirín, a mhíle stóirín cad é an fóirthin dúinn le fáil?"
"M'fhear-sa bheith faoi na fódaibh agus mise ag tórramh do mhná,
Mo chreach's mo mhíle truagh thú, nach pósta leat atáim
M'fhear-sa bheith faoi na fódaibh, agus mise ag tórramh do mhná."

"My Noreen, my *storeen*, my darling,
Can there nothing, be done for your sake?"
— "Till my husband is under the sod,
And till I be at your wife's wake.
My woe and my thousand afflictions,
That your hand is not mine to take,
Till my husband be under the sod,
And till I be at your wife's wake."

In the next a girl calls piteously on her lover to take her away with him, and free her from her unbearable surroundings:

Conas nach dtig tú a Sheóin 's mo thógáil óm mhuintir féin,
Conas nach dtig tú a ghrá bháin 's mo thógáil uathu uile go léir,
An rud sin a bhfuilimid ag trácht air, más i ndán dúinn gan é bheith réidh,
Och! déantar comhra cláir dom, agus fágtar mé sínte san gcré.

Why dost thou not come to me, Shone,
From my people to take me away,
Why dost thou not come, white love,
To save me from all this day.
How long have we spoken of this!
And yet fortune still bars the way!
Och! make me a coffin of boards, then,
And leave me beneath the clay.

In the following lines the heartache of jealousy is simply but forcibly expressed:

'Sí Máire mo chuid is mo stóirín
An cailín ciúin ceolmhar caoin
Is cláirseach is is smóilín ar bord í
Ag seinm go ceolmhar binn
An tráth chím chugam san ród í
'S fear eile ar a láimh san tslí
Is annamh éirím inairde
'S nach spreagann an Bás mo chroí.

Oh Mary's my love and my wonder,
  My beautiful girl of song,
She's a harp or a thrush on the table
  That will sing to us all day long.
When I see her cross over the pathway
  With another beside her than I
Death grips at my heart and stabs it
  Till I feel I must fall and die.

In these songs the lover is never tired of singing the beauty of his loved one in strains of even more than Celtic hyperbole, as:

Dá mba dubh an fharraige,
  'S an talamh bheith 'na pháipéar bán,
Cleití míne geala
  As gach eala ar an tonn ag snámh,
An méid cléireach atá i Sacsana
  Ag an aon chlár amháin,
Agus geanúlacht mo chailín
  Ní scríobhfadh siad go bráth.

If all the sea were ink, love,
  And all the land were paper white,
And every swan that swims, love
  Should give his quills so broad and bright,
And all the clerks in England
  Around one board were set to write,
And half my maiden's sweetness
  It would fail them to indite.

Or, again, in another song: —

Níl aon chrann ins an gcoill
  Nach dtiontódh a bhonn os a bharr,
Ná aon eala ar an tonn
  Nach dtiontódh a chúl leis an tsnámh,
Ná aon tsagart san bhFrainc
  Nach dtug cúl do aifreann a rá
Ach ag feitheamh gach am
  Ar phéarla deas an chléibh bháin.

There is never a tree but would stand
  On its head upside down in the wood,
And never a swan on the strand
  But would turn his back on the flood,
And never a priest in all France
  But would turn his back on the Mass
For the sake of the chance of a glance
  At my own pearl of white should she pass.

The next is more sentimental than adulatory:

> Is é mo léan géar gan mé 'mo lacha beag bán
> Do shnámhfainn go haerach in éadan na tuile 's na trá
> Ag súil le Mac Dé go réiteodh seisean mo chás
> Is go sínfí mo thaobh le péarla deas an chléibh bháin.

> 'T is my grief and my pain that I am not
>   A little white duck on the bay,
> I should rise on the swell of the billows,
>   And drive in the teeth of the spray;
> Still hoping that God may decide
>   In my favour, and me far away,
> That my side may be set by the side
>   Of my white-blossomed pearl some day.

Here follows a very rude strain indeed, though the lover's satisfaction at the reflection that his wife is not of English extraction is amusing if nothing else. From the mention of the minuet and spinnet the piece would seem to have been written, or I should rather say, composed, for I doubt if any of these pieces were ever before on paper, about the reign of Queen Anne or one of the first Georges.

Ní de líne na Sacsanach ná a shamhail cineáil bréagaigh
Do tháinig mo ghrá-sa ach ó scoth fionna Éireann
Do sheinneadh sí an bheidhlín, an spinnéid 's an chláirseach
'S dhamhsódh sí minuet ar leath-fhad (*leithead*) an phláta.

My jewel, my flower of Erin, my girl of wit and of sport,
She is sprung from no Sacsanach line, and from no lying race of the sort;
She can play on the harp and the fiddle, she can play on the spinnet in state,
Or can dance me a minuet lightly upon half of the length of the plate.

In the next piece the lover seems to have been thrown into a dungeon, probably at the instigation of his successful rival, who during his incarceration appears to have married the mistress of the unfortunate prisoner. His prison treatment may be compared with that of our modern MPs. To judge from his description oakum-picking and productive employment of prisoners was in those times unknown, at least he could hardly have done much work with his 'smalls' (wrists, knees, and ancles), 'bolted and locked.'

Do chaith mé naoi míosa i bpríosún ceangailte go cruaidh,
Bhí boltaí ar mo chaolaibh agus míle glas as sin suas,
Thabharfainn-se síthe mar a thabharfadh eala cois cuain,
Nó go sínfinn mo thaobh-sa síos le bean an fhir ruaidh.

Nine months did I spend in my prison, made fast, fettered tightly, and bound,
There were bolts on my wrists and my ancles, there were locks by the thousand
    all round,
Yet I'd rush like the wave of the tide, or I'd leap with the wings of a swan,
Could my side but be set by the side of the bride of the Red-haired Man.

In other pieces a girl sings the despair and melancholy that seize hold of her when she finds herself amongst her husband's people, far away from her home and friends, amid strange faces and strange surroundings.

> Nuair dearcaim-se suas
> Ar ard-mhala an tsléibhe,
> Tagann tuirse mhór orm
>   Agus briseadh croí,
> An neascóid cléibh
> Ar mo chliathán gléigeal
> Arraing ón éag
>   Is mé bheith mo luí.

> When I look up to the frown
> Of the mountains hanging down,
> A weariness comes over me,
>   And I sit apart;
> And there rolls a lump of woe
> O'er my bosom, white as snow,
> And the pains of death come at me,
>   And I break my heart.

Ah! how different was it all from the lovely home of her youth, from Dúiche Uí Bhriain (O'Brien's country — wherever that is), where she used to hear the cattle lowing every morning outside her own 'pleasant, prosperous, long, broad, bright house' in the valley; O'Brien's country — there was no place like that.

> Bíonn an gandal ann 's an bárdal,
> Bíonn ál ag an lachain ann
> Searrach ag an láir ann,
>   Agus leanbh ag an mnaoi.
> Na bric ag éirí inairde,
> 'S an abhainn dul le fáinní,
> 'S nach cúrtha deas an áit í,
>   Bheith i ndúiche Uí Briain.;

> There the drake is and the gander,
> There the duck and ducklings wander,
> There the mare has got her foal,
>   And there the woman has her child.
> There the river's swiftly sweeping,
> There the speckled trout is leaping,
> In O'Brien's pleasant country,
>   All so green, and fair, and mild.

I shall not easily forget the old lady from whom I rescued this song with extreme difficulty. She was clothed in rags and shrivelled with smoke and age like a mummy. She appeared to be nearly a hundred years old, and lived with her daughter, who seemed nearly as old as herself, in a little hut of one room built of sods in the middle of a wet bog, with a hole in the roof for a chimney. When she came to a place in the song where the girl describes her new house on the mountain as a

> Botháinín gan fónamh
> Ag bagairt orm i gcónaí
> Gan aon ghreim beo ann
> Ach an frap atá faoi.

i.e., 'an unprofitable little hut, ever threatening to fall in on me, without a single holdfast in it, but the prop that is supporting it,' she shook with amusement till the tears came into her eyes, and stopped to assure me with bursts of jerky asthmatic laughter, in which her daughter joined, that the girl's house was just like their own. Poor old lady! it was no wonder that the song appealed to her. I found out afterwards that the girl's fate had been her own.

From the specimens which I have now given, the reader will be able to form a pretty good conception of what the love-songs of the Gaelic peasantry — at least of Connacht, for all these songs were collected in that province — are like. It may appear strange, however, that I have only given stray verses instead of translating entire songs. But the fact is that the inconsequentness of these songs, as I have taken them down from the lips of the peasantry, is startling.

Many adjectives have been applied by many writers to the Gaelic genius, but to my mind nothing about it is so noticeable as its inconsequentness, if I may use such a word — a peculiarity which, as far as I know, no one has yet noticed. The thought of the Irish peasant takes the most surprising and capricious leaps. It's movement is like the career of his own goblin, the Pooka; it clears the most formidable obstacles at a bound and carries across astonishing distances in a moment. The folk-song is the very incarnation of this spirit. It is nearly impossible to find three verses in which there is anything like an ordinary sequence of thought. They are full up of charms that the mind must leap, elipses that it must fill up, and detours of movement which only the most vivid imagination can make straight. This is the reason why I have found no popular ballads amongst the peasantry, for to tell a story in verse requires an orderly, progressive, and somewhat slow sequence of ideas, and this is the very faculty which the Gael has not got — his mind is too quick and passionate. We have positively nothing in Gaelic like those splendid ballads of Lowland Scotland.[1] Whenever we do meet with anything like a 'ballad', that is, like a story told in verse, as in 'Tomás Ó Catháin and the Ghost,'[2] we find everything abrupt, wild, and

---

1 Always of course excepting the Ossianic poems, which are probably the work of regular bards in the 9th-12th centuries and which have been orally transmitted amongst the peasantry since then. These poems are half ballad and half epic.

2 See page 232 of my *Leabhar Sgeulaigheachta*.

disordered. The lyric style has always best suited the impetuous and inconsecutive temperament of the Irish Celt.

But even this characteristic of Gaelic thought is insufficient to account for the perfectly extraordinary inconsequentness and abruptness of the folk-songs, as I have found them. I imagine that the cause of this peculiarity is not to be ascribed wholly to the authors of the songs, but also in great part to the medium which the songs passed through before they came to us — that medium, of course, being the various generations of local singers who have perpetuated them. These singers often forgot, as was natural, the real words of the song, and then they invented others, but more frequently they borrowed verses from any other piece that came into their head, provided it could be sung to the same tune, and hence the songs as we have them now are a curious mixture indeed. What between the 'unsequacious' mind of the original makers, the alterations made by generations of singers who forgot the words, and the extraneous verses borrowed from completely different productions, two out of three of the folksongs which I have collected, resemble those children's toys of paper where when you pull a string you get a different pair of legs or a different head, joined to a different body. The most beautiful sentiments will be followed by the most grotesque bathos, and the tenderest and most exquisite verses will end in the absurdest nonsense. This has been done by the singers who have transmitted them. Here for example is a fine verse made by a man upon whom trouble had fallen. Between the first two lines and the second two there is a strong, but, for a Celt, not wholly unnatural ellipsis:

> Mo bhrón! mo dhith! mo dheacair! Nach sínte bhí mé i dtalamh
>   Sula fuair mé scannal faoi mo chuid féin,
> 'S a liacht lá breá fada a dtig úlla cúrtha ar chrannaibh
>   Duilliúr donn ar dair, agus drúcht ar an bhféar.

> It is my bitter hardship I was not dead and buried
>   'Ere scandal and reverses had struck me through and through,
> And all the fine long hours the scented apple flowers
>   And oaks break into foliage and grass a gemmed with dew.

Now these lines are certainly the genuine work of the poet, whoever he was; but what shall we say of the next? It runs:

> Now since I am drunk from continuous drinking of whiskey, &c!

Some singer has done this.

Again, the lines that follow the verse already given:

> They tell me that love is a small thing, &c.,

run

> If I go to Dublin there's no fear I'll ever return.

And I might give a hundred more examples of the same kind. I prefer, however, to give just one specimen of a comparatively perfect folk-song which has not been interfered with. I took it down from the singing of the same old woman from whom I got the song of the disillusioned bride. It is very perfect in its form; and I have not the least doubt that had anyone collected the songs, of which I have here given specimen verses, a couple of generations ago, they could easily have been restored to equal perfection:

  Mo bhrón ar an bhfarraige
   Is é tá mór
  Is é gabháil idir mé
   'S mo mhíle stór.

  D'fhágadh san mbaile mé
   Déanamh bróin,
  Gan aon tsúil thar sáile liom
   Choíche nó go deo.

  Mo léan nach bhfuil mise
   'Gus mo mhíle grá
  Ar bord loinge
   Triall go Meiriceá.

  Mo léan nach bhfuil mise
   'Gus mo mhúirnín bhán
  I gcúige Laighin
   Nó i gcondae an Chláir.

  Leaba luachra
   Bhí fúm aréir
  Agus chaith mé amach é
   Le teas an lae.

  Tháinig mo ghrá-sa
   Le mo thaobh
  Guala ar ghualainn
   Agus béal ar bhéal.

  Oh, my grief on the sea!
   How the waves of it roll!
  For they heave between me
   And the love of my soul.

  Abandoned, forsaken,
   To grief and to care,
  Will the sea ever waken
   My soul from despair?

  Were I and my darling
   (Oh, heart-bitter wound)
  But on board of the ship
   For America bound.

> Oh, my grief and my trouble!
>   Would he and I were
> In the province of Leinster
>   Or county of Clare.
>
> On a green bed of rushes
>   All last night I lay,
> And I flung it abroad
>   With the heat of the day.
>
> And my love came behind me —
>   He came from the south —
> With his breast to my bosom,
>   His mouth to my mouth.

What makes these folk-songs intensely interesting is the fact that they certainly represent genuine passion. The authors of them are long forgotten, but I have not the smallest doubt that each of them is the work of some man or woman who actually felt in his or her own person all that the song represents. That these pieces are not the productions of conscious or professional poets is evident at the first glance, for their whole style is utterly unlike that of bards who use pen and ink. Here is none of the alliteration, adjectives, assonance, and tricks of the professional poet. There cannot be the least doubt that these love-songs are the work of people whom strong passion caused to express themselves in verse. I am sure that any Gaelic scholar who reads these specimens will agree with me in this.

PART III

After the love-songs, perhaps no class of Gaelic folk-poetry is so numerous as the convivial and drinking songs. This is natural, for like his cousin the Frenchman, the Irishman is an eminently social and convivial animal, and there is scarcely any virtue which ranks higher in his eyes than hospitality. 'Is fearr rith maith ná droch sheasamh,' i.e., 'A good run is better than a bad standing,' is one of our most common proverbs, and it is the saying of a light-hearted impulsive people, who have never shown much appreciation of the close-fisted English saw of the pounds and the pence. Here is a verse from a song in eulogy of one 'Josie MacDaniel,' of whom it is said: —

> Tá bord insan alla
>   'Sé scríofa san mballa:
> 'Is cuma cérb as thú
>   Suigh síos is bí 'g ól'.

> He 's a table in his hall,
>   And it written on the wall:
> 'Wherever you're from at all
>   Sit down and be drinking!'

I fancy this would have been just the house to suit the hero of the celebrated song, 'The Pretty Girl milking the Cow,' who, according to his own account of himself, would have been much at home there:

> Do chaith mé seacht seachtain dem shaol
>   Ag ól i dtigh Shéamais Uí Háil,
> Bhí steancán ó phíobaire caoch ann,
>   Agus punch ann ag líonadh ar chlár
> D'fhágadh mé lag marbh sínte
>   Gan cor i mo chois ná 'mo láimh, ₇rl.

> I spent seven weeks of my lifetime
>   In the house of old Shamus O'Hall,
> A blind piper making us music
>   And punch on the table for all;
> And there I was left lying speechless,
>   My feet they refused me to go,
> And that when I should have been rousing
>   My colleen dhas crootha na mo.

Another hero of the tavern gives utterance to a sentiment which, except for the inherent improbability of the thing, would make us suspect that he was acquainted with the famous Latin chanson of the mediaeval ecclesiastic:

Mihi sit propositum in taverna mori, &c.

> Más duine a gheobhas bás mé
>   Ná tráchtaigh cruaidh liom
> Ach fág mé i dtigh an tábhairne
>   Sáite faoi fhorma.
> Mar a gcloisfidh mé fuaim na gcárta,
>   'S na gcluigmid (*sic*) dá mbualadh,
> Óir is binne liom an ceol sin
>   Ná glór binn na cuaiche.

> If I am a man that must die,
>   Then deal not with me in your spite,
> On a tavern's floor let me lie,
>   Thrust under some form out of sight.
> Where the clinking of glasses I'll hear,
>   And the healths being drunk through the day,
> For such sounds were more dear to my ear
>   Than the cry of the cuckoo in May.

Yet with the usual incongruity of these Irish songs, the very next verse begins with the extraordinary asseveration:

It is clearly I would write verses, and I would read the Bible;

a freak of humour which we must ascribe to the interpolator, unless, indeed, we regard it as a sign that our hero was already far gone on his way to a fit of 'the figs.'

Even in a poem in which an outlaw, concealing himself upon the wild mountains, looks down upon the far-away village where lived his love, he mingles his affection for her and his solicitude for himself with fond recollections of the feasting in his true love's hall. He exclaims pathetically:

> Glóir do Rí na ríthe!
>   Na maol-chnoic a n-imím ann,
> Is faide liom lá agus oíche ansin
>   Ná bliain insan mbaile úd thall;
> Is ann nach gcuirfí an t-ionadh
>   Faoi an dílinn dá thonnadh ann,
> Is ar nós na gcopaire buidhe
>   Bhíos líonta lán de lionn.

> To the king of all kings be glory!
>   Through these bald hills I go,
> A night and a day here are longer
>   Than years in the village below;
> It is there that men never would wonder
>   At the waves of the floods of drink,
> And the ale running red from the coppers
>   Full filled to the frothing brink.

It is noticeable that the outlaw should have dwelt so fondly upon his recollections of the ale in particular, for according to all accounts the Irish beer at this time was execrable, and when James and his French soldiers came over here to lose the battle of the Boyne and ruin Ireland, they complained bitterly of the vile stuff the Irish gave them under the name of beer — a stuff flavoured with some detestable herb in place of hops. The concoction probably tasted better to a native throat than it did to James's courtiers. After his wistful recollections of the 'waves of the floods of drink,' his feelings become too powerful for the outlaw, and he cries to his friend:

> A chomráid mo pháirte
>   Tá bás ar mo chroí le tart
> Más tusa féin mo ghrá-sa,
>   Tabhair dom cárta líonta ceart.
> Níl ach aon choróin amháin agam.
>   Bain gach pighinn do recknál as

> Go n-ólfaidh mise sláinte
> Ar chúl álainn mo chailín deas.

> My comrade, my own companion,
>   My heart in my breast will burst,
> Then get me one quart if you love me,
>   There is death on my soul with thirst.
> I have only one crown in this world,
>   Then take it and spend it all,
> Till I drink one full health to that curled
>   Brown head where the ringlets fall.

This song, a long one of some twenty verses, was repeated to me by an old woman on the banks of Lough Gara, in Connacht. She pointed out to me the ruins of the castle where the outlaw's love, one of the Druries, resided. The Druries are gone now, their lands are gone, their castle is gone, and even this song is gone; for the reciter is dead, and I doubt if anyone else knows it. Of all these the song lasted longest, but, like many a hundred other fine songs, it has gone with the Irish language — whatever remains will follow soon.

Even when a rhymer praises a special district, he does not forget to mention as one of its merits that whiskey is cheap and plenty in it. Here is a different and very much later state of things depicted. The verses belong, not like the last to the 17th century, but, I fancy, to the beginning of this. They are said to be by a blind rhymer of the name of Raftery, in the county Mayo. He is praising that county, and his verses give us a good idea of how a thirsty Irishman of that day pictured his *pays de Cocagne*:

> Tá cruithneacht is coirce, fás eorna 'gus lín ann,
>   Seagal breá aoibhinn, arán plúr agus feól (*sic*),
> Lucht déanta uiscebeatha gan license a dhíol ann,
>   Mór-uaisle na tíre ann, ag imirt 's ag ól.
> Tá cur agus treabhadh ann, 's leasú gan aoileach,
>   Is ioma sin ní ar nár labhair mé air fós
> Áthanna 's muilte ag obair gan scíth ann,
>   'S ní híoctar pighinn cíosa ann ná dada dá shórt.

> There is barley and wheat, flax and oats there by acres,
>   There is rye and white flour and meat every day,
> There the whiskey, unlicensed, is sold by its makers,
>   And the country's great men are at drink or at play.
> There is ploughing and sowing, manure is not needful,
>   With many more things that pass out of my mind;
> There the mills and the kilns and the bags are all seedful—
>   Not a penny of rent's paid, or thing of the kind.

It appears that a supply of drink is quite as necessary for the 'country's great men' as for the humbler compeers of the poet. In the next verse we catch a glimpse of the 'upper ten thousand' at drink and at play: —

> Tá an eitilt 's an fia 's gach uile shórt *game* ann,
>   An mada rua ag léimnigh, an broc 's an míol buí
> Ceolta na ngadhar 's an adharc dá séideadh
>   'S le héirí na gréine do thógfá do chroí.
> Marcaigh ar eachraibh is daoine uaisle gléasta
>   Ag fiach tré na chéile go dtige an oích',
> Siléar go maidin arís dá réiteach ann
>   Ól ag na céadtaibh is leabaí le buí (*recte* luí).

> There's the fawn and the deer and game had for the finding,
>   The red dog[3] aleaping, the badger and the hare,
> There's the music of hounds and the horn awinding,
>   With the rise of the sun one's heart leaps to be there.
> There are gentlemen shining and riding on horses
>   All through other hunting till darkness shall frown,
> Then — cellar till morning, arrance (*recte* arrange) the resources,
>   There's drunk for the hundreds and beds to lie down.

But man does not live by bread alone, or even by unlicensed whiskey, *alias, poteen,* and if a locality is to deserve its fame, it needs more than this — the poor must also be looked after and learning duly honoured; for the Irish Celt's hunger for learning is almost proverbial, and he is notably good to his poor. The poet accordingly winds up with the assertion that in this highly favoured locality:

> Faigheann dílleachtaí 's baintreabhaí cabhair is réiteach
>   Slí bídh, agus éadaí, is talamh gan cíos,
> Scoláirí bochta scríobhadh scol agus léann
>   Lucht iarraidh na déirce ann, ag tarraing 's ag triall.

> The orphan and widow get help in their mourning —
>   Food, clothing, and land, without rent, without care;
> Poor scholars get writing and schooling and learning,
>   And the askers of alms from all quarters draw there.

The 'askers of alms' is a pleasant Irish periphrasis for beggars, a word which, such is their great good feeling, the lower classes rarely use. They prefer to speak of 'holy poverty,' and until quite recently the trade of begging carried with it amongst the country people little or no social discredit. Even in the present century many men, well-dressed and accompanied by horses to carry away their plunder, made an ample livelihood from begging. These were the *bocachs*, and fear of being satirised by them was often an additional inducement to make the peasant give. Father English, a renowned poet of the last century, celebrated the trade of begging in some humorous verses, the first of which may be thus translated: —

---

3 i.e., Fox.

> His work or trade let each man boast
> And think his calling fine,
> Mine own is better than the most,
> For asking alms is mine.

The natural result of this is that while in England, the richest country in the world, one man in every twenty of the population is supported by the other nineteen; in Ireland, which is about the poorest land in Europe, the proportion is only one man to seventy or eighty.

But this article has already run to an extravagant length, and I must here conclude it, merely remarking that if anyone feels an interest in these productions of the Gaelic mind of which I have here given a few specimens, he will have to prosecute the study for himself, for in this instance there is no royal road to learning. By gaining the confidence of the peasantry and by learning their language he will find amongst them some rubbish certainly, but very much more real ore, which were it collected would prove of importance to the philosopher, the poet, the comparative mythologist, and even the historian. Unfortunately it is at present almost too late to reap a harvest. The discouragement and the apathy of those who have influence, the attitude of our Press, which would as soon think of advising the people to stand by their language, traditions, and customs as they would of exhorting them to buy the London *Times* and stand by the Government — all these have changed Southern and Western Ireland within a couple of decades in a manner which no outsider can realise, and have rendered it impossible now to collect myriads of interesting relics of a self-developed Aryan people, which could have been amassed without trouble fifty years ago.

It is no exaggeration, although it is a metaphor, to say that the whole of the west and south and north-west coast of Ireland is today strewn thick with dead and dying traditions of the past, as a forest is with leaves after some great storm. The leaves are now gone and the tree is bare; they will never grow again, never — to use the Irish phrase — while grass grows or water runs.

I suppose the people who helped to being this about are glad of it, but for my part I honestly confess that I am heartily sorry.

In this paper I have only given some few specimens, almost at haphazard, of the unknown and unwritten love and drinking songs of the western Gaelic peasant, but upon some future occasion I may glance at some other branches of our folk-poetry.

Some Words on Irish Folk-lore[*]

Irish and Scotch Gaelic stories are, as a living form of literature, pretty nearly by this time a thing of the past. They have been trampled in the common ruin under the feet of the *Zeitgeist,* happily not before a large harvest has been reaped in Scotland, but unfortunately before anything worth mentioning has been done in Ireland to gather the crop which grew so luxuriously there a few years back.

Strange as it may appear there existed until recently in our midst millions of men and women, who, when their day's work was over, sought and found mental recreation in a domain to which few indeed of us who read and write books, are permitted to enter. Man is, after all, pretty much the same all the world over. When he has become tired of the actualities of life he seeks to unbend his mind with the creations of fancy. We who can read betake ourselves to our favourite novelist, and as we peruse his fictions we can almost see our author erasing this, heightening that, and laying on such and such a touch for effect. His book is the product of his individual brain, and some of us or of our contemporaries have been present at its genesis.

But no one can tell us with certainty of the genesis of the folk tale, no one has been consciously present at its inception, and no one has marked its growth. It is in many ways a mystery, part of the flotsam and jetsam of the ages still beating feebly against the shore of the nineteenth century, swallowed up at last in England by the waves of materialism and civilization combined, but still surviving unengulfed on the western coasts of Ireland, where I gathered together some strange bundles of it.

The folk-lore of Ireland, like its folk songs and native literature, remains practically ungathered and unexplored. Attempts have been made from time to time during the present century to collect Irish folk-lore, but these attempts, though interesting from a literary point of view, must too often be pronounced failures from a scientific one. Crofton Croker's delightful book *Fairy Legends and Traditions of the South of Ireland* first published anonymously in 1825, led the way. All the other books that have been published on the subject have but followed in the footsteps of his; but all have not had the merit of his light style, his pleasant parallels from classical and foreign literature, and his

[*] *Providence Sunday Journal,* 24 August 1890. See p. 44.

delightful annotations, which touch, after a manner peculiarly his own, upon all that is of interest in his text. But the word 'text' conveys the idea of an original to be annotated upon, and Crofton Croker is, alas, too often his own original. There lies his weak point, and the weak point of all his successors as well. The form in which the stories are told is, of course, Croker's own, but no one who knows anything of fairy lore will suppose that his manipulation of the original is confined to the form merely. The fact is that he learned the groundwork of his tales from conversations with the Southern peasantry, whom he knew well, and then elaborated these over the midnight oil, with great skill and delicacy of touch, in order to give a readable book thus spiced to the English public.

After Crofton Croker, setting aside the novelists Carleton and Lover, who only published some incidental and largely manipulated Irish stories, the next person to collect Irish folk-lore in a book form was Patrick Kennedy, a native of the county Wexford, who published *Legendary Fictions of the Irish Celts*, and in 1870 his *Fireside Stories of Ireland*, which he had himself heard in Wexford when a boy. Many of the stories which he gives appear to be the detritus of genuine Gaelic folk stories, but they have filtered down through the English language and idiom, and have become stunted and deformed in the transit. Unfortunately, Kennedy does not give the sources from which he derived the stories, so that, as in the case of Croker's stories, we are at a loss to know how much of the book belongs to Kennedy, the bookseller, and how much to the Wexford peasant.

After this come Lady Wilde's (the well-known Speranza of the '48 period) volumes, her *Ancient Legends* and her *Ancient Cures, Charms and Usages*, published a few weeks ago, in both of which books she gives us a large amount of narrative matters in a folk-lore dress. Unfortunately, like her predecessors, she disdains to quote an authority or to give us the least inkling of where such and such a legend or superstition came from, from whence it was obtained, who were her informants, whether peasant or other; in what parishes or counties the superstition obtains, and all the other collateral information which the modern folk-lorist is sure to expect. Unfortunately, also, Lady Wilde is completely ignorant of Irish, through the medium of which alone such tales and superstitions can be properly collected, and she astonishes us with such striking observations as that 'peasants in Ireland wishing you good luck say in Irish the blessing of Bel and the blessing of Samhain be with you, that is of the sun and the moon.' It happens that though I have spoken Irish in every county in Ireland, where it is still spoken, I have never been, nor do I expect to be, so saluted! Lady Wilde's volumes are nevertheless a wonderful and copious record of folk-lore and folk customs, which must lay Irishmen under one more debt of gratitude to the gifted compiler. It is unfortunate, however, that these volumes are hardly as valuable as they are interesting and for the usual reason — that we do not know what is Lady Wilde's and what is not.

Almost contemporaneously with Lady Wilde's last book, there appeared a couple of months ago yet another volume upon the same subject, by Mr Jeremiah Curtin, an American gentleman who came over to England to prosecute his ethnological investigations. He has collected and given to the public, in a dainty volume, a collection of about twenty folk tales, taken down from amongst the oldest, poorest and most retired of the Gaelic-speaking peasantry. He found, as I have done, that it is useless searching for stories amongst the English-speaking people. The Irish language died out or was killed off over three-fourths of Ireland within the last eighty years, and over all that portion of the country there has been made as clean a sweep of folk-lore and folk-tales, as is made of a barn when a new broom sweeps it out. Mr Curtin has certainly approached much nearer to the fountain-head than any of his predecessors, for my own knowledge of folk-lore, such as it is, enables me to see that he has given his stories to us with much less doctoring and manipulation than they. Unhappily, he must have been obliged to collect his tales through the very awkward medium of an interpreter, because his knowledge of Irish is evidently of the smallest, and makes him fall into some amusing mistakes, such as talking of killing and boiling a stork (Irish, *storc* — a bullock), although his ethnological investigations might have taught him the stork was not a Hibernian fowl. Mr Curtin has not done himself justice by the way in which he has given us his delightful stories, because, like Croker, Kennedy, and Lady Wilde, he has neither mentioned where he got them, nor from whom, nor how. Unfortunately, too, he has a literary style of his own, which gives one an erroneous impression of the language of the stories which he has gathered, for his style — to say the very least of it — has no counterpart in the Gaelic from which he has translated.*

Indeed, it is on this rock of ignorance of Gaelic, that all our workers-up of folk-lore split. In most circles in Ireland it is a disgrace to be known to talk Irish, and in the capital, if one makes use of an Irish word to express one's meaning, as one sometimes does of a French or German word, one would be looked upon as positively outside the pale of decency. Hence we need not be surprised at the ignorance of Gaelic Ireland displayed by literateurs who write for the English public, and credit us with modes of speech which we have not got, and idioms they never learned from us. The chief interest in too many of our folk-tale writers lies in their individual treatment of the skeletons of the various Gaelic stories obtained through English mediums, and it is not devoid of interest to watch the various garb in which the sophisticated minds of the ladies

---

* See 'Jeremiah Curtin's Working Methods: the evidence from the manuscripts,' Janet Egleson Dunleavy and Gareth W. Dunleavy in *Éigse* XVIII (1980) 67-86.

and gentlemen who trifled in such matters clothed the dry bones. But when the skeletons were thus padded round and clad, although built upon folk-lore, they were no longer folk-lore themselves, for folk-lore can only find a fitting garment in the language that comes from the mouths of those whose minds are so primitive that they retain with pleasure those tales which the sophisticated invariably forget: for this reason folk-lore must always be presented in an uncertain and unsuitable medium whenever the contents of the stories are divorced from their original expression in language. Seeing how our Irish writers and collectors have treated them hitherto, it is hardly to be wondered at that the writer of the article on folk-lore in the *Encyclopaedia Britannica*, though he gives the names of some fifty authorities on the subject, has not mentioned a simple (*recte*: single) Irish collection. I believe the only attempt ever made — so far — to take down and print their folk stories from the lips of the peasantry, in the exact language in which they uttered them, was made by myself in a modest little volume published last year in the Irish character and language, entitled *Leabhar Sgeulaigheachta* or 'Story Book.' In this little book, besides giving copious notes on the language of my informants, I gave their names and localities — information which must always be the very first requisite of any work upon which a future scientist may rely when he proceeds to draw honey (is it always honey?) from the flowers which we collectors have culled for him. Since these stories have, so far, not been translated into English, a glance at their contents may prove not wholly uninteresting to the student of human nature and antiquities.

I shall begin by roughly dividing all the folk-lore found amongst the Irish into two classes, of which I propose to examine one in this paper, namely, into stories which I believe had a conscious genesis upon Irish ground, and stories which had no such genesis. The first class (which I shall not for the present examine), consists of the remains or detritus of stories which I believe to have been invented by the bards and professional story-tellers to amuse the chiefs, their patrons; and some of these stories which may have been consciously invented — as one of our own novelists will invent — out of the brain of an individual bard, have come down to our own day, and are still told in a ragged and dilapidated condition amongst those few of the peasantry who still speak no language but Irish. The other class, which I propose to treat of here, consists of nature-myths and attempts on the part of prehistoric man to explain the various phenomena of nature personifying them and then telling stories about them when so personified. It consists also of tales meant to inculcate morality, or to show that virtue has its own reward, in the long run, while vice goes to the wall. It consists, in addition to these, of numberless stories on all sorts of things, chiefly on Kings and Kings' daughters, and wizards, and enchanted swans, and talking beasts, and grateful animals, and skilled companions, and hags in the form of weasels and other animals, and mermaids and adventures in lonely woods with giants with one eye, and they are full of reminiscences of cannibalism, of swords of light (evidently a dim recollection of a time when a race of men using bronze or stone weapons came in contact with men using polished steel), of magic apples, of cakes and other inanimate objects that are gifted with speech, of fairy music and fairies who live in the green hills, of pookas who entice men on their back and leap over mountains with them, of elopements, of impossible tasks successfully accomplished, of the strong man whom nothing can kill, of the wicked stepmother who is at last overcome by her suffering stepdaughter, of fiery dragons and unfortunate princesses, and, in a word, of all the paraphernalia of human thought mixed and jumbled and crowded together, that choked the brain of man during the progress of the centuries, and which he has got rid of only in comparatively modern times — only, in fact, since the close of the middle ages.

But perhaps some one, reading all these strange and wonderful legends that have drifted down the centuries, might be tempted to say, 'These stories are very whimsical and wonderful, indeed, but for my part I do not understand why you call them valuable: they are simply stories such as I invent myself, or any of us may invent, to amuse our children, and they can have no higher or more important origin than that.' To make such an apparently natural objection as this, is to display the most consummate ignorance of the science of folk-lore. So far from these stories having been invented in modern times to amuse children, they are themselves so old as to date from the far distant prehistoric ages when man was himself a child. The fact of my finding old Paddy Mulrooney or old Kitty O'Leary able to tell me an Irish story about a prince who is enchanted, and a white pigeon who is his bride, is in itself nothing wonderful, but if we find an Indian ayah in a palace at Calcutta soothing the white child she has charge of by telling him precisely that same story, and again, if going further afield we find the identical tale related amongst the snows of Siberia — this, it must be confessed, puts a very different complexion upon the folk-tale; this forces us to confess whether we will or no, that old Kitty's story is not to be despised as unmeaning nonsense, of which no one can make use except, perhaps, to quiet a child!

The fact is that within the last few years folk-lore (first founded as a science by the brothers Grimm in Germany some fifty years ago) has advanced so rapidly, as the world contracts and scientific people examine the folk-lore of peoples formerly out of reach, that nowadays it has produced and proved some of the most extraordinary results that could be conceived. The Grimms thought it extraordinary enough when they discovered a story in some other European country parallel to one of their own German ones; and finally were forced to come to the conclusion that their folk tales which they found in Germany and Russia and Brittany etc., were so immeasurably old that they had been carried by these various Aryan-speaking races from the early home and cradle from which went forth the various races, Greeks, Romans, Teutons, Slavs, Celts and the Sanscrit-speaking peoples of India, to conquer the peoples they found before them, and to colonize or at least give their language to Europe and India. But at present scientific research has largely extended this result of the Grimms' investigations, and has proved that not amongst Aryan-speaking races in Europe and India alone are there tales to be found, but also amongst the Zulus in Africa, amongst the Mongolians in Asia and amongst the red Indians of America.

It may be urged that man's ideas are but limited, and that these stories might have arisen independently. But that cannot be so with regard to at least some of them, which are so curious and intricate that they must have been invented once and for all, as it can hardly be credited that two independent brains could have hit upon the same story. Here, for instance, is such an example: A young man gets possession of a magic ring. This ring is stolen from him by his enemy, and is recovered by the aid of some grateful heart (*recte* beast) whom he has benefited. His enemy who has stolen the ring, hides it away in his mouth, but the grateful mouse insinuates his tail into the nose of the thief, makes him sneeze, and out comes the magic ring. Now, this story is found in the Punjaub, amongst the Bretons, the Albanians, the modern Greeks, and the Russians, and, it is quite ridiculous to think that these could have all independently invented the same story for themselves. Since Grimm's time, however, the same story has been discovered — young man, ring, mouse and all — amongst savage tribes in America, as widely different from the others, both racially and geographically, as the world would admit of. How the story came there is the mystery which the science of folk-lore has as yet been unable to solve.

The Irish stories, as I have collected them, bear a near resemblance to the German tales which the Grimms collected and rendered popular in every country in Europe. They also bear a close resemblance to the tales of the Norse, and many of them have close parallels in Russian and Slavonic folk stories. It is needless to say that wherever one of the Irish stories has a parallel in the Slavonic, Sanscrit or Teutonic languages, it proves its antiquity at once, as these various races must have carried the tale with them when they set off from their original home to colonise Europe and India in prehistoric times. But some of these stories bear on their faces proofs of extraordinary antiquity, for they are plainly nature myths invented by primitive man to account for the various phenomena of nature. I shall give a few instances of such, collected by myself, for the first time. In a story entitled 'The boy who was long on his mother,' we find evident traces of a sun myth. The hero of this tale is the strong man who cannot be beaten, and who succeeds in everything. He is a regular Hercules, and many of his adventures resemble those of the classic Hercules. He takes service with the King, and the King gives him impossible tasks to perform, and tries to take his life, just as the King in classic story tried to take the life of Hercules. Amongst other things he desires him to drain dry a lake full of water. The lake happens to be in a hollow, with a steep embankment at one side like a reservoir. The hero puts his mouth to a hole which he makes in the embankment and sucks down the water of the lake, with boats, fishes, ships and everything else that it contained, leaving the lake 'as dry as the flat of your hand.' Even a sceptic must admit that this tale is the remains of an Aryan sun myth, and personifies the action of the warm sun in drying up a lake and making it a marsh, killing the fishes and leaving the boats stranded. But the story is suggestive of more than this. Professor Rhys tried to prove, lately, in his Hebbert lectures, that Hercules was a sun god. But our hero is evidently Hercules for, like Hercules, a King tries to kill him by giving him impossible tasks to perform. Like Hercules, he descends into hell and frightens the devils with his club; like Hercules, he accomplishes his tasks successfully, and escapes the death the King intends for him. But the Irish tradition has preserved this trait of draining the lake dry, and thereby identifies our hero with the sun god, the very thing which, on much more slender grounds, Professor Rhys and those who think with him, assert Hercules to have been. If this story is not the remains of a nature myth it is perfectly unintelligible, for no natural person could hope to impose upon even a child by saying that a man drank up a lake, ships and all; and yet this apparently nonsensical story has been with strange conservatism repeated from father to son for thousands of years and must have taken its rise at a time our Aryan ancestors were in much the same rude and mindless condition as the Australian blacks or the Digger Indians are to-day.

Again, in another story we hear of a boat that sails equally swiftly over land and sea and goes straight to its mark. It is so large that if all the men of the world were to enter it, there would remain place for six hundred more, whilst it is so small that it folds up into the palm of the person who has it. But ships do not sail on land, nor grow large and small, nor go straight to their mark, consequently it is plain that we have here another nature myth, vastly old, invented by prehistoric man, for these ships can be nothing but the clouds which sail over land and sea, which are large enough to hold the largest armies and small enough to fold into the hand, and which go straight to the mark. The meaning of this has been forgotten for countless ages, but the story has survived.

Again, in another tale called 'The bird of sweet music,' a man follows a sweet singing bird into a cave underground and finds a country where he wanders for a year and a day, and a woman who befriends him while there, and enables him to bring back the bird, which turns out to be a King's daughter. At the end of the tale the narrator mentioned quite casually that the woman whom he met down there was his mother. But this touch shows that the land where he wandered was the Celtic Hades, the country of the dead beneath the ground, and stamps the tale at once as prechristian.

But there are other stories which, though they do not bear their great antiquity or any appearance of being myths upon their face, nevertheless, when compared with kindred stories found elsewhere, turn out to be old Aryan tales and to contain traces of nature myths. This will be best explained by giving a concrete example of it. For this purpose we will examine an Irish folk-story which I took down in Gaelic word for word from the recitation of an old man, one Shawn Cunningham, who lives in the County Roscommon, on the borders of the County Mayo, in the village of Ballingshuil, on the highroad between Frenchpark and Ballaghadareen.

This story which is called the 'King of Ireland's Son' is a fair specimen of a great many others collected by me amongst the Western peasantry. It begins by giving an account of how the King of Erin's son went out hunting of a snowy day, and how he killed a raven. The raven fell upon snow which was all crimsoned with its blood. The Prince thought to himself how lovely that woman would be whose tresses were as dark as the raven's head, whose skin was as white as the spotless snow, and whose cheeks were as ruddy as the crimson blood. Thereupon he puts himself under geasa, as the Irish phrase is, that is, binds himself under a solemn obligation 'not to eat two meals at one table or sleep two nights in one house, until he should find a woman whose hair was as black as the raven's head, and her skin as white as the snow, and her two cheeks as red as the blood.' He starts off to the western (*recte* eastern) world, where he hears that such a woman exists. Money was not very plenty in Ireland at that time, but he took with him twenty pounds. 'He had not,' says the narrator, 'walked far until he met a funeral, and he said it was as good for him to go three steps with the corpse. He had not walked the three steps until there came a man and left his writ down on the corpse for five pounds. There was a law in Erin at that time that any man to whom another person owed a debt, that if that person who owed the debt was dead that person's people could not bury him without having paid his debts, or without the leave of the person to whom the debts were owed. When the King of Ireland's son beheld the sons and daughters of the dead man crying and wailing because they had no money to pay his debts, he said to himself: 'It's a great pity that these poor people have not money,' and he put his hand in his pocket and he himself paid five pounds for the corpse. After that he said he might as well go as far as the church to see it buried. He had hardly got to the church when there came another man and left his writ on the body for five pounds more. 'Well, as I gave the first five pounds,' said the King of Erin's son to himself, 'it's as good for me to pay the other five, and to let the poor man go to his grave in peace.' He paid the other five pounds. He had only ten pounds then. He had not gone very far until he met a thin, dark man, and he asked him where he was going. He said that he was going looking for a woman in the Eastern world. The thin dark man asked him did he want a servant, and he said he did, and asked what would be the wages he'd be looking for. He said: 'The first kiss of his wife, if he should get her.' The King of Ireland's son promised him that.

They had not gone very far until they met another man and his gun in his hand, and he a levelling it at the black bird that was in the eastern world, that he might have it for his dinner. The thin, dark man said to him it was as good for him to take that man into his service also, if he would take service with him. The son of the King of Ireland asked him if he would come into his service. 'I will,' said the man, 'if I get my wages.' 'And what are the wages you'll be looking for?' 'The place of a house and garden.' 'You'll get that if my journey succeeds with me.'

The King of Ireland's son went forward with the thin, dark man and the gunner, and they had not gone very far until a man met them and his ear laid on the ground, and he listening to the grass growing. 'It's as good for you to take that man into your service,' said the thin, dark man. The King's son asked the man whether he would come with him on service. 'I'll come if I get the place of a house and a garden.' 'You'll get that if the thing I have in my head succeeds with me.'

The son of the King of Ireland, the thin, dark man, the gun-man and the ear-man went forward, and it was not far they went until they met another man, and his one foot on his shoulder, and he keeping a field of hares without letting one in or one out of the field. The King's son wondered, and asked him, 'What was the meaning of his keeping one foot on his shoulder like that?' 'Oh,' says he, 'if I had my two feet on the ground, I should be so swift I would go out of sight.' 'Will you come on service with me?' etc.

The King of Ireland's son, the thin, dark man, the gun-man, the ear-man and the foot-man went forward, and it was not far they went until they came to a man, and he turning round a wind mill with one nostril, and he had his finger laid on his nose, closing the other. 'Why have you your finger on your nose?' said the King of Ireland's son. 'Oh,' said he, 'if I were to blow with the two nostrils I would sweep the mill altogether up out of that into the air.' 'Will you come on hire with me?' etc.

The son of the King of Ireland, the thin, dark man, the gun-man, the ear-man, the foot-man and the blow-man went forward until they came to a man sitting by the side of the road, and he a breaking stones with one thigh, and he had no hammer or anything else. The King's son asked him why it was he was breaking stones with one thigh like that. 'Oh,' says he, 'if I were to strike them with the double thigh, I'd make powder of them.' 'Will you hire?' etc.';

Then they all went forward together, the son of the King of Ireland, the thin, dark man, the gun-man, the ear-man, the foot-man, the blow-man and the man who broke the stones with the side of his thigh, and they would overtake the March wind that was before them, and the March wind that was behind them would not overtake them, until the evening came and the end of the day.

After this the present narrator gives their further adventures at great length, relating all that happened to the company during their expedition to this wonderful woman who lived in the western (*recte* eastern) world. During the long journey thither, the King's son, with the assistance of the thin dark man, becomes possessor of a pair of old slippers, which, when he put them on and wished to be in any place, instantly transported him thither: of an old cap, which, when he put it on his head, enabled him to see everybody without being seen: and of an old rusty sword which would cut through the solid rock as if it were cheese. At last they arrive at the ladies' castle and are put up and hospitably received, but the lady tells him that he must perform three tasks for her or else he must lose his head. She even points him out a stake stuck into the ground, and waiting for his skull to be set up on it. It was the sixtieth stake; fifty-nine had already been decorated with the heads of her suitors. It is unnecessary to mention how he managed by the aid of the thin dark man to accomplish the various tasks, but after they were all accomplished she still said that she never would marry him unless he got a runner to travel with her runner for three bottles of the healing balm out of the well of the western (*recte* eastern) world, and if her own runner should return quicker that his, she said 'his head was gone.'

She got an old hag — some witch — (I am now giving the exact words of my narrator translated) and she gave her three bottles. The thin dark man was bade give three bottles to the man who was keeping the field of hares, and they were given him. The hag and the man started with three bottles each one: and the runner of the King's son was coming half way on his road home while the hag had only got half way to the well. 'Sit down,' said the hag to the foot-runner when they met, 'and take your rest, for the pair of them are married now, and don't be breaking your heart running.' She brought over a horse's head and a slumber pin in it, and laid it under his head and when he laid down his head on it he fell asleep. She spilt out all the water he had in his bottles, and she ran forward then to come home. The thin dark man thought it long until they were coming, and he said to the ear-man: 'Lay your ear on the ground and try are they coming'. 'I hear the hag coming,' said he 'but the foot-man is asleep and I hear him snoring.' 'Look from you' said the thin dark man to the gun-man, 'till you see where the foot runner is.' The gun-man looked and he said that the foot-runner was in such and such a place, and a horse's skull under his head and he sleeping. 'Lay your gun to your eye,' said the thin dark man, 'and smash the skull from under his head.' He put his gun to his eye and he swept the skull from under his head. The foot runner woke up and he found that the bottles which he had were empty, and it was necessary for him to return to the well again.

The hag was coming then and the foot runner was not to be seen. Says the thin dark man to the man who was sending round the windmill with his nostril, 'Rise up and try would you put back that hag.' He put his finger to his nose, and when the hag was coming he put a blast of wind under her that swept her back again. She was coming again, and he did the same thing to her. Every time she used to be coming near them he would be sending her back with the wind he would blow out of his nostril. At last he blew with the two nostrils and swept the hag back to the western (*recte* eastern) world again. Then the foot-runner of the King of Ireland's son came, and the day was won.

The Prince had yet another task to accomplish, which I shall not chronicle here, but briefly remark that the thin dark man saves his life once more by taking his wife aside to give her the first kiss, and there picking out of her body certain serpents which would have stung the Prince to death had he attempted it. The end of all is that the thin dark man takes his leave of the Prince and tells him when departing that he was the man who was in the coffin for whom the Prince had twice paid the five pounds, 'and these people who are with you, they are servants whom God has sent to you.' After that he and his people departed and were never seen again.

So much for this Irish Gaelic story, which is of a fairly common type but which, in its main aspects, must be of unknown antiquity, for we find a close parallel of the plot in the Danish story of the 'Traveller,' where the hero pays all his money to get a corpse buried, which afterwards follows him in the shape of a travelling companion, and helps him to win a King's daughter, and instructs him what to do to save himself on the first night of the marriage, just as the thin dark man picks out the snake in our story.

But while the Danish parallel runs on the same lines with ours, as the 'motivation' — a barbarous but useful word ...[*illegible*]... who take hire with the Prince. We have to go further afield for them. Now on consulting the Czech story of 'George with the Goat' translated last year by Mr Wratislaw in his folk tales from Slavonic sources, we find a very remarkable parallel to these supernatural helpers, which it is best to give at length.

George, the hero, starts, like the Irish Prince, to win the King's daughter, 'and' says the narrator, 'he met a man who had a foot on his shoulder.' George said, 'Why have you your foot on your shoulder?' He replied, 'If I take it off I leap a hundred miles.' 'Whither are you going?' 'I am going in search of service, to see if any one will take me.' 'Well, come with us.' They went on again and met a man who had a bandage on his eyes. 'Why have you a bandage on your eyes?' He answered, 'If I remove the bandage I see a hundred miles.' 'Whither are you going?' 'I am going in search of service if you will take me.' 'Yes, I'll take you, come also with me.' They went on a bit further and met another fellow who had a bottle under his arm, and instead of a stopper held his thumb in it. 'Why do you hold your thumb there?' 'If I pull it out I squirt a hundred miles and besprinkle everything that I choose; if you like, take me also into your service; it may be to your advantage and ours, too.' George replied, 'Well, come, too.'

When George comes to the King's daughter she will not be given to him if he be not able to bring a goblet of water in a minute from a spring a hundred miles off. This is nearly the same as in our tale; what follows resembles it even closer. I give the exact words of the story. 'So George said to the man who had the foot on his shoulder, 'You said that if you took your foot down you could jump a hundred miles?' He replied, 'I'll easily do that,' took down his foot and jumped and was there. But after this there was only a very little time to spare, and by then he ought to have been back. So George said to the second, 'You said that if you removed the bandage from your eyes you could see a hundred miles: peep and see what is going on.' 'Ah, sir! Goodness gracious! he's fallen asleep.' 'That will be a bad job,' said George, 'the time will be up. You, third man, you said if you pulled your thumb out, you could squirt a hundred miles; be quick and squirt thither that he may get up, and you, look whether he is moving or what.' 'Oh, sir, he's getting up now, he's knocking the dust off, he's drawing the water.' He then gave a jump and was there exactly in time.'

It will be observed that in the Irish tale, the gunman plays a double part, that of the man who sees and that of the man who squirts. But the Bohemian story contains evident traces of having been once a nature myth, traces which the Irish story, though much longer and in every way superior, has lost. For, as Mr Wratislaw explains it, 'the man who jumps a hundred miles appears to be the rainbow, the man with bandaged eyes the lightning, and the man with the bottle the cloud.' This exceedingly interesting point has been wholly obscured in our tale, but nevertheless shows pretty plainly what the origin of these incidents was, though it sees to have been improved upon in the course of ages by adding the man who broke the stones, the ear-man, and the blow-man, which, however, I have no doubt many folk-lorists would interpret as the avalanche, the wind and the calm.

I have, however, done enough to show the vast antiquity of these tales as collected from some half starving peasant in a smoky cabin in a Connacht bog, and I hope I have also shown that they deserve some better treatment than to be pooh-poohed and cast aside as old rubbish. For I may well ask, of all that connects the nineteenth century with prehistoric man, of all that couples man as he is with man as he once was, is there anything except a few drilled stones and flint arrow heads that approaches within any measurable distance of these tales.

On Some Indian Folk-lore*

There are many spots in Canada where, despite repeating Winchesters and growth of population, the big game, moose and caribou, are not yet extinct. Such places are to be found all over the province of New Brunswick, especially in the Northern counties. This province is thinly populated, and about four-fifths, or even more, of it is still covered with forest and jungle, interspersed by 'barrens' or pieces of poor, untimbered land, varying from a quarter of a mile to several miles in extent, and forming the feeding ground of the caribou, who live on moss, which they paw up from under the snow, and on a kind of grey lichen, which hangs from the branches of the hackmatack or tamarack (English spruce) trees.

    I had long been endeavoring to secure some folk-lore and old stories from the Milicete Indians, who dwell along the St John and other inland rivers in New Brunswick, but somehow or other the aspect of a stranger in the broad daylight seemed always to have a depressing influence upon them, and they invariably either alleged that they knew no stories, or else that they used to hear them but had now forgotten them. The few Milicete stories, which in the end I succeeded in getting, I must attribute to the caribou, after which I went out hunting with two Indians and two half-breeds. One of these half-breeds was a curious combination of blood, his father having been a Russian Finn and his mother a squaw, yet though the Finns are one of the cleverest races in Europe, it so turned out that he was the stupid one of the party, and could tell no stories outside of a personal adventure or two. The other half-breed was the son of an old Hudson Bay voyageur, who had become so Indianized that he had never spoken anything to his children but Indian, and this man, who had an exuberance of French vivacity in his nature, was, like Mercurius, chief speaker and also chief story teller for the rest of the party. The full bred Indians were more taciturn and did not know English sufficiently well to tell a long story in it, and although I had picked up several hundred words and phrases of Milicete I did not understand it sufficiently to follow a rapidly told story. Accordingly the majority of the stories which I jotted down came from the French half-breed, who, having been born in an English-speaking part of the province of New Brunswick, where his father had settled, spoke Indian

* *Providence Sunday Journal*, 12 April 1891. Subtitled: 'Algonquin Stories'. See pp. 43-4.

and not very fluent English, but strange to say, hardly any French. I may here mention that the northern part of the province contains a large number of French speakers, whose language, far from tending to die out as German is dying in the States seems bent upon holding its place for all time in Canada, and competing with English and Spanish in the linguistic distribution of the new world. Almost two-fifths of Canada is at present French speaking, and as the French population is increasing faster than the English they may soon be equal. The French of the habitans, however, is becoming largely anglicised, and they speak of potatos for *pomme de terre*, post cartes for *cartes de poste*, and what is more remarkable some families of French origin appear to have a mania for translating their names into English; thus numberless Blancs now call themselves Whites or Wites, even though they continue to speak French.

As to the Indian population of New Brunswick, it is probably under a thousand, and is chiefly composed of two different tribes speaking, as far as I could find out, almost totally distinct languages, the Milicetes, the Micmacs. These Indians pull very well with the whites, and men who will walk out of a lumber camp and refuse to work in it if a negro is taken into employment, make not the slightest objection to working with Indians. The men and squaws are saluted still as brother and sister. The red man is, however, decreasing in numbers here as elsewhere, partly from disease, partly from the increasing scarcity of game, and partly through his inability to adapt himself to the new civilisation, though I must confess that the most of those with whom I came in contact appeared as capable of taking care of themselves as anyone need wish, and more than one who had in time past served as guide or hunter to the officers of the regular army — before it was withdrawn from Canada — had completely acquired the offhand manners of the English officer, and uttered passing oaths and planted themselves with their back to the fire and extended legs with all the charming insouciance and polish of club or mess room. The worst of the red man is his improvidence. He spends money as he gets it, and even after great hunting or 'furring' successes and making a coup of several hundred dollars, he always runs through his wealth immediately on getting it in the silliest way, and it seems probable that another generation or two will be necessary to eradicate this failing from the breed.

Of our hunting exploits I am not going to speak; suffice it to say that we pitched our camp in a great thicket, shovelling away the snow, which was about two feet thick, and leaving about three inches of it on the ground; we covered it over with a quantity of fine spruce boughs, and spreading our skins and blankets over them we slept very comfortably, nor did we find it hard to keep the tent warm, although the thermometer stood for several days at 35 below zero. Unfortunately snow had fallen, and changed into a half rain just as we were encamping ourselves, and this, freezing on the top of the snow, made a kind of hard crust, which our snow shoes cracked at every step, so that it became impossible to stalk either caribou or moose, for the noise of the snow crust as it cracked could be distinctly heard for half a mile. We were obliged, accordingly, to remain in camp for about a fortnight, waiting for fresh snow to fall, which would deaden the noise of our snow shoes, and give us an opportunity to creep on the caribou who were in our vicinity. It was during this time that, having nothing better to do, each of us told all the stories he could think of, and I know, for my part, I must have told over thirty. Many of the stories of the half-breed seemed to me to have filtered into Indian from a French Canadian, and some actually from a Scotch Gaelic or Irish source. The most of them he had been told by his father in Indian, others he had picked up round camp fires, but the proportion that seemed to me to be of pure Indian origin was less than half. It was, however, quite natural that his father, having been an old Hudson Bay voyager, should have picked up Scotch Gaelic stories from his fellow hunters, great numbers of whom were Scotch, and afterwards recited them in Indian to his children. Several, indeed, the majority of his stories, were probably of French origin, and many of them were too gross for repetition. Amongst other stories of European origin which he had picked up through the medium of Indian was that of the Merchant of Venice. The story was alleged to have happened in France, no names were given except that the hero was, as usual, Jack, nor was the nationality of the Jew mentioned. Jack wheeled down to his creditor his money in a wheelbarrow, but came later and would have had to pay his pound of flesh, had not the primitive Portia, his wife, not his sweetheart, dressed herself up in an officer's clothes with a sword and threatened to kill the other if he drew blood while taking his pound of flesh. I have not the slightest doubt that this story was derived from an original French source, and would probably have been told to me just the same had Shakespeare never exited. The story itself, which is probably of Eastern origin, is to be found in the great medieval assortment of tales of the Gesta Romanorum, and no doubt some Frenchman carried with him the traditional version which filtered into an Indian and from that into a broken English dress. Another story, undoubtedly of French origin, was that most indecent of all the tales in Boccaccio's *Decamerone*, 'How They Sent the Devil Back into Hell,' the hero of which piece was, as usual, the ubiquitous and mythic 'Jack'.

The genuine Indian stories, however, were, like the stories of every primitive race, of two kinds; the first of war and hunting and personal adventures, the other, and to me the most interesting, consisted of what I may call folk-lore, pure and simple, in which the supernatural or extravagantly impossible plays the largest part, such folk-lore as I gave a sketch of some months ago, in relation to the Irish Gaels. Of the war and hunting stories, the most noticeable was one which I have since heard corroborated by many Indians, and which has frequently been retold me in nearly the same manner, so that I have little doubt of the essential truth of it.

A couple of hundred years ago, more or less, for none of my informants were accurate in matters of time, there arose a great war between the Milicetes on the St John river and the Mohawks or Iroquois, for they are called by both names, who lived farther north in Canada and nearer to the St Lawrence. One time 250 Mohawk warriors started and came down the St John river in flat canoes as far as Little Falls, and when they got there they surprised two Indian women, whose husbands and uncle were out hunting. As the warriors were quite ignorant of the river they took the women prisoners and made them act as guides. In order to keep their band together they lashed their canoes one to the other, so that they made a broad belt of boats almost extending from bank to bank of the stream, which is pretty rapid and about half a mile broad. They questioned the women closely as to the nature of the river, but the women assured them that it was all equally smooth and level until they should come to the Milicete camp. This was not true, for right before them, but many miles away, lay the Grand Falls, a tremendous cataract, which I have heard many over-patriotic New Brunswickers place, in their enthusiasm, on a level with Niagara. However, as night came on, most of the warriors ceased to paddle, and, on the repeated assurances of the women that there was no danger from the river, most of them, including the chiefs, lay down and slept, while the current carried the whole flotilla slowly along. The women, however, who knew the river perfectly, continued to gradually pass over into the end boats, next the shore, and in these they still continued paddling. When the roar of the Grand Falls was at length heard, the few Mohawks who were awake started to their feet, but the women assured them that the noise of the waters came from a great stream which fell into the St John. By this time the centre canoes were well caught in the treacherous current and drawn in towards their destruction. On seeing this, the women leaped into the water, and, being nearer the shore, where the current was less powerful, they managed to gain the land, but the canoes in the centre drew those at the two wings after them, and before the half-sleeping Mohawks could unlash their canoes or grasp their paddles, they were irresistibly drawn to the cataract, shot over it, and perished to a man.

Below the falls many scores of their dead bodies were thrown ashore by the river. The two women scalped all the chiefs and then choosing an enormous pine tree about 100 feet high, they peeled all the greenery off it, leaving on it only a few naked branches, and to these they affixed the chieftains' scalps. They then cut away all the bushes and little trees for about a hundred feet from the trunks, and in this space they danced their war dance round the tree all day and all night. The next day their uncle coming back from hunting heard their cries and following the sound came up with them and seeing the scalps, he joined the dance also. Their husbands came up the next day and they, too, fell to dancing the war dance round the tree, and so those five danced for one fortnight without stopping, the Indians said, but this must be exaggeration. At the end of their wild fortnight's dance they returned home and told the Milicetes how they had been saved by the two women. The tree is standing yet, and the Indians eagerly assured me that if I came with them they could show me the place where not a bush has grown ever since round that grim pine, and where the earth is trodden down in a deep circle all round it by the feet of those savage dancers so long ago.

After this the Mohawks came again with a still greater fleet of canoes to wipe the Milicetes off the face of the earth. After they had come a good way below Grand Falls they encamped, and were espied by three Milicetes, one of whom was sent off to warn the tribe, while the other two paddled their canoe up the river and past the Mohawk camp; then when they had got out of sight of their enemies' encampment they landed on the opposite side of the river, carried their canoes back again on dry land, keeping themselves concealed amongst the trees, and embarking again below their foes they again paddled up river past the camp of the Iroquois, only to land on the other side and do the same thing over again. For three days and three nights they continued to pass by the Iroquois in this fashion and make their enemies believe that canoe after canoe of Milicete warriors had gone up the river to cut off their retreat. This belief induced the Iroquois to come to terms, and when the Milicetes had finally been mustered and encamped opposite to them, both parties remained for several days without any hostilities breaking out. At last a meeting took place between the chiefs on both sides and a treaty of peace was made, and as they did not understand a word of each other's language they solemnly buried their guns and tomahayguns (axes) in each other's presence, and the Mohawks departed again to their homes in Canada. This treaty was renewed every two years, the Milicetes sending at considerable expense and inconvenience a deputation to the Mohawks near the St Lawrence. About 10 years ago, however, the absurdity of renewing this treaty under the altered conditions of affairs, when the slender remnants of either tribe, enclosed and eaten up by a white population, had nothing to fear from the other dawned upon the Mohawks, and they dissuaded the Milicetes from sending ambassadors any more to renew the treaty by saying 'once made, made forever'. And so for the last ten years the custom has been left in abeyance, and probably will be for all futurity, and thus snaps another link binding Canada with a poetic past. The modern spirit of the century was well expressed in my Indian's final comment: 'We Milicetes, we damn fools to send men up around all dat way for nutting.'

The supernatural stories told by the Indians bore a great resemblance to those of the old world, and several of them were close parallels to stories which I had already taken down in Gaelic from the recitation of Irish peasants; one in especial, of which I gave a brief abstract with its Czech equivalent in my last paper on folk-lore, 'The King of Ireland's Son.' I found that the blow man who figures there, and who blew with one nostril so hard that the wind from it would turn a mill, and the foot-man, who, with one foot over his shoulder, was still swift enough to keep a field full of hares from running away, were familiar figures to my Indians, though whence they derived their acquaintance with these worthies, I cannot say, for it may possibly have been from some Gaelic source. On the other hand, I found a pretty close Indian parallel to one of my Gaelic stories, which, from the name of the hero and the nature of the incidents, could never, I think, have been the result of Indian imagination polishing up a white man's tale, but must have been a genuine Milicete story. It was as follows:

There was once an Indian born with a bow and arrow and with a pipe. He grew up and his name was Noval. Because he had been born with the bow and arrow he was a great hunter. He spent all his time in hunting, and one day that he was out he shot a beautiful bird, so beautiful that he had never seen its like before. The King of the Indians had a daughter, and there was no other girl so lovely as she. She saw Noval passing by with the bird in his hand and wished to have it. She said to him, 'Noval, I want to buy that bird from you.' 'You will get it,' said he, 'if you give me the price of it.' 'What do you want for it?' said she. 'I want you to show me your feet as far as the ankles.' 'Oh, Noval,' she said, 'if my father were to see me he'd beat me.' But anyhow she showed him her ankles and got the bird.

It was not long after that till Noval was out hunting again, and he shot a still finer bird. He came to the King's daughter, and when she saw the bird she said, 'Noval,' she says, 'will you sell me that bird?' 'I will,' said Noval, 'if you give me the price I want.' 'What's that, Noval?' 'To let me see your legs up to the knees.' 'Oh, Noval, if my father knew that he'd beat me.' However, she let Noval see her legs up to the knees, and Noval gave her the bird.

It was not long after that till Noval was out hunting again, and he killed the third bird, which was so fine that he nor no one else had ever seen the like of it. It was green and red and blue and black and white. He put the bird on top of his head, and he went past the place where the King's daughter was. The King's daughter called him back, and she said: 'That is the finest bird, yet Noval; I must have it; what do you want for it?' 'I'll give it to you if you let me have the price of it,' said Noval. 'Whatever it is you must get it,' said she. 'I will not give you the bird until I look at you back between your shoulders,' said Noval. 'Oh, Noval, if my father knew that he would beat me.' 'Come into the wood,' said Noval, 'and your father will not know.' She did that and she showed him her shoulders. Now, she had a gold sign behind her shoulders, and a silver sign in front of her knee and Noval saw them both.

It happened that not very long after this the King thought that it was time to marry his daughter, and he let it be known that anyone who could guess what his daughter's sign (totem) was should marry her, but whoever failed to guess it should have his head cut off. When that news went out through the whole country all the chiefs and captains and sachems gathered together to the King, and they were guessing, one one sign, another another, and as fast as they were guessing the King was cutting off their heads because they guessed wrong. At last Noval came, and he guessed that the King's daughter had a silver sign on her knee and a gold sign on her shoulder. When the King heard that he said he had guessed right, and he gave Noval his daughter in marriage.

But when all the sachems and chiefs and big men saw Noval had got the King's daughter, they were jealous of him, and they wanted to kill him, but they did not know how. At last two of them came to Noval one day and asked him to come away picking berries with them. They brought him far away with them picking berries, and at last they left him bogged in a swampy place where they knew there was a great wild bull, and they ran away themselves. Noval was not long in the place, and was trying to find his way out, when he saw the great wild bull making at him, and he thought he saw as good as a dead man when all of a sudden he drew his fife and began to play. As soon as he heard the music the big white bull stopped and he came to Noval and asked him, 'Noval,' says he, 'could you teach me that tune?' 'I could,' says Noval, 'If you come home with me.' The white bull and himself came home together to the King's house, and all that saw him coming and all the chiefs and big men ran away as soon as they saw the white bull. 'Now, Noval,' says the white bull, when they came to the King's house 'what am I to do to learn that tune.' 'Do you stop here in the garden,' said Noval, 'and I'll teach it to you.'

When the two captains saw that they could not get rid of Noval that way, they thought of another plan. The brought him out to pick berries with them to a place where there was a great white stallion that killed everybody that came near him. When they found Noval near where they knew that the stallion was, they hid from Noval and made off home. It was not long till Noval saw the white stallion coming at him to tear him to pieces, but when he was close up to him he pulled out his fife and began to play. The white stallion stopped and began to dance, 'Noval,' said the white stallion, 'do you think could you learn me that tune?' 'Surely,' says Noval, 'If you come home with me I'll learn it to you.' The white stallion came home with him to the King's house, and when he got as far as the garden Noval told him to wait there beside the white bull, and that as soon as he had time he would teach him the tune.

When the men who were jealous of him saw they could not kill Noval in this way, they brought him out with them into another part of the country, where there was a great white bear that nobody could go near. When they got Noval near the place where the bear was they hid and sneaked back home. The bear saw Noval picking berries and he ran at him and both his jaws open. As soon as Noval saw him coming at him he out with his fife and began playing. The bear stopped and after a while began dancing. Then the bear came to Noval and said: 'Noval,' says he, 'could you teach me that tune?' 'I could,' says Noval, 'if you come home with me.' The bear went home with him, and all the people who saw Noval coming with the bear ran away and were afraid to come back. When Noval got as far as the garden he told the bear to remain in the garden along with the white bull and the white stallion, but he himself went into the King's house the same as before.

At the end of a week, as he was passing by the garden, the white bull called to him: 'Noval,' says he, 'I'm getting tired waiting here. What's delaying you from teaching me that tune you promised,' and the white stallion and the white bear called out the same thing. 'All right,' said Noval, 'I'll teach you right away, one at a time. You were the first I promised,' says he to the white bull, 'so come with me first.' The white bull came with him till he brought him a long way off to a big precipice of rock, and then he began to play the fife, and as soon as he began to play the bull faced him and began dancing. He was playing and playing, until he got the bull on the edge of the rock and when he got him there he pushed him over, and he fell into the river below. 'Now, my lad,' says he, 'you won't come to me for a tune again.' And with that he went home. When he came again to the garden the white stallion asked him, 'Where's the white bull?' 'Oh, the white bull has learned his tune long ago, and is gone home again,' said Noval. 'Will you take me and teach me now,' said the stallion. 'Come with me, then,' said Noval. Noval brought the white stallion with him to the top of the precipice and began playing, and when he got the white stallion on the edge of the cliff he pushed him over. 'Now, my boy,' says he, 'you'll want no more tunes.'

When he came back the white bear asked him where the stallion was, 'Oh,' says Noval, 'he's learned his tune long ago and he's gone home with the white bull.' 'Will you teach me my tune now,' said the bear. 'You must wait a couple of days,' said Noval. Noval knew there was no use in pushing the bear over the rocks, for he would only climb up again, so he had to think of some other way of getting rid of him. He chose out a great tall spruce tree, and he climbed up till he was near the top, and he stripped off all the branches, and when he got near the top he took and bored a hole right through the tree and he made a peg to fit the hole. When he was ready he said to the bear, 'Well go up to the top of the tree here, that's the place to teach you the tune. So himself and the bear climbed up to the top of the tree, and when they were there he drew out his fife and began playing. After a while the bear began to get sleepy with the sound of the music, and at last he fell asleep. As soon as Noval got him fast asleep he stuck his tail into the hole that he had made in the tree, and clapped the peg in so that he had the tail wedged in so tightly that the bear could not stir. Then he slid down from the tree and went home, and he hoped he had seen the last of the bear, the bull and the stallion.

After Noval had gone home the bear awoke and tried to climb down the tree, but found his tail was caught. He tried to get it loose by giving it a good pull, but it would not come. He had to remain in the tree three days. At last he was starving and he said to himself, 'It's as good to die one way as another.' With that he got a grip of the tree, gave such a jerk on his tail that since he could not pull it out of the hole in the tree he pulled it out of his own back, and down he fell on the ground half dead. As soon as he awoke he went in search of Noval to tear him in pieces. He met the white stallion and the white bull also, who were going on the same journey, for after being thrown down the rocks they managed somehow to escape and get back again. All three went to Noval's house and when Noval heard they were coming he ran away along with his wife, and the bear, the bull and the stallion pursued them. At last Noval and his wife got into a boggy place, where they could run no longer, and Noval said, 'It's as good for us to wait for our death quietly as to kill ourselves running.' With that he sat down on the ground, and waited for them. But when they saw him sitting down waiting for them they were afraid to come near him for fear he would do them some other harm. 'That's the way he was,' says the stallion, 'when he made music for me and the next thing he did was to push me over the rocks.' 'That's the way he was with me too,' said the bull. 'That's the way he sat above on the tree with me,' said the bear, 'we may as well go home and leave him.' They went away then and left him, and Noval and his wife went home and made a feast and I was there, too, and I drank too much, and they pitched me out of the door, and that's how I got this broken finger.

Such was the Indian story, retold here in all points exactly as I heard it, from numerous notes jotted down during the narration, but the Irish parallel is so curious that I must give at least its conclusion. In the Irish story the beasts are white horse, lion and fox, upon each of which the hero, who is a tailor, has played off a trick, with the intention of keeping them in captivity forever; the lion, for instance, had his tail pegged into a hole, like the bear in the Indian story. They regain their freedom and pursue the tailor, along with 'the King's army from Dublin.' The tale concludes thus: The lion and the fox, and the army of Dublin, went on then, trying to catch the tailor, and they were going till they came to the place where the old white garraun (horse) was, and the old white garraun said to them that the tailor and his wife had been there in the morning, and 'loose me out,' said he, 'I am swifter than ye, and I'll overtake them.' They loosed out the old white garraun then and the old white garraun, the fox, the lion, and the army of Dublin pursued the tailor and wife together, and it was not long till they came up with him, and saw himself and his wife out before them. When the tailor saw them coming he got out of the coach with his wife, and he sat down on the ground.

When the old white garraun saw the tailor sitting down on the ground he said: 'That's the position he had when he made the hole for me, that I couldn't come out of, once I went down into it. I'll go no nearer to him.'

'No,' said the fox, 'but that's the very way he had when he was making the thing for me, and I'll go no nearer to him.'

'No,' said the lion, 'but that's the very way he was when he was making the plough that I was caught in. I'll go no nearer to him.'

They all went from him then and returned. The tailor and his wife came home to Galway. They gave me paper stockings and shoes of thick milk. I lost them since. They got the ford and I the stepping stones. They were drowned, but I came safe.

It is a very noticeable fact that in these two parallel stories the attitude of the hero to the beasts which treat him well and whom he treats badly is unexplained. It is the more curious because folk Marchen are, as a rule, perfectly intelligible and reasonable, but here there is no intelligible moral at all, for not only does the hero treat the beasts badly without a cause, but he escapes from the consequences of his own cruelty.

So much for these scraps of Algonquin folk-lore, picked up at hazard, but to which I may return later on.

The Irish Language[*]

The distinguished Irish author, Dr Douglas Hyde, best known to our Gaelic readers by his nom de plume, 'An Craoibhín Aoibhinn,' met with a warm reception from his brother Gaels in New York, during his present flying visit to this city. On Sunday, June 14th, he was entertained by the Athletic Section of the Gaelic Society, at their country club house, at Tallten, near Woodside, L.I.; and the evening following he was tendered a dinner by the Gaelic scholars of the Society, at their city home, 17 West 28th Street. All the toasts were proposed and responded to in the Irish language; and it may in truth be said that the distinguished guest held the unique position of being the first personage to have the honor of being so received in America. Mr T. O'Neill Russell occupied the chair; and seated around the tables were the principal workers in the Gaelic Language Movement in this and surrounding cities.

Dr Hyde delivered an address upon 'The Irish Language: its present condition and future prospects as a spoken tongue,' before the members of the Society on last Tuesday evening. The President, ex-Commissioner James S. Coleman, occupied the chair, and in introducing the speaker, paid him a high tribute for his labors in the field of modern Irish literature. Dr Hyde spoke for over half an hour in the Irish language, after which he made the following address in English:

I feel rather embarrassed — and at the same time very much flattered — at being called upon to address such a representative and intelligent audience of my countrymen, upon a subject upon which many of you are, doubtless, as competent to form an opinion as I am. When, therefore, it was, to my great surprise, intimated to me, a day or two ago, that the Cumann na Gaedhilge had arranged for me to deliver a lecture upon the present state of the Irish language, I ascribed the honor solely to the fact that I have come later than most of you from the seat of war — or rather of more inglorious peace — and consequently may be supposed to be better acquainted with the recent phases of the struggle, which is not so much a struggle as the steady flowing out of a tide, which we want to see flow in again. At the outset, you must understand that, although connected with several associations whose object is nominally the revival of the Irish language and the Irish spirit, I am on this occasion speaking for myself alone, and am merely giving you my individual view of the situation. I am not here as a partizan or a 'crank,' or a rabid propagator of any particular opinion. The Society has asked me to say a few words about the Irish language and I wish to make them both brief and uncolored.

[*] *The Irish American*, 27 June 1891. See pp. 44-46.

In the first place, then, you must know that the Irish language is not dead, but that it is in a bad state of health. It is not dead, because the last census showed that there are nearly a million of the race who still speak it; yet it is not well, because of that million the majority are over middle age, and belong to a generation which a decade or two will wipe out of existence.

One hundred years ago, Irish, not English, was the language of the Milesians in Ireland, throughout the whole length and breadth of the land, and of every one with the single exception of the semi-English gentlemen of the 'Ascendancy' and the Scotch planters of Ulster. At that time, if only Ireland had a proper constitution, it would have been quite easy to have established the language as the written, spoken and commercial medium of communication of the whole island. Of course you are all sufficiently acquainted with your own history to know that such a scheme as that was never dreamt of as long as Ireland was governed by a little privileged knot of Protestant legislators. But had the French invasion of '98 proved successful and had the slightest effort been made by the Irish chiefs to establish the national language, nothing can be more certain than that the whole of Ireland and a great part of Australia, New Zealand and America would now be Irish-speaking. Perhaps some of you may doubt the fact of this extensive prevalence of the Irish langauge a hundred years ago. If you do, it can only be with respect to Leinster and Ulster; for even as late as sixty or seventy years ago, it is doubtful if there were man, woman or child born in any part of Connacht or Munster who was ignorant of Irish. Now with regard to Leinster, it may astonish you to hear that I have myself met in the County Wicklow, within sixteen or seventeen miles of Dublin, men who, when young, always repeated the 'Rosary' along with their families in Irish, and said that that was the custom there sixty years ago. Again, that most Irish of good Irishmen, Mr Cleaver, who now lives in Wales, told me he met, over thirty years ago, a man from the County Carlow who did not know one single word of English. As for East Meath, many thousand people speak Irish there yet; and as for Kilkenny, I was out, this very winter, hunting moose and caribou with some Indians in the wilds of New Brunswick, and on entering the very last house of the settlement on the edge of the primeval forests which yet clothe a large part of that province, I found an old man who, to the intense astonishment of the Indians and of the other white man who was along with me, answered me, when I addressed him, in the best Irish; and I found out that he was from near the city of Kilkenny, and, though he had been here for forty years, had not forgotten the language of his youth. But I regret to say that, had he remained in Ireland, discouragement, false shame and the growth of West-Britonism would probably have driven the last word of it out of his head.

Now, as to Ulster. The old men who used to walk all the way from

DUANAIRE

NA

NUAḊ-ĠAEḊILGE.

AIR N-A CUR I N-EAGAR TRÉ ĊÚRAM

AN T-SAOI OIRḂIḊNIĠ,

E. D. Mc CLIAḂAIR,

Maille le cúngnaṁ ó Ċoṁairle Ċonḋacṫa na

Gaeḋilge.

• • • • • • • • • • • •

An treas clóḋ ḋe'n leaḃrán ro.
Léiṟ-ċeartuiġṫe le S. P.

• • • • • • • • • • • •

I m-Baile-áṫa-cliaṫ:
Ar n-a ċur i g-clóḋ le P. O'Briain,
Ag Uiṁir 46, i Sráiḋ Ċuffe.

1891.

Anthology published by Rev. Euseby D. Cleaver

ANNALA RIOGHACHTA EIREANN.

ANNALS

OF

THE KINGDOM OF IRELAND,

BY THE FOUR MASTERS,

FROM

THE EARLIEST PERIOD TO THE YEAR 1616.

EDITED FROM MSS. IN THE LIBRARY OF THE ROYAL IRISH ACADEMY AND OF TRINITY COLLEGE, DUBLIN, WITH A TRANSLATION, AND COPIOUS NOTES,

BY JOHN O'DONOVAN, LL.D., M.R.I.A.,

BARRISTER AT LAW.

"Olim Regibus parebant, nunc per Principes factionibus et studiis trahuntur: nec aliud adversus validissimas gentes pro nobis utilius, quam quod in commune non consulunt. Rarus duabus tribusve civitatibus ad propulsandum commune periculum conventus: ita dum singuli pugnant universi vincuntur."—TACITUS, AGRICOLA, c. 12.

SECOND EDITION.

VOL. I.

DUBLIN:
HODGES, SMITH, AND CO., GRAFTON-STREET.
BOOKSELLERS TO THE UNIVERSITY.
1856.

The Annals of the Four Masters

Connacht to Drogheda to take shipping for England to reap the harvest there, have assured me that there was little but Irish spoken round Drogheda at that time. Carleton's stories bear witness to the prevalence of Irish in *his* day all over the centre of the North, and at this hour there are some in Cavan and Tyrone, and many thousands in Donegal, who know no English. When my father was young he never heard the peasantry round Mohill, in the County Leitrim, not far from Longford, speak anything but Irish; and I do not think I am saying too much when I assert that a hundred years ago every man of Milesian stock in Ireland was acquainted with the Gaelic language. Even at the time of the great famine there were about 4,000,000 of Irish, who spoke the native language; that is a population larger than that of the whole of Switzerland. This is only forty-five years ago, and now the proportion has dwindled to less than a million, and in a very few years more, unless an effort be made, and made at once, Irish will be as extinct as Cornish.

Is it not something unexampled that a pure Aryan language like Irish should have been allowed to die without a single hand being held out to save it? If Irish were a poor, mean language, of low capacity and limited vocabulary, with no past to speak of and no literature behind it, I might, perhaps, see it die with more complacency. But when everyone knows, or ought to know that, instead of being a poor, mean, limited language, it is a vast, varied, very opulent one — that it is a pure Aryan language, and, unlike Basque or Magyar, stands upon an equal footing with Greek, Latin and Sanscrit; when everyone know that, instead of being inadequate to the expression of thought, it is, or at least was two hundred years ago, and could easily be made again, as adequate to the expression of thought as Greek or German; when everybody who has given the matter the very slightest thought knows that the enormous mass of Irish literature, which is lying at present in manuscript, has not only never been equalled but never approached either in age, variety, or value by any vernacular language in Europe; when all this is openly known and confessed, I acknowledge that it gives me a pang of sorrow to see the language of the Bards and Brehons, of the Saints and sages, the language of Rory O'More, of Patrick Sarsfield, and Owen Roe O'Neill, the best men that Ireland ever produced, kicked contemptuously aside, crawling away, as it were, with a broken leg to die, like a hunted dog in a ditch, a vile and lingering death.

Perhaps, gentlemen, you may think this language hard or exaggerated; but when we see an O'Connell, wielding a power over the race which no man ever exercised before or since, having the cynicism to address mass meetings of his countrymen in a language which not one in five of his audience understood; when we see that great institution, Maynooth College, turn out young priests by the thousand without any training in the Irish language; when we see the Catholic gentry — even the 'O's and the Mac's' — educated by preference at English schools whenever their parents are wealthy enough, and taught to say as I have often heard them say — I almost blush to repeat it — that Irish is the language of 'cads'; when we find English sermons preached, Sunday after Sunday, in chapels and cathedrals, where at least every second sermon should be in Irish; when we find the proprietors of Irish Catholic newspapers steadily refusing even one square inch for the publication of even an Irish song; when we find all that — and nobody seeks to deny the fact or cloak it — I ask you am I too severe in my condemnation? If you still think that I am, then I pray you to pardon me, and to ascribe it to the natural partiality of anyone for a noble language which he has spoken as a child, and which he sees threatened with contemptuous extinction.

Now, although Irish has probably been the language of the father, grandfather, or great grandfathers of everyone in this room, and of all their ancestry before them, although the very shape of their faces and organs of speech, and perhaps even their tone of thought, have been unconsciously moulded or influenced by it, still I know that I am standing in a practical country amongst practical men, and that you require me to give some adequate reason for continuing to keep alive the Irish language, and, avoiding vague generalities, to state clearly what it is I wish to see done.

Now, I want to see the language kept alive for several reasons: first of all, because it is not good for the Irish, or any other race, to throw sentiment to the dogs; secondly, I want to see the language kept alive as a great national heritage; thirdly, as one of the best bonds to knit together the Irish race, and fourthly, because a bilingual race are infinitely superior to a race that speaks only one language. Here in America, as far as I can see, the one link that binds the Irish together is their Catholicity. In time past that has proved an almost sufficient link, because Irishman and Catholic were synonymous. But that will not be so in the future. The influx of German and Italian and other European Catholics will put an end to that; and if the Irish race is to hold together at all, it will have to cultivate other ties. It will have to again adopt in a foreign land the music, songs, traditions, and games of the race, and all Irishmen should at least know the Irish letters and something of the past history and glories of their land. Do you believe that Americans will think the worse of you for this, or that such a training will unfit you for a place in this vast and glorious Republic? I tell you no — a thousand times no! Respect yourselves and America will respect you. America will greedily assimilate, wants to assimilate, all that is best of the characteristics of the various races that inhabit her soil. How can she respect us if we throw sentiment to the dogs, and hang our heads and give up what every other nation — even little Switzerland, even tiny Denmark, holds most dear. Another reason — because all the world knows, and the experience of the whole world goes to prove, that the bi-lingual races are doubly men, and are double in sharpness and mental capacity. The history of Switzerland and of Holland shows it. In Ireland the people pretend to think it is not so, but experience is against them.

We in Ireland owe a great deal to the Gaels of America; for if it were not for the help we get from them, the Irish Language movement would not have assumed the position it now occupies. We are both thankful and grateful to you for it. We are a people nervously sensitive to the least touch of sarcasm. It is sarcasm that has tended to root out the Irish language; but when we know that you in America, are admiring our efforts to revive it, that does more than anything else to keep the Irish language alive. It is a most disgraceful shame the way in which Irishmen are brought up. They are ashamed of their language, institutions, and of everything Irish. I met two young Irishmen from the County Mayo, coming over here, and asked them where they came from. They could speak Irish well, but they would not. One said at last 'I come from a little village over there called Ireland.' So far from having any regard to their country, their race and their history, hundreds of thousands of them, when they come here, prefer to drop their honorable Milesian names, and to call themselves Stiggins or Hunk or Buggins in preference to the surnames of saints. Of two brothers one calls himself 'Mr Love' while the other remains O'Gara, thereby condescending to remain connected with the patron of the Four Masters and two thousand years of the glorious past. One brother remains a Brehony, showing his descent from one of the very highest and most honorable titles in Ireland, a Brehon, a law-giver and poet; the other 'Mr Judge!' The Mac-Fiachs become 'Hunts,' myriads of the ancient and honorable MacGoverns and MacGowans of the North, have now degenerated into the ugly Saxon monosyllable Smith; hundreds of the O'Shaughnessys are now Chaunceys; the O'Byrnes are Burnses, and so on *ad infinitum*; and the melancholy part of it is that, as far as I am aware, not one single word of warning or remonstrance has been raised against this colossal cringing, either by the Irish press or by Irish public men.

Now, there are only two possible ways, as far as I can see, to keep up the Irish spirit of the people, and a due regard for the language of the past; one of these is to gain Home Rule, and by a vigorous movement, on this side of the Atlantic and at home, to put pressure on the un-Irish Irishmen, to teach Irish history in the schools, to put the Irish language in all institutions and examinations upon the same footing or a little more favorable footing than French, Latin and Greek, and to insist on having Irish-speaking functionaries and schoolmasters in Irish speaking parts of the country. I do not for a moment advocate making Irish the language of the country at large, or of the National Parliament. I do not want to be an impossible visionary or rabid partisan. What I wish to see is Irish established as a living language, for all time, among the million or half million who still speak it along the West coast, and to insure that the language will hold a favorable place in teaching institutions and government examinations. Unless we retain a bilingual population as large as we now have, Irish may be said to be dead, and with it nine-tenths of the glories of the past; for, with modern Irish once dead, adieu to all hope of translating, publishing or understanding that unique glory of our race — our vast Irish literature.

As Home Rule is being deferred and may not, perhaps, be attained either so early as some people think, the only other plan for preventing the imminent extinction of the Irish language appears to me to be that of personally interviewing the bilinguists themselves. Nothing short of a house-to-house canvas will do. Something of the sort of house to house visitation which James Stephens adopted in order to breathe new life into the 'corpse on the dissecting table.' Nothing short of this will do — nothing short of taking a pledge from every Gaelic speaking family in Ireland, that they will speak Irish and Irish only on all occasions when it is understood.

I should earnestly advocate a deputation of Irish-Americans around Ireland for this purpose, to urge them in behalf of their race, in behalf of their countrymen across the Atlantic, for the love of their great forefathers, and for the honor of Ireland to remain Irish-speaking and not to give the English people this last shameful victory over us — that the once great language of the once great Gaelic race should expire in a very few years amid contumely and scorn. I should advocate that medals, as badges of honor, should be struck and given at the end of a year to every family that could conscientiously say that they had kept their word. This sort of thing would do more to elevate the people in their own eyes and the eyes of the world, than a great many thousand speeches by professed politicians. Unfortunately, however, such schemes cost money, and the wealthy men of the race won't give theirs for proceedings like that. Whatever they may pretend, they prefer in their hearts to see us 'Englified' and 'West-Britonised,' and are not one bit ashamed of what they ought to blush for, the rapid degradation, the lack of self-respect and the unmanly cringing of so many of their race — things which we seek to put an end to, and which societies like yours, gentlemen, as I have good reason to know are very influential in stopping.

At the conclusion of the address, Mr Patrick O'Byrne moved and Mr T. O'Neill-Russell seconded a vote of thanks to the speaker of the evening, after which an informal reception was tendered to Dr Hyde, all the members present being anxious to become personally acquainted with him.

The Necessity for De-Anglicising Ireland*

When we speak of 'The Necessity for De-Anglicising the Irish Nation,' we mean it, not as a protest against imitating what is *best* in the English people, for that would be absurd, but rather to show the folly of neglecting what is Irish, and hastening to adopt, pell-mell, and indiscrimatingly, everything that is English, simply because it *is* English.

This is a question which most Irishmen will naturally look at from a National point of view, but it is one which ought also to claim the sympathies of every intelligent Unionist, and which, as I know, does claim the sympathy of many.

If we take a bird's-eye view of our island to-day, and compare it with what it used to be, we must be struck by the extraordinary fact that the nation which was once, as every one admits, one of the most classically learned and cultured nations in Europe, is now one of the least so; how one of the most reading and literary peoples has become one of the *least* studious and most *un*-literary, and how the present art products of one of the quickest, most sensitive, and most artistic races on earth are now only distinguished for their hideousness.

I shall endeavour to show that this failure of the Irish people in recent times has been largely brought about by the race diverging during this century from the right path, and ceasing to be Irish without becoming English. I shall attempt to show that with the bulk of the people this change took place quite recently, much more recently than most people imagine, and is, in fact, still going on. I should also like to call attention to the illogical position of men who drop their own language to speak English, of men who translate their euphonious Irish names into English monosyllables, of men who read English books, and know nothing about Gaelic literature, nevertheless protesting as a matter of sentiment that they hate the country which at every hand's turn they rush to imitate.

I wish to show you that in Anglicising ourselves wholesale we have thrown away with a light heart the best claim which we have upon the world's recognition of us as a separate nationality. What did Mazzini say? What is Goldwin Smith never tired of declaiming? What do the *Spectator* and *Saturday Review* harp on? That we ought to be content as an integral part of the United Kingdom because we have lost the notes of nationality, our language and customs.

* The National Literary Society, Dublin, 25 November 1892. *The Revival of Irish Literature* (Fisher Unwin, London 1894). See Introduction *passim*.

It has always been very curious to me how Irish sentiment sticks in this half-way house — how it continues to apparently hate the English, and at the same time continues to imitate them; how it continues to clamour for recognition as a distinct nationality, and at the same time throws away with both hands what would make it so. If Irishmen only went a little farther they would become good Englishmen in sentiment also. But — illogical as it appears — there seems not the slightest sign or probability of their taking that step. It is the curious certainty that come what may Irishmen will continue to resist English rule, even though it should be for their good, which prevents many of our nation from becoming Unionists upon the spot. It is a fact, and we must face it as a fact, that although they adopt English habits and copy England in every way, the great bulk of Irishmen and Irishwomen over the whole world are known to be filled with a dull, ever-abiding animosity against her, and — right or wrong — to grieve when she prospers, and joy when she is hurt. Such movements as Young Irelandism, Fenianism, Land Leagueism, and Parliamentary obstruction seem always to gain their sympathy and support. It is just because there appears no earthly chance of their becoming good members of the Empire that I urge that they should not remain in the anomalous position they are in, but since they absolutely refuse to become the one thing, that they become the other; cultivate what they have rejected, and build up an Irish nation on Irish lines.

But you ask, why should we wish to make Ireland more Celtic than it is — why should we de-Anglicise it at all?

I answer because the Irish race is at present in a most anomalous position, imitating England and yet apparently hating it. How can it produce anything good in literature, art, or institutions as long as it is actuated by motives so contradictory? Besides, I believe it is our Gaelic past which, though the Irish race does not recognise it just at present, is really at the bottom of the Irish heart, and prevents us becoming citizens of the Empire, as, I think, can be easily proved.

To say that Ireland has not prospered under English rule is simply a truism; all the world admits it, England does not deny it. But the English retort is ready. You have not prospered, they say, because you would not settle down contentedly, like the Scotch, and form part of the Empire. 'Twenty years of good, resolute, grand-fatherly government,' said a well-known Englishman, will solve the Irish question. He possibly made the period too short, but let us suppose this. Let us suppose for a moment — which is impossible — that there were to arise a series of Cromwells in England for the space of one hundred years, able administrators of the Empire, careful rulers of Ireland, developing to the utmost our national resources, whilst they unremittingly stamped out every spark of national feeling, making Ireland a land of wealth and factories, whilst they extinguished every thought and every idea that was Irish, and left us, at last, after a hundred years of good government, fat, wealthy, and populous, but with all our characteristics gone, with every external that at present differentiates us from the English lost or dropped; all our Irish names of places and people turned into English names; the Irish language completely extinct; the O's and the Macs dropped; our Irish intonation changed, as far as possible by English schoolmasters into something English; our history no longer remembered or taught; the names of our rebels and martyrs blotted out; our battlefields and traditions forgotten; the fact that we were not of Saxon origin dropped out of sight and memory, and let me now put the question — How many Irishmen are there who would purchase material prosperity at such a price? It is exactly such a question as this and the answer to it that shows the difference between the English and Irish race. Nine Englishmen out of ten would jump to make the exchange, and I as firmly believe that nine Irishmen out of ten would indignantly refuse it.

And yet this awful idea of complete Anglicisation, which I have here put before you in all its crudity, is, and has been, making silent inroads upon us for nearly a century.

Its inroads have been silent, because, had the Gaelic race perceived what was being done, or had they been once warned of what was taking place in their own midst, they would, I think, never have allowed it. When the picture of complete Anglicisation is drawn for them in all its nakedness Irish sentimentality becomes suddenly a power and refuses to surrender its birthright.

What lies at the back of the sentiments of nationality with which the Irish millions seem so strongly leavened; what can prompt them to applaud such sentiments as:

> They say the British empire owes much to Irish hands,
> That Irish valour fixed her flag o'er many conquered lands;
> And ask if Erin takes no pride in these her gallant sons,
> Her Wolseleys and her Lawrences, her Wolfes and Wellingtons.
>
> Ah! these were of the Empire — we yield them to her fame,
> And ne'er in Erin's orisons are heard their alien name;
> But those for whom her heart beats high and benedictions swell,
> They died upon the scaffold and they pined within the cell.

Of course it is a very composite feeling which prompts them; but I believe that what is largely behind it is the half unconscious feeling that the race which at one time held possession of more than half Europe, which established itself in Greece, and burned infant Rome, is now — almost extirpated and absorbed elsewhere — making its last stand for independence in this island of Ireland; and do what they may the race of to-day cannot wholly divest itself from the mantle of its own past. Through early Irish literature, for instance, can be best form some conception of what that race really was, which, after overthrowing and trampling on the primitive peoples of half Europe, was itself forced in turn to yield its speech, manners, and independence to the victorious eagles of Rome. We alone of the nations of Western Europe escaped the claws of those birds of prey; we alone developed ourselves naturally upon our own lines outside of and free from all Roman influence; we alone were thus able to produce an early art and literature, *our* antiquities can best throw light upon the pre-Romanised inhabitants of half Europe and — we are our father's sons.

There is really no exaggeration in all this, although Irishmen are sometimes prone to overstating as well as to forgetting. Westwood himself declares that, were it not for Irishmen, these islands would possess no primitive works of art worth the mentioning; Jubainville asserts that early Irish literature is that which best throws light upon the manners and customs of his own ancestors the Gauls; and Zimmer, who has done so much for Celtic philology, has declared that only a spurious criticism can make an attempt to doubt about the historical character of the chief persons of our two epic cycles, that of Cuchullain and of Finn. It is useless elaborating this point; and Dr Sigerson has already shown in his opening lecture the debt of gratitude which in many respects Europe owes to ancient Ireland. The dim consciousness of this is one of those things which are at the back of Irish national sentiment, and our business, whether we be Unionists or Nationalists, should be to make this dim consciousness an active and potent feeling, and thus increase our sense of self-respect and of honour.

What we must endeavour to never forget is this, that the Ireland of to-day is the descendant of the Ireland of the seventh century; then the school of Europe and the torch of learning. It is true that Northmen made some minor settlements in it in the ninth and tenth centuries, it is true that the Normans made extensive settlements during the succeeding centuries, but none of those broke the continuity of the social life of the island. Dane and Norman drawn to the kindly Irish breast issued forth in a generation or two fully Irishised, and more Hibernian than the Hibernians themselves, and even after the Cromwellian plantation the children of numbers of the English soldiers who settled in the south and midlands, were, after forty years' residence, and after marrying Irish wives, turned into good Irishmen, and unable to speak a word of English, while several Gaelic poets of the last century have, like Father English, the most unmistakably English names. In two points only was the continuity of the Irishism of Ireland damaged. First, in the north-east of Ulster, where the Gaelic race was expelled and the land planted with aliens, whom our dear mother Erin, assimilative as she is, has hitherto found it difficult to absorb, and in the ownership of the land, eight-ninths of which belongs to people many of whom always lived, or live, abroad, and not half of whom Ireland can be said to have assimilated.

During all this time the continuation of Erin's national life centred, according to our way of looking at it, not so much in the Cromwellian or Williamite landholders who sat in College Green, and governed the country, as in the mass of the people whom Dean Swift considered might be entirely neglected, and looked upon as hewers of wood and drawers of water; the men who, nevertheless, constituted the real working population, and who were living on in the hopes of better days; the men who have since made America, and have within the last ten years proved what an important factor they may be in wrecking or in building the British Empire. These are the men of whom our merchants, artisans, and farmers mostly consist, and in whose hands is to-day the making or marring of an Irish nation. But, alas, *quantum mutatus ab illo!* What the battleaxe of the Dane, the sword of the Norman, the wile of the Saxon were unable to perform, we have accomplished ourselves. We have at last broken the continuity of Irish life, and just at the moment when the Celtic race is presumably about to largely recover possession of its own country, it finds itself deprived and stript of its Celtic characteristics, cut off from the past, yet scarcely in touch with the present. It has lost since the beginning of this century almost all that connected it with the era of Cuchullain and of Ossian, that connected it with the Christianisers of Europe, that connected it with Brian Boru and the heroes of Clontarf, with the O'Neills and O'Donnells, with Rory O'More, with the Wild Geese, and even to some extent with the men of '98. It has lost all that they had — language, traditions, music, genius and ideas. Just when we should be starting to build up anew the Irish race and the Gaelic nation — as within our own recollection Greece has been built up anew — we find ourselves despoiled of the bricks of nationality. The old bricks that lasted eighteen hundred years are destroyed; we must now set to, to bake new ones, if we can, on other ground and of other clay. Imagine for a moment the restoration of a German-speaking Greece.

The bulk of the Irish race really lived in the closest contact with the traditions of the past and the national life of nearly eighteen hundred years, until the beginning of this century. Not only so, but during the whole of the dark Penal times they produced amongst themselves a most vigorous literary development. Their schoolmasters and wealthy farmers, unwearied scribes, produced innumerable manuscripts in beautiful writing, each letter separated from another as in Greek, transcripts both of the ancient literature of their sires and of the more modern literature produced by themselves. Until the beginning of the present century there was no county, no barony, and I may almost say, no townland which did not boast of an Irish poet, the people's representative of those ancient bards who died out with the extirpation of the great Milesian families. The literary activity of even the eighteenth century among the Gaels was very great, not in the South alone, but also in Ulster — the number of poets it produced was something astonishing. It did not, however, produce many works in Gaelic prose, but it propagated translations of many pieces from the French, Latin, Spanish, and English. Every well-to-do farmer could read and write Irish, and many of them could understand even archaic Irish. I have myself heard persons reciting the poems of Donogha More O'Daly, Abbot of Boyle, in Roscommon, who died sixty years before Chaucer was born. To this very day the people have a word for archaic Irish, which is much the same as though Chaucer's poems were handed down amongst the English peasantry, but required a special training to understand. This training, however, nearly every one of fair education during the Penal times possessed, nor did they begin to lose their Irish training and knowledge until after the establishment of Maynooth and the rise of O'Connell. These two events made an end of the Gaelicism of the Gaelic race, although a great number of poets and scribes existed even down to the forties and fifties of the present century, and a few may linger on yet in remote localities. But it may be said, roughly speaking, that the ancient Gaelic civilisation died with O'Connell, largely, I am afraid, owing to his example and his neglect of inculcating the necessity of keeping alive racial customs, language, and traditions, in which with the one notable exception of our scholarly idealist, Smith O'Brien, he has been followed until a year ago by almost every leader of the Irish race.

Thomas Davis and his brilliant band of Young Irelanders came just at the dividing of the line, and tried to give to Ireland a new literature in English to replace the literature which was just being discarded. It succeeded and it did not succeed. It was a most brilliant effort, but the old bark had been too recently stripped off the Irish tree, and the trunk could not take as it might have done to a fresh one. It was a new departure, and at first produced a violent effect. Yet in the long run it failed to properly leaven our peasantry, who might, perhaps, have been reached upon other lines. I say they *might* have been reached upon other lines because it is quite certain that even well on into the beginning of this century, Irish poor scholars and schoolmasters used to gain the greatest favour and applause by reading out manuscripts in the people's houses at night, some of which manuscripts had an antiquity of a couple of hundred years or more behind them, and which, when they got illegible from age, were always recopied. The Irish peasantry at that time were all to some extent cultured men, and many of the better off ones were scholars and poets. What have we now left of all that? Scarcely a trace. Many of them read newspapers indeed, but who reads, much less recites, an epic poem, or chants an elegiac or even a hymn?

Wherever Irish throughout Ireland continued to be spoken, there the ancient MSS. continued to be read, there the epics of Cuchullainn,

Conor MacNessa, Déirdre, Finn, Oscar, and Ossian continued to be told, and there poetry and music held sway. Some people may think I am exaggerating in asserting that such a state of things existed down to the present century, but it is no exaggeration. I have myself spoken with men from Cavan and Tyrone who spoke excellent Irish. Carleton's stories bear witness to the prevalence of the Irish language and traditions in Ulster when he began to write. My friend Mr Lloyd has found numbers in Antrim who spoke good Irish. And, as for Leinster, my friend Mr Cleaver informed me that when he lived in Wicklow a man came by from the County Carlow in search of work who could not speak a word of English. Old labourers from Connacht, who used to go to reap the harvest in England and take shipping at Drogheda, told me that at that time, fifty years ago, Irish was spoken by every one round that town. I have met an old man in Wicklow, not twenty miles from Dublin, whose parents always repeated the Rosary in Irish. My friend Father O'Growny, who has done and is doing so much for the Irish language and literature at Maynooth, tells me that there, within twenty miles of Dublin, are three old people who still speak Irish. O'Curry found people within seven miles of Dublin city who had never heard English in their youth at all, except from the car-drivers of the great town. I gave an old man in the street who begged from me, a penny, only a few days ago, saying, 'Sin pighin agad,' and when he answered in Irish I asked him where he was from, and he said from *Newna (n' Eamhain)*, *i.e.*, Navan. Last year I was in Canada and out hunting with some Red Indians, and we spent a night in the last white man's house in the last settlement on the brink of the primeval forest; and judging from a peculiarly Hibernian physiognomy that the man was Irish, I addressed him in Gaelic, and to the intense astonishment both of whites and Indians we entered into a conversation which none of them understood; and it turned out that he was from within three miles of Kilkenny, and had been forty years in that country without forgetting the language he had spoken as a child, and I, although from the centre of Connacht, understood him perfectly. When my father was a young boy in the County Leitrim, not far from Longford, he seldom heard the farm labourers and tenants speak anything but Irish amongst themselves. So much for Ulster and Leinster, but Connacht and Munster were until quite recently completely Gaelic. In fact, I may venture to say, that, up to the beginning of the present century, neither man, woman, nor child of the Gaelic race, either of high blood or low blood, existed in Ireland who did not either speak Irish or understand it. But within the last ninety years we have, with an unparalleled frivolity, deliberately thrown away our birthright and Anglicised ourselves. None of the children of those people of whom I have spoken know Irish, and the race will from henceforth be changed; for as Monsieur Jubainville says of the influence of Rome upon Gaul, England 'has definitely conquered us, she has even imposed upon us her language, that is to say, the form of our thoughts during every instant of our existence.' It is curious that those who most fear West Britainism have so eagerly consented to imposing upon the Irish race what, according to Jubainville, who in common with all the great scholars of the continent, seems to regret it very much, is 'the form of our thoughts during every instant of our existence.'

So much for the greatest stroke of all in our Anglicisation, the loss of our language. I have often heard people thank God that if the English gave us nothing else they gave us at least their language. In this way they put a bold face upon the matter, and pretend that the Irish language *is* not worth knowing, and has no literature. But the Irish language *is* worth knowing, or why would the greatest philologists of Germany, France, and Italy be emulously studying it, and it *does* possess a literature, or why would a German savant have made the calculation that the books written in Irish between the eleventh and seventeenth centuries, and still extant, would fill a thousand octavo volumes.

I have no hesitation at all in saying that every Irish-feeling Irishman, who hates the reproach of West-Britonism, should set himself to encourage the efforts which are being made to keep alive our once great national tongue. The losing of it is our greatest blow, and the sorest stroke that the rapid Anglicisation of Ireland has inflicted upon us. In order to de-Anglicise ourselves we must at once arrest the decay of the langauge. We must bring pressure upon our politicians not to snuff it out by their tacit discouragement merely because they do not happen themselves to understand it. We must arouse some spark of patriotic inspiration among the peasantry who still use the language, and put an end to the shameful state of feeling — a thousand-tongued reproach to our leaders and statesmen — which makes young men and women blush and hang their heads when overheard speaking their own language.[1] Maynooth has at last come splendidly to the front, and it is now incumbent upon every clerical student to attend lectures in the

---

1   As an instance of this, I mention the case of a young man I met on the road coming from the fair of Tuam, some ten miles away. I saluted him in Irish, and he answered me in English. 'Don't you speak Irish,' said I. 'Well, I declare to God, sir,' he said, 'my father and mother hasn't a word of English, but still, I don't speak Irish.' This was absolutely true for him. There are thousands upon thousands of houses all over Ireland to-day where the old people invariably use Irish in addressing the children, and the children as invariably answer in English, the children understanding Irish but not speaking it, the parents understanding their children's English but unable to use it themselves. In a great many cases, I should almost say most, the children are not conscious of the existence of two languages. I remember asking a gossoon a couple of miles west of Ballaghaderreen in the Co. Mayo, some questions in Irish and he answered them in English. At last I said to him, *'Nach labhrann tú Gaedheilg?'* (i.e., 'Don't you speak Irish?') and his answer was, 'And isn't it Irish I'm spaking?' 'No *a-chuisle*,' said I, 'it's not Irish you're speaking, but English.' 'Well then,' said he, 'that's

Irish language and history during the first three years of his course. But in order to keep the Irish language alive where it is still spoken — which is the utmost we can at present aspire to — nothing less than a house-to-house visitation and exhortation of the people themselves will so, something — though with a very different purpose — analogous to the procedure that James Stephens adopted throughout Ireland when he found her like a corpse on the dissecting table. This and some system of giving medals or badges of honour to every family who will guarantee that they have always spoken Irish amongst themselves during the year. But, unfortunately, distracted as we are and torn by contending factions, it is impossible to find either men or money to carry out this simple remedy, although to a dispassionate foreigner — to a Zeuss, Jubainville, Zimmer, Kuno Meyer, Windisch, or Ascoli, and the rest — this is of greater importance than whether Mr Redmond or Mr MacCarthy lead the largest wing of the Irish party for the moment, or Mr So-and-So succeed with his election petition. To a person taking a bird's-eye view of the situation a hundred or five hundred years hence, believe me, it will also appear of greater importance than any mere temporary wrangle, but, unhappily, our countrymen cannot be brought to see this.

We can, however, insist, and we *shall* insist if Home Rule be carried, that the Irish language, which so many foreign scholars of the first calibre find so worthy of study, shall be placed on a par with — or even above — Greek, Latin, and modern languages, in all examinations held under the Irish Government. We can also insist, and we *shall* insist, that in those baronies where the children speak Irish, Irish shall be taught, and that Irish-speaking schoolmasters, petty sessions clerks, and even magistrates be appointed in Irish-speaking districts. If all this were done, it should not be very difficult, with the aid of the foremost foreign scholars, to bring about a tone of thought which would make it disgraceful for an educated Irishman — especially of the old Celtic race, MacDermotts, O'Conors, O'Sullivans, MacCarthys, O'Neills — to be ignorant of his own language — would make it at least as disgraceful as for an educated Jew to be quite ignorant of Hebrew.

We find the decay of our language faithfully reflected in the decay of our surnames. In Celtic times a great proof of the powers of assimilation which the Irish nation possessed, was the fact that so many

---

how I spoke it ever'! He was quite unconscious that I was addressing him in one language and he answering in another. On a different occasion I spoke Irish to a little girl in a house near Kilfree Junction, Co. Sligo, into which I went while waiting for a train. The girl answered me in Irish until her brother came in. 'Arrah now, Mary,' said he, with what was intended to be a most bitter sneer; 'and isn't that a credit to you!' And poor Mary — whom I had with difficulty persuaded to begin — immediately hung her head and changed to English. This is going on from Malin Head to Galway, and from Galway to Waterford, with the exception possibly of a few spots in Donegal and Kerry, where the people are wiser and more national.

of the great Norman and English nobles lived like the native chiefs and took Irish names. In this way the De Bourgos of Connacht became MacWilliams, of which clan again some minor branches became MacPhilpins, MacGibbons, and MacRaymonds. The Birminghams of Connacht took the name of MacFeoiris, the Stauntons became MacAveelys, the Nangles MacCostellos, the Prendergasts of Mayo became MacMaurices, the De Courcys became Mac Patricks, the Bissetts of Antrim became MacEóins, and so on. Roughly speaking, it may be said that most of the English and Norman families outside of the Pale were Irish in name and manners from the beginning of the fourteenth to the middle of the seventeenth century.

In 1465 an Act was passed by the Parliament of the English Pale that all Irishmen inside the Pale should take an English name 'of one towne as Sutton, Chester, Trym, Skryne, Corke, Kinsale; or colour, as white, black, brown; or art or science, as smith or carpenter; or office, as cooke, butler; and that he and his issue shall use this name' or forfeit all his goods. A great number of the lesser families complied with this typically English ordinance; but the greater ones — the MacMurroghs, O'Tooles, O'Byrnes, O'Nolans, O'Mores, O'Ryans, O'Conor Falys, O'Kellys, &c. — refused, and never did change their names. A hundred and thirty years later we find Spenser, the poet, advocating the renewal of this statute. By doing this, says Spenser, 'they shall in time learne quite to forget the Irish nation. And herewithal,' he says, 'would I also wish the O's and Macs which the heads of septs have taken to their names to be utterly forbidden and extinguished, for that the same being an ordinance (as some say) first made by O'Brien (*Brian Borúmha*) for the strengthening of the Irish, the abrogation thereof will as much enfeeble them.' It was, however, only after Aughrim and the Boyne that Irish names began to be changed in great numbers, and O'Conors to become 'Conyers,' O'Reillys 'Ridleys,' O'Donnells 'Daniels,' O'Sullivans 'Silvans,' MacCarthys 'Carters,' and so on.

But it is the last sixty years that have made most havoc with our Milesian names. It seemed as if the people were possessed with a mania for changing them to something — anything at all, only to get rid of the Milesian sound. 'Why,' said O'Connell, once talking to a mass-meeting of Lord Chancellor Sugden, 'you wouldn't call a decent pig Sugden.' Yet he never uttered a word of remonstrance at the O'Lahiffs, O'Brollahans, and MacRorys becoming under his eyes Guthrys, Bradleys, and Rogerses. It is more than a little curious, and a very bad augury for the future independence of Ireland, that men of education and intelligence like Carleton the novelist, or Hardiman, author of the History of Galway and the *Irish Minstrelsy*, should have changed their Milesian names, one from that of O'Cairellan, who was ancient chief of Clandermot, the other from the well-known name of O'Hargadain. In Connacht alone I know scores of Gatelys, Sextons, Baldwins, Foxes,

Coxes, Footes, Greenes, Keatings, who are really O'Gatlies, O'Sesnans, O'Mulligans, O'Shanahans, MacGillacullys, O'Trehys, O'Honeens, and O'Keateys. The O'Hennesys are Harringtons, the O'Kinsellaghs, Kingsleys and Tinslys, the O'Feehillys Pickleys, and so on. O'Donovan, writing in 1862, gives a list of names which had recently been changed in the neighbourhood of Cootehill, Co. Cavan. These Irish names of MacNebo, MacIntyre, MacGilroy, MacTernan, MacCorry, MacOscar, MacBrehon, O'Clery, Murtagh, O'Drum, &c., were becoming, or had become, Victory, Victoria, Callwell, Freeman, King, Nugent, Gilman, Leonard, Godwin, Goodwin, Smyth, Golderich, Golding, Masterton, Lind, Crosby, Grosby, Crosse, Corry, Cosgrove, Judge, Brabacy, Brabazon, Clarke, Clerkin, Cunningham, Drummond, Tackit, Sexton, and Mortimer[2] — not a bad attempt at West-Britonising for one little town!

2 The following are a few instances out of hundreds of the monstrous transmographying of Gaelic names into English. The Gillespies (Giolla-Easbuig, i.e., Bishop's servant) are Archbolds or Bishops. The Mackeys (Mac Aodha, i.e., son of Ae or Hugh) are Hughes. The Mac Reevys or Mac Culreevys (Mac Cúil-Riabhaigh, i.e., son of the grey poll) are Grays. The Mac Eóchagáins instead of being all Gahagans or Geoghegans have — some of them — deformed their name into the monstrosity of Goggin. The Mac Feeachrys (Mac Fhiachraidh) are Vickors or even Hunters. The Mac Feehalys are often Fieldings. Mac Gilleesa (mac Giolla Íosa, i.e., sons of Jesus' devotee) are either Gillespie or Giles. The Mac Gillamurrys (Mac Giolla-Mhuire, i.e., son of the Virgin's devotee) is often made Marmion, sometimes more correctly Macilmurray or Mac Ilmurry. Mac Gillamerry (Mac Giolla Meidhre, i.e., son of the servant of merriment) is Anglicised Merryman. Mac Gillaree (Mac Giolla-righ, i.e., son of the King's servant) is very often made King, but sometimes pretty correctly Mac Gilroy or Mac Ilroy — thus the Connemara people have made Kingston of the village of Ballyconry, because the *ry* or *righ* means a king. The Mac Irs, sons of Ir, earliest coloniser of Ireland, have, by some confusion with *geirr*, the genitive of *gearr*, 'short,' become Shorts or Shortalls, but sometimes, less corruptly, Kerrs. The honourable name of Mac Rannell (Mac Raghnaill) is now seldom met with in any other form than that of Reynolds. The Mac Sorarans (Mac Samhradháin, the clan or tribe of the Mac Gaurans or Mac Governs) have become Somers, through some fancied etymology with the word *samhradh*. The Mac Sorleys (Mac Samharlaigh) are often Shirleys. The honourable and poetic race of Mac-an-Bháirds (sons of the bard) are now Wards to a man. The Mac-intleevys (Mac an tsléibhe, i.e., sons of the mountain) are Levys or Dunlevys. The Macintaggarts (Mac an tsagairt, i.e., son of the priest) are now Priestmans, or occasionally, I do not know why, Segraves. The Macgintys (Mac an tsaoi, i.e., son of the sage) are very often Nobles. The Macinteers (Mac an tsaoir, i.e., son of the carpenter) instead of being made MacIntyre as the Scots always have it, are in Ireland, Carpenters or Wrights, or — because *saor* means 'free' as well as Carpenter — Frees and Freemans. Many of the O'Hagans (Ó h-Aodhgáin) are now Fagans, and even Dickens's Fagan the Jew has not put a stop to the hideous transformation. The O'Hillans (Mac Uí Iollain, i.e., sons of Illan, a great name in Irish romance) have become Hylands or Whelans. It would be tedious to go through all the well-known names that immediately occur to one as thus suffering; suffice it to say, that the O'Heas became Hayses, the O'Queenahans, Mosses, Mossmans, and Kinahans, the O'Longans Longs, the O'Naghtens Nortons, the O'Reardons Salmons, the O'Shanahans Foxes, and so on *ad infinitum*.

Numbers of people, again, like Mr Davitt or Mr Hennessy, drop the O and Mac which properly belong to their names; others, without actually changing them, metamorphose their names, as we have seen, into every possible form. I was told in America that the first Chauncey who ever came out there was an O'Shaughnessy, who went to, I think, Maryland, in the middle of the last century, and who had twelve sons, who called themselves Chauncey, and from whom most of or all the Chaunceys in America are descended. I know people who have translated their names within the last ten years. This vile habit is going on with almost unabated vigour, and nobody has ever raised a protest against it. Out of the many hundreds of O'Byrnes — offshoots of the great Wicklow chieftains — in the city of New York, only four have retained that name; all the rest have taken the Scotch name of Burns. I have this information from two of the remaining four, both friends of my own, and both splendid Gaelic scholars, though from opposite ends of Ireland, Donegal and Waterford. Of two brothers of whom I was lately told, though I do not know them personally, one is an O'Gara, and still condescends to remain connected with the patron of the Four Masters and a thousand years of a glorious past, whilst the other (through some etymological confusion with the word Caraim, which means 'I love') calls himself Mr Love! Another brother remains a Brehony, thus showing his descent from one of the very highest and most honourable titles in Ireland — a Brehon, law-giver and poet; the other brother is John Judge. In fact, hundreds of thousands of Irishmen prefer to drop their honourable Milesian names, and call themselves Groggins or Duggan, or Higgins or Guthry, or any other beastly name, in preference to the surnames of warriors, saints, and poets; and the melancholy part of it is, that not one single word of warning or remonstrance has been raised, as far as I am aware, against this colossal cringing either by the Irish public press or public men.

With our Irish Christian names the case is nearly as bad. Where are now all the fine old Irish Christian names of both men and women which were in vogue even a hundred years ago? They have been discarded as unclean things, not because they were ugly in themselves or inharmonious, but simply because they were not English. No man is now christened by a Gaelic name, 'nor no woman neither.' Such common Irish Christian names as Conn, Cairbre, Farfeasa, Teig, Diarmuid, Kian, Cuan, Ae, Art, Mahon, Eochaidh, Fearflatha, Cathan, Rory, Coll, Lochlainn, Cathal, Lughaidh, Turlough, Éamon, Randal, Niall, Sorley, and Conor, are now extinct or nearly so. Donough and Murrough survive in the O'Brien family. Angus, Manus, Fergal, and Felim are now hardly known. The man whom you call Diarmuid when you speak Irish, a low, pernicious, un-Irish, detestable custom, begot by slavery, propagated by cringing, and fostered by flunkeyism, forces you to call Jeremiah when you speak English, or as a concession, Darby. In like manner, the indigenous Teig is West-Britonised into Thaddeus or Thady, for no earthly reason than that both begin with a T. Donough is Denis, Cahal is Charles, Murtagh and Murough are Mortimer, Dómhnall is Daniel, Partholan, the name of the earliest coloniser of Ireland, is Bartholomew or Batty,[3] Eoghan (Owen) is frequently Eugene, and our own O'Curry, though he plucked up courage to prefix the O to his name in later life, never discarded the Eugene, which, however, is far from being a monstrosity like most of our West-Britonised names; Félim is Felix, Finghin (Finneen) is Florence, Conor is Corney, Turlough is Terence, Éamon is Edmond or Neddy, and so on. In fact, of the great wealth of Gaelic Christian names in use a century or two ago, only Owen, Brian, Cormac, and Patrick seem to have survived in general use.

Nor have our female names fared one bit better; we have discarded them even more ruthlessly than those of our men. Surely Sadhbh (Sive) is a prettier name than Sabina or Sibby, and Nóra than Onny, Honny, or Honour (so translated simply because Nóra sounds like *onóir*, the Irish for 'honour'); surely Una is prettier than Winny, which it becomes when West-Britonised. Mève, the great name of the Queen of Connacht who led the famous cattle spoiling of Cuailgne, celebrated in the greatest Irish epic, is at least as pretty as Maud, which it becomes when Anglicised, and Eibhlin (Eileen) is prettier than Ellen or Elinor. Aoife (Eefy), Sighle (Sheela), Móirin (Moreen), Nuala and Fionnuala (Finnoola), are all beautiful names which were in use until quite recently. Maurya and Anya are still common, but are not indigenous Irish names at all, so that I do not mind their rejection, whilst three other very common ones, Suraha, Shinéad, and Shuwaun, sound so bad in English that I do not very much regret their being translated into Sarah, Jane, and Joan respectively; but I must put in a plea for the retention of such beautiful words as Eefee, Oona, Eileen, Mève, Sive, and Nuala. Of all the beautiful Christian names of women which were in use a century or two ago Brighid (Breed), under the ugly form of Bridget, or still worse, of Biddy, and Eiblin under the form of Eveleen, and perhaps Norah, seem to be the only survivals, and they are becoming rarer. I *do* think that the time has now come to make a vigorous protest against this continued West-Britonising of ourselves, and that our people ought to have a word in season addressed to them by their leaders which will stop them from translating their Milesian surnames into hideous Saxon, and help to introduce Irish instead of English Christian names. As long as the Irish nation goes on as it is doing I cannot have much hope of its ultimately taking its place amongst the nations of the earth, for if it does, it will have proceeded upon different lines from every other

---

3 It is questionable, however, whether Partholan as a modern Christian name is not itself an Irishised form of Bartholomew.

nationality that God every created. I hope that we shall never be satisfied either as individuals or as a society as long as the Brehonys call themselves Judges, the Clan Govern call themselves Smiths, and the O'Reardons Salmons, as long as our boys are called Dan and Jeremiah instead of Donal and Diarmuid, and our girls Honny, Winny, and Ellen instead of Nóra, Una, and Eileen.

Our topographical nomenclature too — as we may now be prepared to expect — has been also shamefully corrupted to suit English ears; but unfortunately the difficulties attendant upon a realteration of our place-names to their proper forms are very great, nor do I mean to go into this question now, for it is one so long and so difficult that it would require a lecture, or rather a series of lectures to itself. Suffice it to say, that many of the best-known names in our history and annals have become almost wholly unrecognisable, through the ignorant West-Britonising of them. The unfortunate natives of the eighteenth century allowed all kinds of havoc to be played with even their best-known names. For example the river Feóir they allowed to be turned permanently into the Nore, which happened this way. Some Englishman, asking the name of the river, was told that it was *An Fheóir*, pronounced In n'yore, because the F when preceded by the definitive article *an* is not sounded, so that in his ignorance he mistook the word Feóir for Neóir, and the name has been thus perpetuated. In the same way the great Connacht lake, Lock Corrib, is really Loch Orrib, or rather Loch Orbsen, some Englishman having mistaken the C at the end of Loch for the beginning of the next word. Sometimes the Ordnance Survey people make a rough guess at the Irish name and jot down certain English letters almost on chance. Sometimes again they make an Irish word resemble an English one, as in the celebrated Tailtin in Meath, where the great gathering of the nation was held, and, which, to make sure that no national memories should stick to it, has been West-Britonised Telltown.[4] On the whole, our place names have been treated with about the same respect as if they were the names of a savage tribe which had never before been reduced to writing, and with about the same intelligence and contempt as vulgar English squatters treat the topographical nomenclature of the Red Indians. These things are now to a certain extent stereotyped, and are difficult at this hour to change, especially where Irish names have been translated into English, like Swinford and Strokestown, or ignored as in Charleville or Midleton. But though it would take the strength and goodwill of an united nation to put our topographical nomenclature on a rational basis like that of Wales and the Scotch Highlands, there is one thing which our Society can do, and that is to insist upon

---

4 For more information about Tailtin, see an article by me incorporated in the 'Rules of the Gaelic Athletic Association,' recently published.

pronouncing our Irish names properly. Why will a certain class of people insist upon getting as far away from the pronunciation of the natives as possible? I remember a Galway gentleman pulling me up severely for speaking of Athenree. 'It's not Athenree,' he said, 'it's called Athenrye.' Yet in saying this he simply went out of his way to mispronounce the historic name, which means the 'King's ford,' and which all the natives call *-ree*, not *rye*.[5] Another instance out of many thousands is my own market town, Ballagh-a-derreen, literally, 'the way of the oak-wood.' Ballach is the same word as in the phrase *Fág a' bealach*, 'clear the way,' and 'derreen' is the diminutive of Derry, an oak-wood. Yet the more 'civilised' of the population, perhaps one in fifty, offend one's ears with the frightful jargon Bálla-hád-hereen. Thus Lord Iveagh (Ee-vah) becomes Lord Ivy, and Seana-guala, the old sholder, becomes Shanagolden, and leads you to expect a mine, or at least a furze-covered hill.

I shall not give any more examples of deliberate carelessness, ineptitude, and West-Britonising in our Irish topography, for the instances may be numbered by thousands and thousands. I hope and trust that where it may be done without any great inconvenience a native Irish Government will be induced to provide for the restoration of our place-names on something like a rational basis.

Our music, too, has become Anglicised to an alarming extent. Not only has the national instrument, the harp — which efforts are now being made to revive in the Highlands — become extinct, but even the Irish pipes are threatened with the same fate. In place of the pipers and fiddles who, even twenty years ago, were comparatively common, we are now in many places menaced by the German band and the barrel organ. Something should be done to keep the native pipes and the native airs amongst us still. If Ireland loses her music she loses what is, after her Gaelic language and literature, her most valuable and most characteristic possession. And she is rapidly losing it. A few years ago all our travelling fiddlers and pipers could play the old airs which were then constantly called for, the *Cúis d'á pléidh, Drinaun Dunn, Roseen Dubh, Gamhan Geal Bán, Eileen-a-roon, Shawn O'Dwyer in Glanna*, and the rest, whether gay or plaintive, which have for so many centuries entranced the Gael. But now English music-hall ballads and Scotch songs have gained an enormous place in the repertoire of the wandering minstrel, and the minstrels themselves are becoming fewer and fewer, and I fear worse and worse. It is difficult to find a remedy for this. I am afraid in this practical age to go so far as to advocate the establishment in Cork or Galway of a small institution in which young

---

5   In Irish it is Beul-áth-an-righ contracted into B'l'áth-'n-righ, pronounced *Blawn-ree*.

and promising pipers might be trained to play all the Irish airs and sent forth to delight our population; for I shall be told that this is not a matter for even an Irish Government to stir in, though it is certain that many a Government has lavished money on schemes less pleasant and less useful. For the present, then, I must be content with hoping that the revival of our Irish music may go hand in hand with the revival of Irish ideas and Celtic modes of thought which our Society is seeking to bring about, and that people may be brought to love the purity of *Siúbhail Siúbhail*, or the fun of the *Moddereen Ruadh* in preference to 'Get Your Hair Cut,' or 'Over the Garden Wall,' or, even if it is not asking too much, of 'Ta-ra-ra-boom-de-ay.'

Our games, too, were in a most grievous condition until the brave and patriotic men who started the Gaelic Athletic Association took in hand their revival. I confess that the instantaneous and extraordinary success which attended their efforts when working upon national lines has filled me with more hope for the future of Ireland than everything else put together. I consider the work of the association in reviving our ancient national game of *camán*, or hurling, and Gaelic football, has done more for Ireland than all the speeches of politicians for the last five years. And it is not alone that that splendid association revived for a time with vigour our national sports, but it revived also our national recollections, and the names of the various clubs through the country have perpetuated the memory of the great and good men and martyrs of Ireland. The physique of our youth has been improved in many of our counties; they have been taught self-restraint, and how to obey their captains; they have been, in many places, weaned from standing idle in their own roads or street corners; and not least, they have been introduced to the use of a thoroughly good and Irish garb. Wherever the warm striped green jersey of the Gaelic Athletic Association was seen, there Irish manhood and Irish memories were rapidly reviving. There torn collars and ugly neckties hanging awry and far better not there at all, and dirty shirts of bad linen were banished, and our young hurlers were clad like men and Irishmen, and not in the shoddy second-hand suits of Manchester and London shop-boys. Could not this alteration be carried still further? Could we not make that jersey still more popular, and could we not, in places where both garbs are worn, use our influence against English second-hand trousers, generally dirty in front, and hanging in muddy tatters at the heels, and in favour of the cleaner worsted stockings and neat breeches which many of the older generation still wear? Why have we discarded our own comfortable frieze? Why does every man in Connemara wear home-made and home-spun tweed, while in the midland counties we have become too proud for it, though we are not too proud to buy at every fair and market the most incongruous cast-off clothes imported from English cities, and to wear them? Let us, as far as we have any influence, set our faces against this aping of English dress, and encourage our women to spin and our men to wear comfortable frieze suits of their own wool, free from shoddy and humbug. So shall we de-Anglicise Ireland to some purpose, foster a native spirit and a growth of native custom which will form the strongest barrier against English influence and be in the end the surest guarantee of Irish autonomy.

I have now mentioned a few of the principal points on which it would be desirable for us to move, with a view to de-Anglicising ourselves; but perhaps the principal point of all I have taken for granted. That is the necessity for encouraging the use of Anglo-Irish literature instead of English books, especially instead of English periodicals. We must set our face sternly against penny dreadfuls, shilling shockers, and still more, the garbage of vulgar English weeklies like *Bow Bells* and the *Police Intelligence*. Every house should have a copy of Moore and Davis. In a word, we must strive to cultivate everything that is most racial, most smacking of the soil, most Gaelic, most Irish, because in spite of the little admixture of Saxon blood in the north-east corner, this island *is* and will *ever* remain Celtic to the core, far more Celtic than most people imagine, because, as I have shown you, the names of our people are no criterion of their race. On racial lines, then, we shall best develop, following the bent of our own natures; and, in order to do this, we must create a strong feeling against West-Britonism, for it — if we give it the least chance, or show it the smallest quarter — will overwhelm us like a flood, and we shall find ourselves toiling painfully behind the English at each step following the same fashions, only six months behind the English ones; reading the same books, only months behind them: taking up the same fads, after they have become stale *there*, following *them* in our dress, literature, music, games, and ideas, only a long time after them and a vast way behind. We will become, what, I fear, we are largely at present, a nation of imitators, the Japanese of Western Europe, lost to the power of native initiative and alive only to second-hand assimilation. I do not think I am overrating this danger. We are probably at once the most assimilative and the most sensitive nation in Europe. A lady in Boston said to me that the Irish immigrants had become Americanised on the journey out before ever they landed at Castle Gardens. And when I ventured to regret it, she said, shrewdly, 'If they did not at once become Americanised they would not be Irish.' I knew fifteen Irish workmen who were working in a haggard in England give up talking Irish amongst themselves because the English farmer laughed at them. And yet O'Connell used to call us the 'finest peasantry in Europe.' Unfortunately, he took little care that we should remain so. We must teach ourselves to be less sensitive, we must teach ourselves not to be ashamed of ourselves, because the Gaelic people can never produce its best before the world as long as it remains tied to the apron-strings of another race and another island, waiting for *it* to move before it will venture to take any step itself.

In conclusion, I would earnestly appeal to every one, whether Unionist or Nationalist, who wishes to see the Irish nation produce its best — and surely whatever our politics are we all wish that — to set his face against this constant running to England for our books, literature, music, games, fashions, and ideas. I appeal to every one whatever his politics — for this is no political matter — to do his best to help the Irish race to develop in future upon Irish lines, even at the risk of encouraging national aspirations, because upon Irish lines alone can the Irish race once more become what it was of yore — one of the most original, artistic, literary, and charming peoples of Europe.

The Gaelic Revival

EDITORIAL NOTE

In his autobiography *Mise agus an Connradh* (1937) Douglas Hyde, referring to the activities of Conradh na Gaeilge in 1905, says:

'Bhí sé ag síneadh amach ins an mbliain anois agus bhí easpa mhór airgid orainn. Do cheap an Conradh go mba cheart dom féin dul amach go hAmericeá agus iarracht do dhéanamh ar níos mó airgid d'fháil dóibh ansan. Do chuireamar amach Tomás Bán romham. Do ghlac mo chara Seán Ó Cuinn chuige é, agus thug sé isteach ina thigh féin é' (147-8).*

Hyde's *Mo Thurus go hAmerice* (1937) is dedicated to this Seán Ó Cuinn, John Quinn, New York lawyer and patron of the Arts, and begins with the author's recollection of their first encounter which took place on 26 August 1900 at the grave of Raftery in Cillínín (Killeenan) on the occasion of the inauguration of an inscribed memorial stone in memory of the poet. Also present were Edward Martyn, W.B. Yeats, and the instigator of the monument, Lady Gregory. Subsequently Quinn had written to Hyde inviting him to New York, promising to assist him in his work, and renewed the invitation in person during a visit to Ireland in 1904. He had performed a similar service for W.B. Yeats some years earlier. The death of his father in 1905 had left Hyde, who had been President of Conradh na Gaeilge since its inception, free to accept the invitation. The Conradh then arranged to have a circular distributed throughout the United States announcing Hyde's visit and asking all Irish-Americans to welcome and support him. Tomás Bán Ó Coincheanainn, from Inis Meáin of the Aran Islands, who had lived and worked in North America, preceded Hyde as Advance Agent in October preparing the ground in the various cities and states on his strenuous itinerary, under the guidance and advice of John Quinn who also organised a highranking committee to formally receive Dr Hyde and his wife when they arrived on the Majestic in New York, on 15 November 1905, after a tumultuous send-off from Ireland the previous week.

* It was well out into the year now and we were in great need of funds. The Conradh thought that I myself should go out to America and try to obtain more money there for them. We sent Tomás Bán in advance of me. My friend John Quinn received him, and took him into his own house.

Their first four days were spent at the Manhattan Hotel, meeting the Press, before John Quinn transferred the Hydes to his own residence at 120 Broadway.

Harvard and Yale were the venues for Hyde's first two public speaking engagements. At Harvard, on 20 November, he spoke on Irish folklore to an audience of approximately 500, and at Yale his subject was the mind and philosophy of Conradh na Gaeilge. A very cordial meeting and lunch with President Roosevelt at the White House followed, before his first major and crucial public appearance in New York city. He himself relates:

Anois tháinig an lá mór a raibh bua nó bris i ndán dom. Ba é sin an lá a raibh cruinniú mór le bheith agam ins an Carnegie Hall. Bhí sé ullmhaithe le fada an lá roimh ré. Díoladh ar candáil an chéad rang de na boscaí, roimhe sin, ag an Hoffman House, agus tugadh a lán airgid isteach. A bhuíochas sin ar Mhac Uí Chuinn. Do chruinnigh sé na daoine le chéile agus chuir sé Peadar Fionnlaigh Ó Duinn, fear a raibh aithne air ar fud Americeá, mar 'Mister Dooley', ag díol na mboscaí. Ach nuair nár fhéad seisean teacht, fuaireadar fear mór eile lena ndíol. Tugadh suas le trí céad dollar ar chuid de na boscaí.*

When finally the moment arrived for his own address to the packed auditorium, he says, 'bhí mo chroí ag bualadh agus ag preabarnaigh ionam le neart sceoin'.**

The *Gaelic American*, which devoted several of its pages to the event, introduced its report as follows:

The meeting that greeted Douglas Hyde in Carnegie Hall last Sunday evening was in every respect the finest that ever greeted an Irishman in New York. It was a most pronounced success from every point of view — in the number, character and standing of those present, the tactful opening speech of Judge Keogh, the masterly address of Bourke Cockran, the clear, convincing and simply eloquent plea for the Gaelic League by Douglas Hyde; the enthusiasm of the audience and the financial result, it was by long odds the most remarkable Irish gathering ever held in New York. No missionary from Ireland ever before commenced an American tour under such favourable circumstances, and the complete success of that tour is already assured.[1]

---

* Then arrived the big day on which triumph or failure lay in store for me. That was the day when I was to have a great meeting in the Carnegie Hall. It had been arranged well in advance. The first row of the boxes had been previously sold by auction at Hoffman House, and much money had been taken in. This was thanks to Mr Quinn. He had gathered the people together and put Peter Finley Dunne, known throughout America as 'Mister Dooley', to selling the boxes. But when he could not come, they found another well-known figure to sell them. Up to three hundred dollars was paid for some of the boxes.

** My heart was beating and leaping inside me with fright.

1 *Gaelic American*, 2 December 1905. Passages from the *GA* commentary are shown in *italics*. The tour itself was a great financial success, bringing in a total of £12,400.

DR. DOUGLAS HYDE

WILL LECTURE AT

CARNEGIE HALL,

Seventh Avenue and 57th Street,

NEW YORK CITY,

SUNDAY EVENING, NOVEMBER 26, 1905,

ON

"THE GAELIC REVIVAL."

Hon. MARTIN J. KEOGH will preside, and
Hon. W. BOURKE COCKRAN will deliver an introductory address.

Mr. Patrick O'Shea, of Dublin, who is generally considered the best Irish singer in Ireland, will sing in Irish and English, and there will be music by a selected orchestra.

All those interested in the Irish National Revival are earnestly urged to attend this meeting, and to put forth their best efforts to make it one of the greatest meetings ever held in the City of New York.

Tickets for the lecture are on sale at the following places:

McBride's Ticket Agency, 71 Broadway, New York City.
Brentano's, Union Square, New York City.
McPartland & O'Flaherty, 629 Eighth Avenue, between 40th and 41st Streets, New York City.
Irish Counties Athletic Union, 341 W. 47th St., New York City.
Irish-American Athletic Club, 163 E. 60th St., New York City.
Irish National Club, 241 West 57th Street, New York City.
Vanderbilt Hotel, 42d St. and Lexington Ave., New York City.
Mr. Thomas J. O'Sullivan's place of business, 257 Hudson St., New York City, and at all Branches of the Gaelic League in Brooklyn and New York.

MARTIN J. KEOGH, Chairman.
VICTOR J. DOWLING, Treasurer.
JOHN QUINN, Secretary.
Douglas Hyde Reception Committee of New York.

THIS ADVERTISEMENT IS INSERTED FREE.

Tomás Ó Concheanainn

Douglas Hyde addressing crowds in Dublin, 1903

After a speech of welcome lasting over half an hour by the noted orator W. Bourke Cockran and the rendering of some Irish songs by Patrick O'Shea, the Supreme Court Justice Martin J. Keogh, who presided, introduced the evening's honoured guest and principal speaker:

> 'Now, Ladies and Gentlemen, it gives me unspeakable pleasure to present to you the right arm, the brain and soul of the Gaelic revival in Ireland, patriot and scholar, Dr Douglas Hyde.' (Great applause.)
>
> When Douglas Hyde stepped forward he received a great ovation. Every man and woman in the audience rose and a good old-fashioned Irish cheer went up that left no doubt in An Craoibhín's mind that the crowd in front of him and around him was Irish to the core. The cheer was renewed again and again, the men in evening dress on the platform and in the boxes doing their part as lustily as those in the body of the hall and on the galleries, and the ladies waving their handkerchiefs. This continued for several minutes, and the leader of Irish-Ireland stood there, looking half abashed until the storm of applause had subsided.
>
> Then his first words were in Gaelic, and the frequent bursts of applause and words of approval shouted to him in the old tongue showed unmistakably that a large part of the audience understood every word he uttered. This so pleased and warmed him up that he prolonged the Irish part of his address until at last he feared that those who had no knowledge of Irish imagined he was going to tell them nothing in English at all. Then he jokingly reassured them and delivered his address in the language understood by the majority of those present.

HIS SPEECH IN GAELIC*

Dr Hyde's speech in Gaelic was in part, as follows:

A dhuine uasail atá san gcathaoir, a mhná uaisle, a dhaoine uaisle agus a chairde go léir, — tá bród agus áthas orm sibhse fheicsint anso anocht, agus aithne do chur ar Ghaelaibh na cathrach móire seo. Is mór an sásamh dhom é agus mé 'mo strainséara in bhur measc i bhfad ó bhaile, éadan geanúil Gaelach d'fheicsint arís, agus dar liomsa níl ins an halla mór so anocht ach Gaeil agus fíorÉireannaigh. Táimid cruinnithe anso anocht le buille do bhualadh ar son na sean-bhean bhoichte (*sic*) d'fhágamar in ár ndiaidh in Éirinn — ach, dar mo lámh! ní sean-bhean bhocht atá inti inniu, ach cailín óg croíúil a bhfuil na mílte agus na mílte ag titim i ngrá léi. Tá sí ag cromadh arís ar spóirt agus ar aoibhneas, tá sí ag cromadh arís ar rinceannaibh agus damhsa, ar cheol agus ar

---

* Mr Chairman, ladies and gentlemen and friends, I am proud and happy to see you all here to-night, and to meet the Irish people of this great city. It gives me great satisfaction, a stranger in your midst and far from home, to see a kindly Irish face again, and it seems to me there is no one in this great hall but true Irish people. We are gathered here to-night to strike a blow for the poor old lady (Shan Van Vocht) which we left behind us in Ireland — but, by my hand, it isn't a poor old woman she is to-day, but a young hearty girl with whom thousands and thousands are falling in love. She is beginning again to sport and play, she is beginning to dance, to play music

amhráin. Tá sí bocht go fóill, ach má tá féin, tá sí óg álainn deas dathúil, agus tá ruda ann níos measa ná an bochtanas! Ach, bocht nó saibhir, is í ár nÉire féin í, agus táimid dul dá tógáil. Agus táimid dá tógáil. Níl lá san mbliain nach bhfuilimid ag déanamh rud éigin le maise do chur uirthi. Fuaireamar í dhá bhliain dhéag ó shin ina cúige — ní hea, ach ina contae Shacsanaigh — ina rubaillín beag gránna, agus táimid 'déanamh náisiún di. Táimid ag tabhairt ar ais di a nósa agus a béasa féin, agus ag díbirt na ndrochnós Gallda amach aisti. Táimid ag tabhairt ar ais di a teanga féin, a ceoil féin, a rinceanna féin, agus gach aon ní dá raibh aici nuair bhí sí 'na náisiún dáiríre.

Ní obair éadrom í seo. Ach tá fhios agam go maith chomh maith agus thuigfeas sibhse in Americea créad táimid 'dhéanamh san mbaile, go ndéarfaidh sibh go bhfuil an ceart againn, agus is le cur i gcéill agus i dtuigsint daoibhse créad tá ar siúl againn d'fhág Tomás Bán agus mé féin Éire agus thángamar anso.

Tá difir mhór idir an Éirinn do bhí againn dhá bhliain dhéag ó shin agus an Éire atá ann inniu. Ní raibh le feicsint an uair sin in Éirinn ach an dá pháirtí amháin, na tiarnaí talúna agus na daoine ag bualadh, ag léasadh agus ag plancadh le chéile. Ach, buíochas le Dia, tá an troid sin beagnach socraithe anois, nó ar shlí do bheith socraithe. Tá na daoine ag fáil seilbh ar thalamh na hÉireann arís, agus tá na tiarnaí ag éirí i

and to sing. She is still poor, but even so, she is young and beautiful, and there are worse things than poverty! But, poor or rich, she is our own Ireland, and we are going to set her aright. And we *are* setting her aright. There's not a day in the year when we are not doing something to enhance her appearance. We found her twelve years ago and she a province — nay, but an English shire — a little ugly tailpiece, and we are making a nation out of her. We are returning to her her own customs and habits, and banishing the bad Anglicised practices from her. We are restoring to her her own language, her own music, her own dances, and every thing which she had when she was truly a nation.

This is not an easy task. And I am well aware how much you in America understand what we are doing at home, that you will say that we are right, and it is to bring it home to you, and to make you understand what we are about, that Tomás Bán and myself left Ireland and came here.

There is a great difference between the Ireland we had twelve years ago and the Ireland of to-day. There were only two parties to be seen in Ireland at that time, the landlords and the people striking, thrashing, fighting with one another. But, thanks be to God, that quarrel is now almost settled, or on the way to being settled. The people are gaining possession of the land of Ireland again, the landlords are becoming far more Irish than they were, when they relinquish their lands.

We now have the time and the opportunity to look around at our country, and we now understand that the land question is not the only question in Ireland. There is another question as important, or more important, namely, is Ireland going to be an ugly shire, a little anglified tailpiece or a nation as she always was. I say this much to you: an Ireland which merely contained the speech, music, sports, dances and customs of the English would be of no interest to me. It wouldn't matter to me whether it was high up or low down, because that country would not be Ireland, but an English county, and furthermore, rather than be in it I would far prefer to be in England itself.

bhfad níos Gaelaí ná mar bhíodar nuair scarann siad lena gcuid talún.

Tá am agus uain againn anois le breathnú thart ar ár dtír agus tuigimid anois nach í ceist na talún an aon cheist amháin in Éirinn. Tá ceist eile ann chomh trom léi, nó níos troime, agus is í sin, bhfuil Éire le bheith ina contae gránna, ina rubaillín beag gallda, nó ina náisiún mar bhí sí ariamh. Adeirim libh an méid seo: Éire nach mbeadh inti ach caint, ceol, spóirteanna, rince agus béasa na nGall, ba chuma liomsa í bheith ann nó as, ba chuma liom í bheith in uachtar nó in íochtar, óir ní Éire do bheadh ins an tír sin ach contae Shacsanach agus b'fhearr liom i bhfad a bheith i Sacsana féin ná inti leis.

WHAT HE SAID IN IRISH[2]

Following is the substance of what he said in Irish.

Mr Chairman, Ladies and Gentlemen — It gives me very great pleasure to be with you to-night. When I see this great gathering around me and when I hear your voices, I feel as if I had never left Ireland, or if I did, that I had merely transplanted myself from one Ireland to another Ireland. There is this difference, however, between the two Irelands; that those at home understand the Gaelic League; they understand the work that we are doing; they understand its full significance, and they see the result of our work every day of their lives. I fear that you here do not understand it yet, and the task that I have put before me this evening is to explain to you the full significance of our movement.

What are we doing? I will tell you in one word. We are creating a new nation among the nations of the world. We are making the people self-confident, self-reliant. We are restoring the strength and the heart, the mind and the brain of Ireland as it was in the free and happy days of long ago. We are bringing back her own tongue that was half-dead; her own music that was half-forgotten; her own habits and her own customs that were dying day by day. We are putting a new soul into the people, and as I have said, in one word, we are creating a new nation on the map of Europe.

Douglas Hyde's Address

After concluding his address in Irish, Dr Hyde commenced jocosely in English amid peals of laughter. He said:

I saw, when I looked around that time, a shade of apprehension on the expressive face of the Judge (referring to Judge Keogh) and I saw a trace of a panic down there, too (referring to the audience). You thought I was going to speak Irish all night (laughter). Well, a very witty, and, faith, a very wicked, Irishman too, said once: "To be intelligible," says

---

2 Compare with my translation given in footnote pp. 175-6.

he, "is to be found out." I do not care if I am found out. The Gaelic League in Ireland and America only wants to be found out, and when you find us out, you will stick to us (applause).

I am not exaggerating when I say that I look upon the moral support of the Irish in America to be the most valuable asset that the Gaelic League at home could have; because every man and woman in Ireland to-day has a relative — many of them have a dozen relatives — here in the United States; and the immense reflex influence which you here in America can wield if you wish to wield it, upon Irish opinion is, in my opinion, of more importance for us to possess ourselves of, than any other asset whatsoever. I would sooner have the moral support of the Irish in America than a quarter of a million of dollars poured into the Gaelic League to-morrow (applause).

I am here to-night to explain to you the life and death struggle upon which we are engaged in Ireland. I see that the more sympathetic of the New York papers say that this is the last grand struggle of the Irish race to preserve their language. Oh, gentlemen! it is ten times, it is a hundred times, it is a thousand times more far-reaching than that! It is the last possible life and death struggle of the Irish race to preserve their national identity (applause).

We have now opened the eyes of the Irish race to the awful yawning chasm which gaped beneath us, over which a single false footstep would have taken us — the awful chasm of Anglicization, which, believe me, is only another name for national extinction, and when you in America understand that — and I shall fail in my mission to-night if I don't make you understand it — then, I know you will join us in saying to the devouring demon of Anglicization whose foul and gluttonous jaws have swallowed everything that was hereditary, natural, instinctive, ancient, intellectual and noble in our Irish people — our language, our songs, our industries, our dances, and our pastimes — I know and say that you will plant your feet firmly and you will say, 'Not one step more, demon! Back, demon! You shall never swallow one single mouthful more of the possessions of Irish Nationhood (applause).

A GREAT NATIONAL MOVEMENT

The movement on which we are engaged to-night is not the movement of a few faddists. It was thought to be so. That time has long gone by. So far is our movement from being a movement of insignificant faddists that papers in Dublin, which are at daggers drawn amongst themselves, are at one in championing our cause. Churchmen like the Archbishop of Dublin and the Cardinal Archbishop of Armagh are with us; even the organ of the independent Orangemen who seceded from the main body said the other day, just before I left Ireland, that it was a movement which no Orangeman or Protestant need be ashamed to join (applause). The Protestant Bishop of Derry (applause) at a church conference spoke to the Northern Protestants most sympathetically about us only the other day. The leader of the Irish Parliamentary Party has himself on many occasions spoken of the importance of our work, and, what is better, his own children are learning Irish.

One of the most remarkable of the Gaelic League festivals ever held in Ireland was held in August at a place where you know the River Bann runs into the sea, Toome Bridge, that for generations upon generations had been the battleground of Catholic and Orangeman; and what do we find? Under our aegis, Catholic and Orangeman came into that place in a spirit of brotherhood unexampled in that part of the world ever before, and I could not tell which was the most numerous at it (applause).

So you see that we are no clique, we are no faction, we are no party. We are above and beyond all politics, all parties and all factions; offending nobody — except the anti-Irishman (laughter and applause). We stand immovable upon the bedrock of the doctrine of true Irish nationhood — an Ireland self-centred, self-sufficing, self-supporting, self-reliant; an Ireland speaking its own language, thinking its own thoughts, writing its own books, sings its own songs, playing its own games, weaving its own coats, and going for nothing outside of the four shores of Ireland that can possibly be procured inside them (applause).

The Gaelic League is founded not upon hatred of England, but upon love of Ireland. Hatred is a negative passion; it is powerful — a very powerful destroyer; but it is useless for building up. Love, on the other hand, is like faith; it can move mountains; and, faith, we have mountains to move (laughter and applause).

BASED ON SOUND PHILOSOPHIC PRINCIPLES

The philosophy of the Gaelic League is this: that Ireland cannot compete with England in the things that come naturally to England and that come unnaturally to us. We cannot, for instance — well, we cannot play cricket as well as Englishmen (laughter). Ah, but sure, we can beat the world at hurling (laughter and applause). Upon our clay floors, we cannot dance the waltzes gracefully; but, sure, we can smash them at a jig or a reel (laughter). We cannot sing 'Johnny, Get Your 'Air Cut', in the Coster pronunciation, but I defy an Englishman to whistle the Maidrín Ruadh (laughter). In one word, we aim at the de-Anglicization of Ireland.

Now it has been objected to me that that word, which I coined long ago for want of a better, *de-Anglicization*, contained in it something harsh, something virulent, something rebellious; and that it was calculated to alienate the good will of many people who would, otherwise, be our supporters; and, as that may possibly be so, and especially in a cosmopolitan city like New York, I desire to say, to set myself right before I go any further, that any ladies and gentlemen of English sympathies who may be here tonight (loud laughter) — never mind, sure, there might be — well I honor and respect everything that is good in the great English race. I yield to no man in my appreciation of their perseverance, their business faculties, their practical qualities. They have colonized many countries; they have called into existence scores of great cities; factories where the unceasing roar and hum of production are never silent. Theirs are the harbors thronged with their forests of masts, theirs, pre-eminently, are the mart and the counting house and the mercantile navy of the world. Wealth, power and the teeming fruits of industry are theirs; and those are things that mankind, in every age, and every race, have, rightly or wrongly — and, upon my word, I think very often wrongly — (laughter and applause) conspired to reverence and admire. Yes; whilst England can point to such advantages as those, she may laugh at those who would belittle her; and, in the history of the world, she has made her mark deeply. Her enemies may hate her — they do hate her; but they cannot despise her.

And yet, and yet, there exists there at her very doors an ancient nation whose half-deserted streets resound ever less and less to the roar of traffic, whose mills are silent, whose factories are fallen, whose very fields are studded only with ruined gables — memories of the past; and yet, around that nation, morality of life, purity of sentiment, unswerving devotion to faith, and to fatherland, and to language, have shed a halo in the eyes of Europe that is all its own (applause). It is a halo, too, that is unstained by oppression of any man, untarnished by avarice of anything, and undimmed by murder (applause).

Well, the characteristics of this Irish race of ours are lightness, brightness, wit, fluency and an artistic temperament. The characteristics of the Teutonic race are an intense business faculty, perseverance and steadiness in details; and in America you have elicited a magnificent blend of both qualities in that free and noble race whose sons or whose adopted sons and daughters I see before me tonight. But mark this: neither race can, with any success whatsoever, cut itself adrift from its own past and throw itself in imitation of the other into habits of life and thought and manners into which God never intended it to be thrown (applause).

THE CURSE OF ANGLICIZATION

But, alas! that is the very thing which the Irish race at home and abroad, dazzled by the material prosperity of the great country to which we are tied — many of them unwillingly tied — that is, I say, the very thing that the Irish race have been doing. This folly, this madness, this suicidal mania (for I cannot call it anything else) of rushing to adopt pell-mell and indiscriminately everything that is English, not because it is good, but because it is English, has been bad for all parties. It has been bad for Irish Nationalists; it has been equally bad for Irish Unionists. It has been bad for our own country, and it has been worse for the country with which we are connected. The more divergence of thought and genius, of natural aptitudes, the better, because, I tell you, there is an individuality in nationalities exactly as there is in persons — and to attempt to mould or crush everything into one particular type has invariably been fatal to the people that attempted it.

In our case, gentlemen, that attempt has been fatal. If you take a bird's-eye view of Ireland today and compare it with what it was you must be struck by the fact that the nation which was at one time the most classically learned and cultured nation in Europe is now one of the least so — how a nation which was one of the most reading and literary peoples in the world is now one of the least reading and the most unliterary, and how the art products of one of the quickest, most sensitive, and most artistic of all populations are now distinguished only by their hideousness!

The causes of this ghastly failure may all be summed up in one word; we have ceased to be Irish without becoming English (applause). It is to this cause that I attribute more than to anything else our awful emigration and impoverishment. Irishmen leave Ireland today because they have ceased to feel that they have a country. They will not accept England as their country, and yet in the Ireland that the Gaelic League found before it, there was nothing to suggest to them anything else than an imitation England, and the public mind had become hopelessly confused and Irishmen had no standard to live by and they emigrated in their thousands.

I want to show you tonight hard facts; I want to show you that in Anglicizing ourselves we have thrown away with a light heart the best claim, the only true claim, that we can make upon the world's recognition of us as a separate nationality. What did Mazzini say? What is Goldwin Smith back there in Canada, never tired of declaring? What does the *Spectator* and the English *Times* harp upon in every issue almost? Why, that we should be content in Ireland to become a big English county, because we have lost the notes of our nationhood, our language and our customs.

What is the answer to that? Have you any answer for it? I declare to God I see no answer to it except to take to our bosoms again the things we have discarded, our language and our customs, and to build up out of them an Irish nationhood anew (applause).

LANGUAGE AN ESSENTIAL OF NATIONALITY

I cannot understand for the life of me how it is that Irish sentiment sticks in a kind of half-way house (laughter). Why does it continue to say that it hates the English and at the same time continue to imitate them? (Applause.) Why does it clamor for recognition, noisily clamor for recognition as a separate nationality when at the same time it throws away with both hands the only thing that would make it so? Why, if Irishmen only went a little further, they would become very good Englishmen in sentiment also. And why don't they do it? Because, whether we regret it or not — some of us regret it; others don't — but whether we regret it or not, the very people that adopt English habits and copy English in every way, still continue to talk of their oppressed country and to sing 'Paddies Evermore' and 'The Green Above the Red,' and if I were to plant a Union Jack over their houses, they would brain me with a lump of a stone (laughter and applause).

And, strange as it may appear, I see no signs at all of their thinking any way differently; and it is perfectly certain to my mind — whether we like it or don't like it — that so long as England refuses Irishmen the right to govern themselves, so long they will continue to dislike her, and movements like Young Irelandism and Fenianism and Land Leagueism and Parliamentary obstruction — all those things will crop up time and again, time and again. And that is why I say since they won't become proper Englishmen, then let them become proper Irishmen; and that since they won't become the one thing, Englishmen in sentiment, then, in God's name, let them become the other thing — let them come in with us and built up an Irish-Ireland! (Applause.)

Now, if you say that Ireland has not prospered under English rule, why it is only a truism. All the world admits it. England itself does not deny it! But, of course, the English retort is ready: 'You did not come in like the Scotch and form part of the Empire'.

'Twenty years of good grandfatherly government,' said a late well-known Prime Minister, 'will solve the Irish question.' Well, I think the gentleman made the time a little too short (laughter). But suppose now with me to-night, suppose — a thing that is impossible — that a series of Oliver Cromwells were to arise in England not for a space of twenty years, but for a space of one hundred years — able administrators of the Empire; careful rulers of Ireland, developing to the utmost our national resources, whilst they unremittingly stamped out every spark of the national feeling, leaving Ireland a land of wealth and factories; leaving us, after a hundred years of good government, fat, wealthy, populous, prosperous, but with all our chacteristics gone; with every external that differentiated us from them lost or dropped; our Irish names of people and places changed into English ones; the Irish language completely extinct; the O's and the Mac's dropped; our Irish intonation changed by English schoolmasters into something English; the names of our rebels and our martyrs blotted out; our battlefields and traditions forgotten; the fact that we were not of Anglo-Saxon origin dropped out of mind and memory — and now let me put the question to you. How many Irishmen are there who would accept material prosperity at such a price as that? (Shouts of None, and great applause.)

It is exactly such a question and the answer that you gave me to it that mark the difference between the two races, a difference as wide as the grave; for I believe that nine Englishmen out of ten would jump to accept it, and I equally believe that nine Irishmen out of ten would indignantly refuse it (great applause).

FORGOT THEY HAD A BIRTHRIGHT

Well, that Anglicization that I pictured to you had everywhere eaten like a disease through Ireland. Nobody noticed it; nobody was told of it; but when Irishmen know, then Irish sentiment becomes a power in the land and refuses indignantly to relinquish its birthright. An, but the Irish had forgotten the fact that they had a birthright at all. That is the truth of the matter. They had forgotten that they were Irishmen in any sense of the word. The old race, the Mac's and O's and those who should have Mac's and O's before their names — those are the descendants of the men who Christianized and who civilized Western Europe, the descendants of the men who, for three centuries, amid the horror and the darkness and confusion of the Middle Ages held aloft the torch of learning and of piety unto every race of mankind. They are the men, Mr Chairman, who now for the first time since the Battle of the Boyne, have been appealed to through their Milesian instincts. And Mr Bourke Cockran marvelled that it brought about this great change in Ireland; and I tell you it is because the men who were crushed at the Battle of the Boyne have been appealed to through their Milesian instincts by the Gaelic League that you see the old Irish race rising on its feet to accept the new doctrines, ever new and ever old (applause).

Those are the men of whom our farmers and our artisans and our shopkeepers consist, and in whose hands is today the making or the marring of the Irish nation. But they are just on the point of recovering the possession of their own land, and their sons and daughters, please God, will have it after them and it is now more necessary than at any time before for these men to decide what will they be. On this side, an Irish nation built up again as it is being built up within our own recollection; on the other side an imitation England (applause).

When the Gaelic League started up, we found that these men were losing everything that connected them with the Christianizers of Europe, that connected them with the era of Cuchullainn and Oisin; that connected them with Brian Boroimhe and the heroes of Clontarf; that connected them with the O'Neills and the O'Donnells; that connected them with Rory O'Moore and with the Wild Geese; that connected them with the men of '98 (applause). They had lost all that those others had, language, traditions, music, genius and ideas; and now, just at the moment when we are becoming masters again of our own land, we find ourselves despoiled and robbed of the old bricks of our nationality, and we must set to work to make new bricks of new clay in a new kiln, to build it with.

Do you believe in burning new bricks of new clay for the old Irish house? I do not believe in it. I believe in going here and there throughout the entire island and gathering together, here and there, every relic of the past upon which we can lay our hands and gathering them together into one great whole and building and enshrining every one of them in the temple that shall be raised to the godhead of Irish nationhood (applause).

ANGLO-IRISH LITERATURE A MISTAKE

The rise of O'Connell and the establishment of Maynooth — Maynooth is now, you will be glad to hear, the most Irish spot in Ireland (applause), the rise of O'Connell and the establishment of Maynooth synchronized with the decay of Irish Ireland. The Irish race, the fathers of the present race of Irish-Americans, really lived in the closest contact with the traditions of the past and the national life of nearly eighteen hundred years, until the beginning of the nineteenth century. Not only so, but during the whole of the dark penal times they produced amongst themselves a most vigorous literary development.

Thomas Davis and the Young Irelanders came just at the parting of the ways, when the nation was, as it were, still in a state of flux and capable of being turned either to one side or the other.

Thomas Davis — that Irishman without fear and without reproach, whose name shall live forever in the grateful hearts of his countrymen — and the Young Irelanders generally, produced a new literature throughout the country. It was a literature in which they strove to compete with England herself upon England's own lines. The effect was enormous for a time, but it cannot be said to have been enduring. The fact is that the bark had been so recently stripped off the stem of the Irish tree that this attempt to replace it by a new bark, stuck on, as it were, with English gum and glue and stick-fast, failed to incorporate itself with the ancient stem, and finally fell off from it, as it were, in flakes. English gum is no substitute, and never can be a substitute for Irish sap. Fifty years of bitter experience have taught us that the Young Ireland heroes did not arrest, and to my thinking could not arrest, the denationalization of Ireland by a literature which, rousing and admirable as it was, was still only a literature written in the Engish language and largely founded upon English models. Remember, I am not saying one word in disparagment of the Young Ireland movement or of the splendid men who created it. If we had been in their place, God knows we might have pursued exactly the same tactics. But I claim that our fifty years of experience should now be made use of and that we go a step farther than they went and allow the natural bark, the Gaelic bark, thin though it may be at first and slender though it may be, to grow with the growth of nature upon the trunk of the ancient Irish elm.

The greatest misfortune that ever befell Ireland has been the loss of her language. I often heard people thank God that if England gave us nothing else, she gave us at least her language. Certainly (turning to Bourke Cockran) I have heard one of the most eloquent expositions of its power to-night that I have ever heard in my life or ever hope to hear again (applause). Well, in that way people put a happy face on it, and have pretended that the Irish language is not worth anything, and that it has no literature. And if the Irish language is worth nothing, why have I met professor after professor from Denmark, from France, from Germany, studying in the mountains of Connacht in order to learn the language that is there banned by the people themselves? (Applause). And it does possess a literature, or why would a German have calculated that books produced in Irish from the tenth to the seventeenth century, and still extant, would fill a thousand octavo volumes? (Applause.)

EVIDENCES OF NATIONAL DEGENERACY

Now do not think, please, that I am exaggerating in any way when I say Ireland was threatented with national extinction if the Gaelic League had not stepped into the breach. I will tell you some instances which first drew my attention to the appalling state of public opinion in the Irish-speaking country. I remember the first thing that opened my eyes was one day that as I was going from the fair of Tuam. I was selling cattle there (laughter and applause). I am not ashamed of it; all Irishmen sell cattle when they have them to sell; and very glad to have them (laughter), I overtook a young man driving a cow before me and I spoke to the young man in Irish, and as I was speaking in Irish he was answering in English (laughter), and at last I said to him, 'Don't you speak Irish?' And what was his answer? 'Well, I declare to God, sir, that neither my father nor my mother has one word of English and still I can't spake and I won't spake Irish.' (laughter). And I, who had just left Professor Georges Godet, of Brittany, France, and Professor Hakon, of Copenhagen, in Denmark, and Kuno Meyer (applause), of Germany, living on buttermilk and potatoes on the mountain sides in the houses of the peasantry to learn to speak the language that this reptile was discarding — to tell you the honest truth I lost my temper (laughter and applause). I lost my temper and I stood out from him, and to tell the honest truth, I hit him one kick. And, mind you, it just shows you what the loss of your native language does for you, the poor, unfortunate devil, he didn't have courage enough to turn around and knock me down (laughter and applause).

I remember another day, I was about six miles from my own house passing along the road when the children came trooping out of what is commonly called a National School; and there was a little 'gossoon' there that I was talking Irish to. I had some questions to ask about people in the neighbourhood, and as I talked to him in Irish he answered me in English. At last, I said to him, 'Don't you speak Irish?' What was the answer?' And isn't it Irish I'm speaking?' (Laughter.) 'No, *a chuisle*,' said I, 'it is not Irish you are speaking.' 'Then this is how I spoke it ever!' says he. That meant that poor little boy coming out of a National School was so densely, darkly and brutally ignorant that he did not know that I was speaking to him in one language and he was answering me in another. This is what passes for Government education in Ireland, but it won't pass in future for Government education, or for any kind of education (applause).

I remember another day, in the County of Sligo, the first of these instances happened in Galway, the second in Mayo, and this in Sligo. I went into a house to wait for a train and there was a pretty little girl at the fireside, and I sat down on a 'creepy' stool and began to talk to her, and, after her first shyness, she began talking Irish very nicely to me, and we were having a pleasant conversation when a dirty little unwashed red-headed brother stuck in his nose, out of a door, and he cocked his nose at her and said (imitating), 'Now, Mary, isn't that a credit for ye?' and not a word could I get out of Mary from that time on (laughter). You laugh, gentlemen, and, God forgive me, I laughed too; but when I went home and thought over it, I swear to you that I cried, because I saw it was the tragedy of a nation in a nutshell (applause).

A WONDERFUL GALWAY PEASANT

I passed through the County Galway a few months ago, and I came across a man who could neither read nor write nor speak English (applause). Quite right, gentlemen; it was all his luck. An ordinary English tourist would put that man down as a mere brute; but what a mind that man had! What a memory! What a wealth of song! What a fund of story! What a variety of information! I wrote down from him at one sitting an Ossianic poem of four hundred lines never before printed or heard of! (Applause).

He had a marvellous fund of folk tale, remainders of Ossianic lays, of religious poems, of songs, parodies, proverbs — in a word, everything that could go to enrich the mind and the moral nature. And all *that* must die with him! And what were we going to replace it with in his son? We were going to replace it with the Third Reading Book, and I would as soon have a lump of ashes choked down my throat as the Third Reading Book of the National Schools. (Applause.)

Now the Gaelic League is engaged upon a grand, reconstructive policy, the policy of creating a new nation upon the old lines, and before we can build up, it is necessary for us to place our finger on the blots.

Well, first, there is the language question of which I have spoken; but a number of other things hang from that language question. And first, strangely enough, comes the question of our own names. It has always seemed to me that a man's own name is part and parcel of himself. I am quite sure that if you changed my name tomorrow I would feel that I was changed myself; I would not understand it. And yet, within the last sixty or seventy years, Irishmen undergoing this awful process of national extinction, have been greedy to change their honorable, ancient, proud Milesian names into some abominable monosyllable because it sounded like something English. Some of the O'Connors became Conyers; the MacRorys, Rogers; the O'Donnells, Daniels; the MacCarthys, Carters and so on.

CHANGING THEIR FINE OLD IRISH NAMES

I remember Daniel O'Connell once, at a great mass meeting, speaking against an opponent of his, Lord Chancellor Sugden. 'Why', said O'Connell, in his best O'Connellite manner, 'you wouldn't call a decent pig Sugden,' and yet he never uttered one word of remonstrance when he saw the McGraths, the Brannigans and the McRorys changing their names before his very eyes to Guthries, Brodericks and Rogers. And the melancholy part of it was that not one single word of warning was ever addressed to the Irish race by their public men, or by their papers, to put a stop to this colossal attempt at vulgarity and degradation until we arose to-day at the eleventh hour. Look at our Christian names. I would have thought the names that were good enough for my grandfather and great-grandfather before me should be good enough for me. Where are our magnificent names of men and boys, Cathair and Domhnal and Angus and Fergus and Cormac and Diarmuid, and so forth. Where do you meet those names now? The man that you call Diarmuid when you speak Irish, an anti-Irish, degrading custom, begot by slavery, propagated by cringing, and fostered by flunkeyism, forces you to call

Jeremiah, Jer-em-i-ah (laughter and applause). Where are our beautiful female names, Nora and Una and Eibhlin and Moirin and Brighid? Where are they? A woman said to me not so long ago, 'God forbid,' said she, poor thing, 'God forbid that I should handicap my child in life by calling her Bridget!' (laughter.) She was wrong! She did handicap her child in life, but it was when she taught her to be ashamed of the patron saint of her own country (applause). There are ten, twenty thousand honest Irish girls whose mothers christened them Bridget at home, who, the moment they touch American soil, call themselves Bride, and Bridie, and Delia and Bedelia (laughter and applause). The spirit of Irish nationality as it speaks through the Gaelic League will never be appeased so long as our boys are called Daniel and Jeremiah, instead of Domhnal and Diarmuid, and our girls Helen and Julia, instead of Eibhlin and Sidhle.

Take our music. After all, the bagpipes, though you may not love its sound, was an artistic instrument; no man but an artist could play upon it. The violin is an artistic instrument; no man without a soft touch, a fine ear, and artistic feeling can play upon the violin. The violin and the bagpipes were in every parish when I was young. Where are they to-day? What has taken their place? What grand, artistic instruments have taken the place of the bagpipes and the violin? Here they are (imitates the playing of the accordeon and the concertina.) (Loud laughter.) Or, if it isn't that, then this has taken its place (imitates the motion of playing the hand organ). (Renewed laughter and applause.) That is called, I suppose, being an Irish nation. Ah! where is the venerable custodian of Ireland's song and music, the man who always commanded a welcome at the peasant's fireside as he trudged through the bogs and over the mountains and through the woods of the country? He sleeps with his green bag beside him under the green sward. In his place have come upon the village stage that quintessence of all vulgarity and all abomination, known throughout the world as 'the stage Irishman'. Gentlemen, your action in dealing with that monster in New York gave me a greater gratification and impressed upon me the imperishability of the Irish character, the possibility of welding our race together, more than any other thing that I remember reading in the American papers (applause).

WORK ACCOMPLISHED BY THE LEAGUE

Well, I said at the outset that I would have failed in my mission to-night if I did not convince you that Ireland was really threatened with national extinction in the most far-reaching and vital sense of the word; and I think I have shown you that it was. I said I would put my finger on the blots, and now you will ask me what have we done to fill them?

I will tell you. A dozen years ago, Irish was taught in less than a dozen schools; six years ago it was taught in 105 schools; to-day it is taught, more or less, in something over three thousand of the eight thousand schools of Ireland (applause). Between public and parochial schools, between colleges and convents, there cannot be less than a quarter of a million people now studying to read and write the language (applause). Six years ago, in intermediate education only 260 pupils passed in Irish; last year over two thousand.

Six years ago no stranger coming to Ireland would have seen anything to tell him that he was not in a big, vulgarized English county. Now, in many of the large towns, and in Dublin, the capital, you see the names of the streets put up and the names of the roads, and the names of the towns printed in Irish capitals at the corner of the streets, and you know that you are not in England (applause). Six years ago, scarcely a paper printed a word of our language. Now all the national daily papers and very many of the weekly papers print columns of it. Six years ago, an Irish book was a rarity that appeared only at intervals of many months. Now not a week goes by but a new book printed in Irish is issued from the press, and the distribution of books and pamphlets from our own office alone, not to speak of the booksellers, has been something over a quarter of a million for every year of the last four (applause).

Six years ago, if you spoke Irish as well as Owen Roe and wrote it as well as Geoffrey Keating it would not be worth a *tráithnín* to you. Now you cannot obtain a place under the Corporation of Dublin, under the Corporation of Limerick, under the County Councils of Cork or Mayo, and a dozen other places, unless you know the language of your country (great applause). Six years ago if the products of Irish hands and Irish brains were to find a market they had to come back with the hall mark of London or of Paris on them. To-day we are rearing and raising a race of men whose one object will be that the article that they buy shall bear the hall mark of 'Made in Ireland' (applause); and the results have been amazing.

We have enormously increased the output of our weaving mills. We have doubled the output of our other factories. Other industries in Ireland have been helped immensely. In every big town in Ireland there is an exhibition of our local industries.

We have two training schools, one in Munster and one in Connacht, to teach the people how to teach. We have a school of higher Irish learning which Kuno Meyer and Professor Strachan, the greatest masters of old Irish and of phonetics in the world, are teaching, and in which they are doing what Trinity College, with all its wealth, refused to do — training up a race of Irish scholars that will take rank among the foremost scholars of the world (applause). We have a fine place of our own in Dublin. We have only twenty paid officers. We have a weekly paper and a monthly magazine. We have organizers who work night and day, Sunday and Monday, at their hard task of persuading the people to be Irish again, and who work and sweat themselves to death at a miserable wage that here you would not offer to a fifth-rate stenographer. And they have a corps of two hundred teachers with them. Wherever they go they bring with them a whiff of ancient Ireland. They teach not the language and the music alone, but the traditions, the dances, and the history of the race.

THE HOPE OF NATIONHOOD

To my mind the existence of Ireland, a nation, depends upon this — whether we can keep those men doing the work or whether we cannot keep them (applause).

And now you will ask me how we manage all this. Where do we get the money for it? Well, it has not been out of the pockets of the great or of the rich in Ireland, I assure you. Who was it that gave us our first legacy, more than five years ago? Who was it that saw floating before his dying eye, as it were, the vision of an Irish nation? Who but a hard working gunsmith, Patrick Mullins, here in New York (applause). He left us by his will ten thousand dollars, and never before did Ireland get, and never again will she get, as much value for money received. And I desire here, on behalf of every Gael in Ireland, to thank Patrick Ford and the *Irish World* (applause); to thank John Devoy and the *Gaelic American* (applause and cheers); to thank that magnificent body of Irishmen, the Ancient Order of Hibernians, and to thank one and all, papers and societies and individuals, who have tried to assist us in the hour of our weakness.

Now we make an appeal every year to our fellow-countrymen, during the week in which falls St Patrick's Day, and our countrymen contribute, almost entirely in pennies and sixpences and shillings, a sum of between three thousand and four thousand pounds, and we make ourselves a sum of between three and four thousands pounds from the sale of our books, pamphlets and newspapers; and with that money we are reviving the soul of Ireland (applause).

But, alas! our work is circumscribed; it must necessarily be circumscribed; we are a poor country; we are an impoverished people. The pennies and the shillings of the poor do not go very far. We are accomplishing our great work, as it were, from hand to mouth. One thing and one thing alone has saved the Irish nation, and it has been the gallant self-sacrifice and devotion of the men who are engaged in this task. I could point to man after man broken in health, broken in wealth, who lay down and died in the cause of what they believed was Irish nationhood, as truly martyrs to the cause as if you had placed them up against that wall and fusiladed them with a file of soldiers. And without that devotion, a million of pounds could have worked no miracle (applause).

Ah! if we only had an intellectual headquarters for the Irish race; if we only had an assured position but for ten short years; oh, if we could only send an organiser into every single diocese in Ireland — then the Irish nation would be saved beyond any shadow of doubt!

THE WORK AHEAD

Well, it is getting so late, I do not want to speak any more, but I had a lot more to say to you (applause and laughter and cries of 'Go on'). Well, just remember this: the Irish language, thank God, is neither Protestant nor Catholic (applause). It is neither a landlord nor a tenant; it is neither a Unionist nor a Separatist; and, in taking it for our platform, we have achieved what is to my mind the supreme and crowning glory of the Gaelic League, because, for the first time in Ireland within my recollection, Catholic and Protestant, Unionist and Nationalist, landlord and tenant, priest and parson, came together, all working hand in hand in the interest of Ireland's life and intellectuality, and we are realizing for the first time, the glorious dream of Thomas Davis (applause),

'How every race and every trade
Should be by love combined.'

We are working together in a common cause, in a spirit of good fellowship. Mr Chairman, that word is not strong enough; in a spirit of loving brotherhood, which has, of recent years, been unexampled in Ireland; and we are not engaged in doing anything that is impossible. It is perfectly possible, and we know it, and we see it.

But I tell you that there is no royal road to the recovery of our nationality. It is a difficult, it is an arduous task, and it demands self-sacrifice. If we are in earnest and have behind us the moral support and the good wishes of America, we must succeed. If we are only playing at being in earnest — and that is a game Irishmen are very good at (laughter) — then we shall fail and the whole world will deride us, and the historian will take his tablets and write the words; *Finis Hiberniae* — the end of Ireland.

The Gaelic League is in earnest. It knows what it is asking and it knows why it is asking for it. It will abate no jot and no tittle of its demand. The oftener it is knocked down the more vigorously will it rise up again. It will accept no defeat. We have upon our side, right, justice, reason, the memory of the dead (applause), and, though it may seem a strange thing to utter it in this town of roaring commerce, yet I believe in my heart that the dead are often more potent than the living.

We have the sympathy of the scholars of Europe. We have the good will of all well-wishers of Ireland, and against us we have only race hatred, anti-Irish bigotry, and Trinity College, Dublin (laughter and applause), and the time has gone by when that combination, from which nothing constructive ever yet emanated — the time has gone by when they shall win any more batties in Ireland (applause).

Pardon me for having kept you so long. Pardon me for speaking to this late hour of the night. I shall end. But I earnestly implore every one of you, whether he be a Nationalist or a Unionist — whatever his politics may be — for this is surely no political matter — to do his best to help the Irish race to develop upon Irish lines, because on Irish lines alone can the Irish race once more become what it was of yore — one of the most original, artistic, literary and charming peoples in Europe (great applause).

Mr J. C. Lynch, in a Gaelic address, presented Dr Hyde with an illuminated set of resolutions, also in Gaelic, which will be printed in the Gaelic American *next week. Justice Keogh then thanked the audience and brought the meeting to a close.*

The Great Work of the Gaelic League*

Knowing the anxiety of the readers of the *Leader* to have at first hand something of the origin, purpose and effect of the Gaelic League from Dr Douglas Hyde, a representative of this paper [Father Yorke] called on the distinguished Irish scholar at his apartments in the St Francis, on Wednesday, and was accorded a most delightful interview. Dr Hyde was extremely anxious to give the *Leader* readers a complete history of the Revival Movement to date, and did so as follows:

The *Leader*— 'The readers of the *Leader* would like to hear from you a brief explanation of the philosophy of the Gaelic League.'

Dr Hyde— 'The philosophy of the Gaelic League is based principally on this, that there is a fundamental distinction between different races of mankind, and between no two races, perhaps, does there run a broader line of radical distinction than between the English and the Irish race. Any attempt of the Irish race to imitate the English on lines that are natural and instinctive to the English, but that are the reverse of natural to ourselves, is bound to end in failure, and has in the past been nothing but a failure. The philosophy of the Gaelic League Movement is that all imitation is barren; and we in Ireland were unfortunately imitating not what was good, but what was worst in English civilization. On the other hand, if we allow Ireland to develop upon National and racial lines, why she may go ahead indefinitely. We need place no bounds to what she may achieve on her own lines in art, literature, commerce and manufactures. On the other hand, an imitative Ireland was an impotent Ireland, and its limbs (*recte* limits?) have been set already, through the mere fact that it was an imitation — an imitation which would never equal the thing imitated.'

The *Leader*— 'A number of people seem to think or say that the Gaelic League is merely a Language Movement; that you are substituting an obsolete language for a tongue which is almost universal, and which has developed with modern civilization.'

NOT TRYING TO ABOLISH ENGLISH

Dr Hyde— 'If you mean to say that we are trying to get rid of the

*From the San Francisco *Leader*, 17 February 1906.

English language in Ireland, I am glad that you have given me an opportunity to point out that we are doing no such thing. We look upon the English language as a commercial necessity, and if I had a friend in Ireland who did not know the English language, I would be the first to teach it to him. But we look upon the Irish language as a National necessity, and a National necessity is just as urgent as a commercial necessity can be. A third language, if we had it, I would designate as an accomplishment, but we are bent upon this, that Ireland shall know both Irish and English. A time may come, but certainly not in our time, when the inhabitants of Ireland could gain all that would be necessary for them from their own language alone, but that time has not come yet, and for that reason I consider English a necessity for this generation.

The *Leader*— 'How does Irish literature compare with English literature.'

Dr Hyde— 'Unfortunately the English literature that finds its way into Ireland and is read by the masses is not literature at all, in the true sense of the word. The English press, as I think Mr Yeats once graphically expressed it, "is pelting us with the mud off its streets." Our people, when they threw away their own native literature and native language, did not turn to Shakespeare, or Tennyson, or Matthew Arnold. They turned to the cheapest English weeklies and the insipid papers that are really sucking the brains out of the people, and this to them represents "the great Engish literature." On the other hand, the literature which we are introducing into Ireland is the literature of the poets, the literature of the saints and shanachies, the old songs, the old folk tales, the old histories full of the old ideas and enthusiasms, and charged full of the spirit of manhood and nationhood, but we are not relying on this alone. We thoroughly understand that in the twentieth century a people cannot subsist on its poems, and its folk tales, and its ancient histories. We are producing a modern literarure built upon these and a rational continuation of these, a literature of modern stories, essays, dramas and poems, which are thoroughly Irish in their origin and conception, but at the same time are as much up to date as the like productions of any other nation in Europe.'

GAELIC WRITERS OF TODAY

The *Leader*— 'Mention a few of the leading writers of the present day.'

Dr Hyde— 'To mention any at all would be invidious, for I would be bound to leave out many whose names deserve to be mentioned, but undoubtedly the greatest writer that the South of Ireland has produced is Father Peter O'Leary, parish priest of Castle Lyons, County Cork, shanachie, grammarian, dramatist and story teller. I look upon his novel, *Séadna*, as the most original piece of work produced during the last ten years, and one which is bound to live in the future.

'Perhaps the voluminous and untiring of all our Munster writers is Father Patrick Dinneen. He has edited poet after poet from among the Munster bards of the seventeenth and eighteenth centuries. His work in producing the first handy Irish dictionary that was ever published has been a God-send to the movement. He has written original novels and essays and plays, and he is also a poet.

'Conán Maol, whose real name is O'Shea, is another Southern writer of great power and quality. His essays on Irish history are brilliant performances.

'Mr J. J. Doyle, who is better known under the name of Beirt Fhear, is a writer of delightful dialogues and stories.

'Mr J. J. O'Kelly, who often writes under the pen-name of Sgeilg, is another excellent writer of Irish, and his work on the Irish saints and scholars on the continent is a most instructive one.

'Nor must I forget my friend, Tadhg O'Donoghue, who writes under the pen-name of 'Torna,' and who is the present editor of the *Gaelic Journal*. His muse is the true traditional one, and his volume of poems, "Leoithne Andeas" or "Zephyrs from the South," is most remarkable for its melody and imagination.

'All of these writers belong to the South of Ireland, which has also given us a dozen others whom I would like to mention, but it would take up too much time.'

THE WEST'S AWAKE

The *Leader*— 'What has the Western Province done for this Movement?'

Dr Hyde— 'In Connacht our chief writers are O'Malley of Coramona, and his brother, the organizer.

'O'Neachtain of Connemara and Michael Breathnach (or Welsh in English), who did splendid work for Irish-Ireland as principal of our little college in Connacht, at which we train teachers how to teach Irish.

'Seamus O'Mulloy is another Connacht poet whose pieces I like very much, but he has not published any volume of writings.

'My friend, Father Healy of Ballinrobe, has also published a useful book on Biblical History, and we have others who write for the local papers and the magazines.

'Dr Henry, one of the leading grammarians of the Movement, is another storyteller. His books on the Irish language and its teaching are, I should think, about the best things of the kind that the movement has yet produced. He is a physician of eminence, who lives in London, and was born in County Sligo. His work in behalf of the Gaelic League has been for years untiring.'

The *Leader*— 'What province do you come from, Dr Hyde?'

Dr Hyde— 'I am a Connacht man myself, but my grandfather was the first of the family who left Munster to settle in Connacht, so I am in a way connected with both provinces.'

ULSTER AND LEINSTER

The *Leader*— 'What has Ulster done?'

Dr Hyde— 'Ulster has not produced as many writers as the other two provinces, but I will name Padraig O'Beirne, the poet. He is a Donegal man, and one of the earliest pioneers in the language movement, as was his friend, Mr Ward, of Killybegs.'

'Seamus O'Ceallaigh, another pleasant writer of considerable humour, is, I think a Tyrone man. John MacNeill, Vice-President of the Gaelic League, and, in my opinion, its original founder, comes from the Glens of Antrim, but indeed it would be impossible for me to give anything like a full list of our writers in Irish. I dare say I am leaving out some of the best, simply because I cannot remember them on the spur of the moment.

'Miss Una O'Farrelly, one of the leading spirits of the Irish movement, and perhaps one of the most active members of our executive committee, has written admirable stories and descriptions, and she is a native of the County Cavan. So, you see the North has not been idle either.

'Miss Mollie O'Kennedy, who has written plays in Irish, is a Dublin girl, and Miss Norma Brothwick, whose *Ceachta Beaga* have been of great advantage to learners, and who knows Irish perfectly, is, I think, not of Irish birth at all, but came over from London to live amongst us. Her mother, I believe, was a Scotch Highlander, so that you see the attraction of our new-born nationality is absorbing even persons from the outside.

'Mr J. J. Lloyd, our greatest authority on Irish typography and the author of the book of Place Names, is, I think, a Leinster man. I think Mr P. J. Ryan, another writer of plays and stories, is either a Leinster man or from its borders, and Leinster is producing quite a crop of active workers, so you see all the provinces are fairly represented in our movement.

The *Leader*— 'What are the prospects of the Language Movement?'

Dr Hyde— 'My dear man, for mercy's sake, do not ask me to prophesy in this Movement. I have never looked forward certainly not with a view of prophesying. If we had done so at any time during the past ten years, what could we have forseen but failure? — and yet we have secured nothing but success upon success. I distrust all prophecy, and I distrust taking stock of the future. The work of the day is sufficient for us, but I will say this much, that when, with almost every power in Ireland and every educational institution, except the Christian Brothers, arrayed against us, and when we had the immense inertia of the people themselves to combat, we have, nevertheless, succeeded so far beyond the wildest dreams, it should not be difficult for us, now that we have broken down so much of the educational opposition to us, and dispelled the inertia, to reach almost any height.'

THE SCHOOL FEES QUESTION

The *Leader*— 'Would you explain the action of the late Tory Government in cutting off the school grants for the teaching of Irish?'

Dr Hyde— 'A few years ago the Government consented to allow results fees, as they are called, to be paid for children who passed in Irish — as in French, mathematics and other subjects. That means that for every boy and girl who passed in Irish the schoolteacher who taught him received each year a sum of two dollars and a half. At first this did not amount to very much, but, as the Movement grew the fees grew with it, until they amounted to $60,000.

'The Government, apparently taking alarm, gave due notice that they would cut off these fees. Now, I want you to observe that $60,000 is just about the one hundred and fiftieth part of the money that Ireland is taxed for her own education. We remonstrated, and asked why they were doing this. The answer was that they were acting from motives of economy. It is an answer that nobody believed or believes, because that money was actually spent upon other things. I wish, moreover, to point out that the country almost unanimously protested against this change. It protested through every elective agency in its power, Boards of Guardians, County Councils, District Councils, Urban Councils and finally through the Committee of Catholic School Managers for the whole of Ireland; and still the Government remained obdurate. I would just call your attention to this fact, that when a nation with practical unanimity desires to have the one hundred and fiftieth part of the money which it is taxed for its own education spent upon a particular thing — especially when that thing is the National language of the country — and the Government refuses it, then plain men have a plain name for that kind of treatment.'

The *Leader*— 'How do you think the Liberal victory will affect the school question as regards the teaching of Irish?'

Dr Hyde— 'Oh, of course it will mean that we shall get back that money. How on earth could any Government calling itself 'Liberal' refuse the united demand of the country to expend its own money in its own way on its own education? Not alone must we get back that money, but I expect that we shall get the control, as we desire, of our own educational primary system. Otherwise, the so-called Liberal Government would be nothing but a tyranny. If they do not give us this, they may as well renounce their title of "Liberal," as far as Ireland is concerned.'

The *Leader*— 'Would they not see a danger ahead?'

Dr Hyde— 'Danger? What danger? This is an educational movement. It is an educational movement, pure and simple. It aims at giving an effectual education instead of an ineffectual one. It aims at interesting the people and arousing their self-respect. There is nothing political in it. How could there be, when many of the leading Gaelic Leaguers are men and women whose politics are noticeably at variance with that of the bulk of the people? No; there is no danger in it to anybody, but I suppose that the shoneens and the imitation-English will not like it, simply because it is an Irish Movement.'

IRELAND NEEDS A NATIONAL UNIVERSITY

The *Leader*— 'That brings us to the University Question, Doctor. Have the Irish people at present any real University education?'

Dr Hyde— 'No, indeeed, they have not. If by the Irish people you mean the Catholic majority. You see, they will not go to Trinity College or the Queen's Colleges. The hierarchy is opposed to it, and there is no other to which they can go. There is, indeed, a thing that is called the Royal University, but it is merely an examining body. It does its work as well as any examining body could do, I think, but it is a farce to call a thing like that a University. Why, the entire essence of University education consists in this, that students from different parts of the country, of different characteristics, of different minds, of different tones of thought, of different aptitudes, meet one another, jostle with one another, and rub off each other's angles. It is to my mind enormously important that at the formative age of a man's mind he should be free to meet and discuss with his fellow in the playground, in the classroom and in his own apartments, politics, ethics, morals, literature, art, religion and the thousand and one impressions that come to a man or woman between the years of eighteen and twenty-five. An examining body only registers your amount of book knowledge, and mere book knowledge is not education.

'What we want in Ireland is a National University, which will bring students together and educate them upon National lines. There is only one real University in Ireland today, and that is Trinity College, Dublin, and it, I should say, takes, if anything, pride in denationalizing its students. I know that up to a year or two ago there was not, in its whole curriculum, a single book or anything else to teach a student that he belonged to any country; and its Irish professor — for it has a thing that goes by the name of an Irish professorship — is appointed and paid by a society for the conversion of Roman Catholics to Protestantism through the medium of their own language. This Irish professorship has been in existence for about fifty years, and, despite the magnificent collection of manuscript literature stored up in the underground rooms of Trinity College library, it has never published nor edited a single text nor trained up a school of scholars to do so. Now, we want an Irish University for many reasons, for national reasons, for commercial reasons, for social reasons, but, above all, for this reason, to insure that every class in the country and every creed shall have the same advantages in Ireland as every other. Until that is done I fear a more or less bitter feeling will always exist that one class or creed is having advantages of which, for certain reasons (whether right or wrong, upon this point I will say nothing), the others cannot avail themselves.'

The *Leader*—'You look, then, upon a Catholic University as a necessity?'

Dr Hyde— 'I fear that the University Question has been greatly set back and much damaged by the nomenclature used about it, and by having the Irish demand generally known as a demand for 'a Catholic University," whereas, if I understand the question rightly — of course, I am only giving my own opinion here, and not speaking of anybody else — what we desire is a National University, to which both Protestant and Catholic shall be equally free to go, and against which no possible ethical or religious objections can be urged by any one. In planning the Irish University of the future, its National nature must be steadily kept in view, and nothing else will satisfy the new-born instincts of the country.'

Index

A
America 8, 44, 52n, 79, 157, 171
Antrim 53, 84, 159, 196
Arnold, Matthew 27, 194
Aryan 95-6, 98-101, 103, 121, 127-9, 149

B
bataí scóir 19, 33
Beside the Fire 21, 42
Bible 22, 27, 35
Bourke, Canon Ulick 19, 60
Brooke, Charlotte 24, 27
Bubbero songs 67, 84
Burns, Robert 105-6

C
Cailín Deas Crúite na mBó 83, 105, 117
Carleton, William 99, 123, 149, 159, 162
Castlerea, Co. Mayo 7
Catholic(s) 18n, 22, 27, 49, 149-50, 179, 191, 197, 199
Céitinn, Seathrún 28, 44n, 54, 62, 189
Celt(ic) 27-9, 33, 36, 68, 7., 75-7, 88, 90, 94, 98, 100, 102-3, 107, 110, 114, 120, 127, 129, 156-7, 161, 168-9
Cleaver, Rev. Euseby 50n, 146-7, 159
Commissioners of National Education 17-8, 20, 30, 33, 79
Comyn, David: see Ó Coimín, Dáithí
Conradh na Gaeilge 8, 17, 38, 45-6, 49, 51-2, 171-2, 178-9, 181, 183, 185, 187-8, 191, 193, 196, 198
Contemporary Club 36, 51

Continental scholars 28, 49, 75, 103, 156, 159-61,185, 189
Corkery, Daniel 21n, 18n
Crofton, Croker 99, 122-4
Cúchulainn 156-8, 183
Curtin, Jeremiah 124
Curtis, Edmund 13, 14

D
Davies, Sir John 15-16
Davis, Thomas 29-30, 92, 106, 158, 169, 184, 191
Davitt, Michael 50n, 101, 164
de Brún, Pádraig 22
de Fréine, Seán 21
Devoy, John 30, 190
Dowden, Prof. Edward 36
Draighneán Donn 71, 83, 105, 167
Dublin University Review 36, 66, 74

E
Encyclopaedia Britannica 98, 125

F
Famine 21, 30
Fenians 30, 33, 45, 154, 182
Fleming, John: see Pléimeann, Seán
Frenchpark, Co. Roscommon 7, 33, 129

G
Gaelic Athletic Association 50n, 108
Gaelic Journal: see *Irisleabhar na Gaeilge*
Gaelic League: see Conradh na Gaeilge
Gaelic Union 33n, 34-5, 38n, 49

INDEX

Gallagher's *Sermons* 56, 58
Greece/Greek 81, 94-8, 100, 127, 149, 151, 155, 157, 161
Greene, Prof. David 12, 20n, 33, 52n
Grimm 97-8, 103, 126-7

H

Hardiman, James 14n, 27, 67, 162
Healy, T.M. 50, 101
Henry VIII 13-4
Hercules 95 , 127-8
Home Rule 30, 38, 151-2, 161

I

Irishman, The 34, 55, 65
Irish Ecclesiastical Record 49-50
Irish National Literary Society 11, 45, 49, 51
Irish National Teachers Organisation 17, 33
Irisleabhar na Gaeilge 34, 46n, 51n, 52

K

Keating, Geoffrey: see Céitinn, Seathrún
Kennedy, Patrick 99, 123-4

L

Lady Gregory 7, 171
Lady Wilde 50n, 99, 123-4
Land League 101, 154, 182
Land, Andrew 96-7
Lavin, John 33, 35
Leabhar Sgeulaigheachta 38-9, 41, 113n, 125
Learned societies 28, 30
Lee, Prof. Joseph 18
Lhuyd, Edward 22-3
Literary History of Ireland 20, 52
Lucerna Fidelium 58, 61
Lydon, Prof. J. F. 12-13

M

Mac Aingil, Aodh 22
Mac Beill, Eoin 22, 45, 47, 48, 50, 52, 196

McPherson, James 27
Mahaffy, John P. 20
Maynooth 46n, 50, 149, 158-60, 184
Mazzini 153, 181
Mise agus an Connradh 46, 171
Moody, T. W. 28
Moore, Thomas 27, 68, 92, 106, 169
Murphy, Prof. Gerard 7
Müller, Max 81, 96-7

N

Napoleon 69, 91
Nation, The 20, 30n, 29, 37, 43, 92, 104n
Nationalist(s) 156, 170, 181, 191-2
National Schools 17, 33, 50, 186-7, 189
New Brunswick, Canada 43, 135-6, 146, 159
New York 44-5, 46n, 50, 79, 145, 171-2, 178, 180
Nibelungenlied 81

O

Ó Beirn, Pádraig 44, 152, 196
O'Brien, William 51
O'Carolan, Turlough 37, 66, 82, 106
Ó Coimín, Dáithí 34, 54, 62n, 64
Ó Concheanainn, Tomás 171, 174, 176
O'Connell, Daniel 29, 102, 149, 158, 162, 169, 184, 187
O'Connor, Charles 27, 75
Ó Cuív, Prof. Brian 13, 14n, 52n
O'Curry, Eugene 28, 75, 82, 159
Ó Dálaigh, Seán 30-1, 67
O'Daly, John: see Ó Dálaigh, Seán
O'Donovan, John 28, 75
O'Donovan Rossa 30, 44
Odyssey 81, 95
Ó hAilín, Tomás 28
(O') Hart, Seamas 34
Ó hEoghusa, Bonaventura 22

Society for the Preservation of
   the Irish Language 33-5, 49
Spencer, Edmund 15, 162
Spencer, Herbert 97
Stanihurst, Richard 13-5
Statutes of Kilkenny 12-13
Stephens, James 45, 152, 161

T
Teuton(ic) 68, 88, 90, 99, 127, 180
Trevelyan, George 17
Trinity College, Dublin 8, 20, 22, 36, 54, 192, 198-9
Tudor monarchs 13-4

U
Unionists 153-4, 156, 170, 181, 191-2
United Ireland 79, 99, 101-2

V
Vallencey, Charles 27

W
Wagner, Pro. Heinrich 18
Walker, Joseph Cooper 26-7
Wordsworth, William 67, 77

Y
Yeats, W. B. 36, 42, 51, 171, 194
Young Ireland 29-30, 51, 154, 158, 182, 184

Z
Zeuss, J. C. 28, 103

Ó Fiaich, Tomás 14
Ó Gramhna, Eoghan 46n, 48-9, 158
Oisín 27, 30, 66, 77, 101-2, 104, 106, 157, 159, 183, 187
Oldham, Charles 36
Ó Maolchonaire, Flaithrí 22
O'Neill Russell, Thomas 44-5, 56, 64, 45, 152
Orangemen 178-9
Orpen, Charles 18

P
Parnell 7, 36, 52
Pearse, P.H. 19
Percy, Thomas 27, 105
Petrie, George 75
Pléimeann, Seán 48-9
Protestant(s) 22, 29, 36, 49, 53, 146, 179, 191, 199

Q
Quinn, John 171-2

R
Raftery, Anthony 35, 37, 119, 171
Rafroidi, Prof. Patrick 28-9
Rolleston, T.W. 37
Romantic Movement 29
Rousseau 74

S
Shakespeare 77, 92, 137, 194
Shan Van Vocht 69-70, 175
Sigerson, Dr. George 20, 30n, 51n, 156